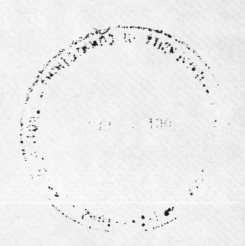

The FORWARD MOVEMENT
of the FOURTEENTH CENTURY

The FORWARD MOVEMENT of the FOURTEENTH CENTURY

EDITED BY FRANCIS LEE UTLEY

Ohio State University Press
Columbus

For our predecessors and teachers

GEORGE H. MCKNIGHT

EDGAR H. MCNEAL

HANS SPERBER

CONTENTS

Editor's Introduction 3

HARRY BOBER: *A Reappraisal of Rayonnant Architecture*.... 9

GEORGE P. CUTTINO: *A Reconsideration of the "Modus tenendi parliamentum"* 31

GRACE FRANK: *French Literature in the Fourteenth Century.* 61

ASTRIK L. GABRIEL: *The College System in the Fourteenth-Century Universities* 79

ALAN GEWIRTH: *Philosophy and Political Thought in the Fourteenth Century* 125

Notes on the Contributors............................. 165

ILLUSTRATIONS

(following page 86)

PLATE

   I. Laon, Cathedral, choir.

  II. Chars, Parish Church, interior of nave looking toward choir.

 III. Saint-Denis, Abbey Church, interior.

 IV. Beauvais, Cathedral, detail of choir.

  V. Chartres, Amiens, and Reims, Cathedrals, nave elevations.

 VI. Saint-Urbain-de-Troyes, choir.

 VII. Albi, Cathedral, interior.

VIII. Toulouse, Church of the Jacobins, interior.

 IX. Boulogne-Billancourt, Notre-Dame-des-Menus, interior.

  X. Montpellier, Cathedral, interior.

 XI. Strasbourg, Cathedral, detail of west façade.

 XII. Séez (Orne), Cathedral, choir.

XIII. Saint-Thibault, Priory Church, detail of choir wall.

XIV. Saint-Sulpice-de-Favières, Church, choir.

 XV. Rouen, Abbey Church of Saint-Ouen, interior of nave looking toward choir.

XVI. Rouen, Abbey Church of Saint-Ouen, interior of nave looking toward choir.

XVII. Exeter, Cathedral, interior looking east.

XVIII. Celles-sur-Belle, Church, interior.

XIX. Narbonne, Cathedral Saint-Just, ambulatory.

XX. Paris, Eglise Saint-Severin, ambulatory.

XXI. Courtyard of the College of Lemoine.

XXII. New College, Oxford.

XXIII. Pembroke College.

XXIV. Pierre d'Ailly, Grand Master of the College of Navarre.

XXV. Inspection of the books in the library of Ave Maria College.

The FORWARD MOVEMENT
of the FOURTEENTH CENTURY

EDITOR'S INTRODUCTION

The fourteenth century in Western Europe is a bridge which links twelfth-century gains to sixteenth-century triumphs. Its glory is both in its political, philosophical, and artistic promise, and in its achievement—Dante, Chaucer, the Gothic cathedrals, and the universities. It is at once the height of the Middle Ages and the beginning of the Renaissance.

Indeed, these conventional terms blur when we adhere to chronology: the very mediaeval Petrarch opens our eyes to the new humanistic ideals; the very mediaeval Chaucer and Boccaccio turn men's minds to a world of men not wholly transitory, and suffused with a love for human fame and action; the very mediaeval Marsilius of Padua and Wycliffe provide the stimulus to new liberties from oppression. Cola di Rienzi and Dante revive ideas of Roman liberty which, though caught in a cultural lag, will be actualized in succeeding centuries. The mediaeval concept of natural law, with its axiom "all men are by nature free," leads in France to the legal freeing of the serfs. Though the myths of agrarianism remain in *Piers Plowman* and Chaucer, the bourgeoisie is already leading one vanguard to a newer myth by its practical victories; and the proletariat, aroused out of its calm by the failure of the feudal ideal in a time of strife and pestilence, is making its first bid for amelioration. In *Piers Plowman* and in the English parliament the common people begin to emerge as a recognizable force in the commonwealth. The call for Church reform is not limited to the Lollards and the Spiritual Franciscans and their continental brethren; Gerson and Trent are anticipated by the orthodox Richard Fitzralph and a host of sermon-writers.

In art the Sienese school is breaking ground which will bear rich fruit in the later Roman and Venetian schools, and the creative spirit north of the Alps is discovering itself. The decline of the great ages of romance and lyric virility is as deceptive as the decline of the twelfth-century monastic reforms; new genres are on the way, and new reforms in the making. Chrétien's "make it new" is matched by the work of Chaucer and the Gawain-poet; and Italy, under the impact of Dante, broadens the base of literary accomplishment. Music flourishes with Machaut and the sophisticated composers of the Court of Burgundy. The drama, after its long evolution from a casual trope, is culminating in the

great biblical cycles; and playwrights and actors are slowly learning the professional techniques which will lead to the triumphs
of sixteenth- and seventeenth-century Spain, France, and England.

At Oxford and Paris the foundations of modern science are
being laid with a new attitude toward the facts of experience and
new theories of motion and mechanics, to which, perhaps, Kepler
and Galileo are indebted. Some of the most exciting logical specu-
lations of our time find their only predecessors in the fourteenth
century, when quantitative aspects of logic are stressed for the
first time. A characteristic empirical skepticism anticipates the
twentieth century, though the goals are strikingly different; and
the reaction against a heavy reliance on rationalism also recalls
our own time. One must not distort historic truth, yet there are
parallels between the fourteenth century and our own which
explain its appeal to us. Man moved then, as now, tortuously,
but with both promise and achievement.

This is a statement of the theme of the conference in mediaeval
studies held at Ohio State University on October 31 and November 1, 1958, sponsored by the Faculty Mediaeval Club. With full
awareness of the risk of historical generalization involved, and
of the bias which might surround any one man's view of history,
the committee planning the conference sought for a thematic
approach to the century which might unify the work of our lecturers—a view not limited to one man's idiosyncracies but one
which would at least call upon a working consensus of diverse
specialists, and allow those who discussed the century to agree or
disagree heuristically.

We were fully aware that in attempting to understand another
epoch, we might merely reveal our bondage to our own century,
that our judgments of history might be the reflection of our
own historical circumstance and personal bias. Collingwood has
reminded us that the theory of progress of Herder, to whom
modern theories of social *telos* owe much, was actually tied completely to his own race and culture, and was indifferent to the
statics and dynamics of other human groups. And Kant's gloomy
view of the past led to exaggerated hopes for the future: "A profound knowledge of history would have taught him that what has
brought progress about has not been the sheer ignorance or the
sheer badness but the concrete actuality of human effort itself,
with all its good and bad elements commingled." [1]

It may be, therefore, that the fourteenth century, with all its tyrannies, looks good to us because it looks so much like the twentieth. In appreciating the virtues of another epoch, we may only reaffirm our allegiance to our own. That we are bound in time may cause us to magnify the present for its resemblance to the past, or the past for its resemblance to the present. So may we likewise magnify when we attribute our present follies to a subversive crisis produced by either Ramus, Rousseau, or Marx. There is value in a cyclic theory like that of Vico, the brilliant enemy of "magnificent opinions concerning antiquity," the bias of the historian in favor of his subject matter.

Within human limitations our lecturers have avoided this error of magnificence or magnification. Their instrument is the microscope, but the microscope brings to light the flaws in strength as well as the tensile structure. A better case for fourteenth-century literature could have been made by calling on great names like Dante and Chaucer, and Grace Frank made this point when she accepted the task of revealing the best features of the century in France. Nevertheless, she has shown us that the momentarily hesitant France, exhausted from the two great preceding centuries, still had something to contribute. Giving the theory of war as an inhibitor of literature some content beyond the bare cliché, she shows that war was accompanied by cynicism and religious schism and the emptiness of the nostalgic Gallic chivalry. She traces new forces—the rising bourgeoisie, Machaut's *Voir Dit* which gives romance new substance, Froissart's light grace and serenity in the presence of shifting values, and Deschamp's satirical sense of responsibility. Her strongest claim is for the drama, for the scope and variety of character in *Miracles de Nostre Dame,* for the cyclic anticipations of *Palatine Passion,* for the touch of proletarian realism in *Le Jour du Jugement.* Though the work of the professional man of letters revealed a dependence on fixed, traditional sources and effects, the drama of the citizenry "had a forward movement, a potentially dynamic vitality."

Harry Bober likewise turns to the nations north of the Alps, where he discovers the source of the insights gained by Giovanni Pisano and even the unique Giotto, Jean Pucelle's transcendence of the best of the earlier Gothic painting, and the antecedents of Van Eyck's exploitation of the individual and particular. His major contribution is a reassessment of French Rayonnant architecture, which is usually compared unfavorably with the late

Gothic of England and Germany. Bober argues that Rayonnant had new architectural problems to solve, that it solved them, that it played a genuine part in the evolution of the Gothic, and that it leads without interruption to the better regarded Flamboyant of the next century.

In his article on mediaeval education, Father Astrik Gabriel finds educational expansion and idealism in both the fourteenth century and our own; each century has its new elite and its waves of reform. Some eighty-seven colleges were founded in the fourteenth century, as contrasted with some twenty-five in the thirteenth and some thirty-three in the fifteenth. Father Gabriel sheds light on college finances and antipluralism, on the career professor known as Buridan, who could jest at a pope, and on the domestic facilities and atmosphere of the colleges and their autonomy in Germany and England. He reveals the personality of the masters, the enthusiasm of the students, and the virtues of scholastic disputation within the frame of argument and the frame of college walls. The colleges fostered new architecture in the quadrangle and the library and new art in the chapels. "The moral integrity of the college administration was an encouraging example in a period of strong competition for benefices. No power—king, pope, bishop, ecclesiastical or lay authority—ever attempted in this century to press its own candidates for college fellowships." Academic freedom, assailed as it always has been, has its roots in solid history. For the mediaeval administrators were also teachers, though even then Alain could compare their organization to "une raison mécanique. Tout y est sans reproche, et tout y est inhumain." A warning to modern administrators, caught in the cross-currents of a mass civilization, with heavy pressures from all sides forcing them to emulate Caesar's wife rather than Caesar or Brutus.

This discussion of the colleges, which were not so cloistered as they seem, leads us to consider the encompassing role of the state. With George Cuttino and Alan Gewirth we move into the area of politics, which conditions both education and art without destroying their autonomous resistance to outside tyranny.

Cuttino finds in the English *Modus tenendi parliamentum* a document that is in some respects more remarkable than the *Defensor pacis,* on which his fellow lecturer Alan Gewirth has lavished such penetrating analysis. He confirms Galbraith's date of 1316-24 and the hypothesis of William Airmyn's authorship, and provides a newly wrought biography which demonstrates Airmyn's status and parliamentary expertise. Thus he delivers a coup de grâce to the Maitland-McIlwain theory that the parliament of that time was essentially judicial in nature and function—in the *Modus* it is as political as it is today. Although the *Modus* is reformist and "advanced" in so far as it was written by an orderly administrator, who was enthusiastic for parliament to be the center of the realm but was plagued by the delinquencies of human nature, especially that found in aristocratic bodies, an early date for the work is not impugned. To establish a community of the realm, it is necessary that the magnate not merely possess the name *magnate* but that he attend the sessions of the ruling body: those who work attain the power. Thus the author of the *Modus* was a realist and no airy projector; if the barons are invited and refuse to appear, they cannot chain parliamentary action. Abstention is a doubtful weapon in true rule. The barons and the prelates are "still here, very much here as countless struggles attest, but the die had been cast." Cuttino lets the text speak for itself, and it speaks loudly for an institution about which we grow dangerously cynical today when passivity toward those who choose to act is more prevalent than in any preceding century.

In his article, Gewirth turns to the relationship of philosophy and practical politics. He selects "a concrete historical period, in which political conflicts took a very sharp form and evoked an extensive body of writings at once theoretical and polemical from men who were philosophers as well as publicists." Modern parallels tempt us: William of Ockham and mathematical logic, Nicholas of Autrecourt and Hume, Thomas Bradwardine and natural philosophers like Copernicus and Galileo. Even more tempting are parallels in the strict realm of politics: Dante and world government, Egidius of Rome's *plena potestas* and modern totalitarianism, the ties of Marsilius of Padua with Machiavelli, Hobbes, Luther, Erasmus, Rousseau,[2] and Marx.

Gewirth, however, seeking something deeper than these obvious parallels, chooses Martin Grabmann's famous correlation between philosophy and politics and subjects it to a historical and philosophical critique. Grabmann argues that the Christian Aristotelians, like Thomas Aquinas, made Church and State autonomous but parallel because they held reason and faith to be self-sufficient, that the Latin Averroists like Siger of Brabant and Marsilius of Padua derived their antipapalism from their preference for reason over faith, and that the traditionalist Augustinians, like St. Bonaventura and Egidius of Rome, favored temporal power for the pope because they subordinated reason to faith. Yet to make the pope Faith and the emperor Reason is, Gewirth would argue, a self-evident absurdity. There are papalist Aristotelians and antipapalist Augustinians. Wycliffe and Luther are notable examples of the latter possibility, and an Averroist like John of Jandun is a quasi-papalist who almost paradoxically elaborates philosophic reason as a twin truth to religious faith. Yet we need not deny *in toto* the relevance of philosophy to politics. Though the Augustinian Wycliffe and the Averroist Marsilius are both antipapal, life in their ideal states would indeed be different, for Wycliffe remains religious and Marsilius secular in emphasis. So Gewirth rounds the circle with a clear assertion that mind plays its part in politics through no dialectical determinism, but through the subtle variations which individual temper, historical situation, and creativity provide.

In his own way, each of our lecturers seems to have confirmed the "themes" of the conference. Thus, although France's literary advance is limited and sporadic; although the artistic advances north of the Alps are controversial; although the college system has human frailties which hamper its intellectual and material leaps; although parliament moves forward only to encounter a major conflict with the despots of the Renaissance; and although political theory retrogresses as well as advances, we may say that human striving makes appreciable gains in a century still conscious of its agrarian and feudal roots. An idea of progress which considers the goal achieved or soon achievable with some simple formula is empty enough; but history may yet be redemptive and not tragic. "Man moved then, as now, tortuously, but with both promise and achievement."

1. R. G. Collingwood, *The Idea of History* (New York, 1956), pp. 68, 92, 102.

2. Marsilius seems to me not so much an apostle of "natural goodness" as a defender of a republican notion that the "people" is always the best authority on its own desires and sufferings. As Gewirth puts it in his *Marsilius of Padua: The Defender of Peace* (New York, 1950 and 1956), II, xli: ". . . The people's will, far from being subject to the vagaries of shifting appetites and partisan advantage, is inevitably directed to the common benefit." The elites who find multiple arguments against this basic assumption of democracy may be always questioned for their *cui bono.*

A REAPPRAISAL OF RAYONNANT ARCHITECTURE

HARRY BOBER

According to one of the oldest general propositions in the historiography of art, modern painting began in fourteenth-century Italy with Giotto. This majestic simplification is still held to be essentially correct, for it is certainly true that from the beginning of the *trecento* Italian painting shifted its course away from the mediaeval line and toward the Renaissance, and initiated fundamental changes which had direct consequences on the entire future of Western art. The modernity and novelty of Giotto's paintings were fully apparent to his contemporaries, and early testimony to this effect is abundant. The most familiar to all is Dante's acclaim of this painter's art as the *dernier cri*: " . . . And now Giotto hath the cry, so that the fame of the other [Cimabue] is obscured." [1] This early enthusiasm was heightened in the middle of the fifteenth century by the addition of a historical element in Ghiberti's assertion that Giotto "introduced the new art." [2] It was on this theme that Vasari elaborated a hundred years later in his famous *Lives,* in which he hailed Giotto as the one who "threw open the gates of the true way to those who afterwards exalted the art to that perfection and greatness which it displays in our age." [3]

A critical perspective on the past is claimed as one of the higher virtues of modern historical scholarship, but it appears that it has added nothing to what the early writers had to say about the *trecento*. This is true not only of the broad lines of the development of painting that they traced, but also for the valuations they placed upon the individual artists. Those masters who were great in the eyes of Ghiberti and Vasari hold much the same places of relative esteem in modern criticism. If anything, such names as Giotto, Duccio, and Simone Martini are more widely and commonly known today than ever before. The work of these artists and the judgment of their contemporaries constitute one of the most indelible marks made by the fourteenth century on all sub-

9

sequent cultural history, and in the very fact of that historical self-consciousness which led the early critics to these valid appraisals may be read an equally significant tribute to their historiographical modernity. Such attainments are considerable even though they are limited by being operative only within the geographically circumscribed sphere of Italy. In their views on the rest of Europe, these early writers were as insular as any ancient Greek for whom an unquestionably superior self stood at the center of the world, while the rest was indiscriminately lumped together as variously and barbarically foreign.

If the scholarship of the past two centuries has had little to add to the profound intuitions about Italy of the *trecento,* it has had much to say about the wealth and diversity of art north of the Alps. For the early Renaissance writers there shone only the light of Italy and ancient Rome. For them Byzantine art of the Greek East loomed dark and harsh, and the art of the "barbarous Goths" to the north allegedly stagnated amid the deep shadows of a millennial eclipse which had brought the "true art" of classical antiquity to a close. It was only with the mediaeval revival of the eighteenth century that Gothic art was discovered for us as a positive and benign affair.[4] The recovery first came about in England, where architectural historians saw in Gothic their own national style, and its worth was placed on a par with the long approved Renaissance and Classical works. The name "Gothic," no longer a stigma of opprobrium or defensive apology, became the badge of enthusiastic nationalism and ubiquitous revivalism. Even Gothic painting and sculpture, which had lagged behind architecture in this restoration, became fully reinstated by the end of the nineteenth century. It was only in our own half-century, however, that historical studies were freed from nationalistic antiquarianism and pietistic romanticism, and a proper picture of Gothic art was more clearly and completely formed. The fourteenth century, of all the phases of Gothic art investigated, remained the last to attract concentrated attention. Now, however—especially in the field of painting—we have advanced to a position from which this area of Northern art may be viewed in a balanced relationship to developments in the rest of Europe.[5]

It is the main purpose of this paper to bring into focus one major area of fourteenth-century art that is still very much slighted, and is the subject of serious injustice in criticism. I refer to the architecture of the North—mainly that in France—which is perhaps the most unfortunate victim of old prejudicial taste. Its neglect may be due to the depleted energies of scholarship, exhausted after the hundred-years war of revival of mediaeval art. Although it would be of interest to examine in their entirety the broader lines of the newly formed picture of the general relationships between the North and the Italian *trecento,* these may be touched upon only superficially, and only as a setting for the architectural problem proposed.

Although less familiar than the Italian masters of the same period, the North had its major and minor painters and sculptors, the stars and constellations of a brilliant Northern hemisphere of art. The names of Jean Pucelle, Jean Bondol, André Beauneveu, Jacquemart de Hesdin, Melchior Broederlam, and others, suffice to remind us of the high degree of artistic individuality and creativity of this area.

While the Byzantine teachers of the first Italian painters were given some acknowledgment—even if oblique—by Ghiberti and Vasari, the Northern Gothic schools and masters were practically ignored. Today, the Northern element in the Italian *trecento* is generally recognized. It is clear, for instance, that Giovanni Pisano's works reveal conscious French Gothic inspiration.[6] His ivory "Virgin and Child" of 1299 (Pisa) must have been indebted directly to such works as the *trumeau* figure of the Virgin and Child in the portal of the north transept of Notre Dame in Paris (*ca.* 1260). Even in Giotto, whose break with the inherited tradition is the most significant and impressive fact, there is a recognizable Gothic denominator in his basic concept of the figure as a modeled shell of outer form.[7]

The course followed in the development of painting shows that the dominant currents flowed from Italy to the North.[8] Florentine and Sienese innovations in spatial representation and narrative expression afforded solutions to problems which were also of interest to the Northern artists. This pattern of derivation is already overwhelmingly patent in the work of Jean Pucelle, the dominant artistic personality in French painting of the second quarter of the fourteenth century. The formal and dramatic means by which he was able to transcend even the finest of earlier Gothic painting in his miniatures for the *Hours of Jeanne d'Evreux* (*ca.* 1325) were derived from Siena.[9] Similar instances of Italian priority may be traced through the rest of the fourteenth century and into the early

fifteenth. Best known among the examples from the end of this
interval is the miniature of the "Presentation of Christ" in the *Très
riches Heures* at Chantilly (*ca.* 1411), painted by one of the
brothers Limbourg. It is thoroughly Italianate and almost a miniature replica of a painting of the same subject by Taddeo Gaddi.[10]

But if Northern painting developed in the wake of Italian developments during the *trecento,* the painters were far from being
docile recipients of new formulas. It is ever apparent that the
Northerners absorbed and assimilated their Italian sources, adapt-
ing them to their own purposes and traditions. Jean Pucelle's
style, for example, for all its indebtedness to Sienese art, could
hardly be confused with the latter. Essentially and primarily,
Pucelle belongs to the line of Gothic continuity running from the
late thirteenth century; and it is that tradition which he trans-
forms, without departing from it. He carries Gothic painting from
a style in which silhouetted figures and architecture are set against
an opaque background to a phase in which architecturally defined
perspective interiors serve to contain or articulate a unified narrative presentation. In the work of Jean Bondol, this line of development may be observed at a later stage, which may be illustrated
by the dedication miniature from the *Bible of Charles V* in The
Hague, which was signed and dated by the artist in 1371.[11] Here,
the whole picture area has been integrated in spatial terms which
subsume even the more obvious Italianate elements, such as the
perspective floor. The total effect is entirely different from the
rational Italian system of structured space and sculptured figures,
especially when we compare this miniature with contemporary
works by the followers of Giotto. In the Bondol miniature, the
whole is primarily a factor of light and the way it plays in the
illusory spatial unit of the scene. All the elements are bound
together in the soft luminosity of a tonal envelope. In place of
figures that are sculptured volumes, there are delicately textured
gradations of minute light particles. Even the fleur-de-lis backdrop
suggests a tonal screen, rather than a delimiting barrier, and
implies a potential luminous extension of the space.

By the end of the fourteenth century, there is a remarkable convergence between Italy and the North in the so-called International Style.[12] (Paintings of that period are still the subject of
footnote controversies, in which they are attributed and re-attrib-
uted, back and forth, between Italy, Paris, and other places.)
However, in the midst of that convergence and exchange, and

out of it, came the famous parting of the ways after about 1400, in which Italy turned, with conscious deliberation, to classical examples and principles, around which her further exploitation of naturalism was oriented. In the North, the now rampant interest in nature reached a climax of another kind, one that was recognizably different from the Italian. Gothic naturalism, founded in the thirteenth-century scholastic discovery of the world of man's surroundings, was sharpened and made more individual in fourteenth-century nominalism and in art. Every single thing and all of its accountable parts that were accessible to the senses were newly fascinating to the painter and sculptor.

Thus by different roads North and South reach what appears to be the same point. It is for this reason that we find such striking affinities between the "Adam and Eve" of the Ghent altarpiece (1432) by the brothers Van Eyck, and those in Masaccio's "Expulsion" in the Brancacci Chapel (1426-28), although Masaccio proceeds from classicizing principle and idealism, and Jan Van Eyck is intent upon the individual and the particular. In this difference lies the profound basis for the divergence in the subsequent history of these two powerful, independent, although at times interacting, artistic movements. From this point on, both North and South share equally as determinants of the future of painting. The same phenomenon may be observed in the sculpture of this period, the development of which parallels what we know of painting, though it has not yet been so thoroughly explored. It may be sufficient, therefore, to turn to that critical point of convergence and divergence at about 1400 for an illustration. Donatello's "St. Mark" of about 1416 [13] arrives at the new ideal naturalism of the Renaissance out of generalizing humanistic principle which is deeply classical in sympathy. The North arrives at an analogous, and equally consequential, modernity in the art of Claus Sluter. His "Isaiah," from the "Well of Moses" (ca. 1400),[14] also shows a startlingly convincing grasp of the whole, which is supported by an authoritative command of the parts. But Sluter's realism is not that of abstract and general humanistic principle. It is rather an achievement of pictorial totality, which is attained by a painstaking record of empirical observations of the surface; he proceeds from the individual particles of visible matter, in an almost microscopic geography, whose sum is the reconstituted whole.

Architecture alone appears to be isolated and exceptional in this larger context, and it is indeed remarkable that it offers nothing which is recognizably comparable to the phenomenon of convergence in painting and sculpture. Renaissance architecture has been vaguely set against that of the late Gothic of the North, especially that of the Flamboyant style, as a complete antithesis. Brunelleschi's Church of the Santo Spirito (1435 ff.), for example, is rational and mathematical in method, classical in its elements, and humanistic in scale and compositional principle.[15] Man, the observer and participant, provides the key unit of proportion by which the whole is related and harmonized. A fifteenth-century church in France, such as Celles-sur-Belle (Deux-Sèvres) (Plate XVIII), is the opposite in principle and in detail. In that church, man is dwarfed, perhaps lost, in measureless, uninterrupted space, mysterious light, and continuous movement.

The original and distinctive character of fifteenth-century Northern architecture has, by now, been rather generally recognized. But in the historical studies of art, there is a telling void, for most writers, in one way or another, cut or taper off the history of Gothic architecture with the late thirteenth century. At best, they make an apologetic allusion to its decline, or fall, in the fourteenth century before proceeding to an enthusiastic epilogue for the more spectacular monuments of the fifteenth. The only exception is made in the case of England; France is left in limbo. France especially, says Pevsner, "did not wake up to the spatial and ornamental implications of the Late Gothic style until the end of the fifteenth century."[16] Exceptions are admitted,[17] but the great creative drive of the fifteenth century in the North is seen in England and, more especially, in Germany. (The *Waldleben* style of Germany is well illustrated by the Church of St. Georg in Dinkelsbühl [1448-92],[18] whose richly elaborate vaulting textures the spatial progression, making Celles-sur-Belle seem barren.) Such a general picture is misleading and more than unjust, however, for we are asked to believe that once the great cathedrals of the thirteenth century had been completed, the original creative drive was totally exhausted, and Gothic architecture petered out or degenerated inconsequentially at the very center of its origin in the Île de France. The presumed decline is usually loosely connected, in a causal way, with the Hundred Years' War, the Black Death, and other disasters, which are convenient in time.[19] Without even troubling to invoke catastrophic disruptions, students report that the decline simply continues in the fifteenth century.

The point at which this decline from riches to poverty supposedly occurred falls somewhere in the last quarter of the thirteenth century, at the time when the style shifts from High Gothic
to what the French scholars have named *le style rayonnant*.[20] I
think we can and should offer a much better explanation of what
happened than the mere assertion that Gothic architecture had
completed all its purposes in France by the second half of the
thirteenth century, and that afterward it merely spread, radiating
over the rest of Europe.[21] If proponents of the Rayonnant credit
this architecture with a modicum of virtue as a style on the
plateau of diffusion, other critics dismiss it without any allowance.
Against the outline of what had been sought and attained in the
pictorial arts of fourteenth-century France, we have the flat declaration by the authoritative English historian, Francis Bond, that
thirteenth-century French architecture "died without an heir." [22]
There is nothing inherently impossible in the proposal that an
architectural decline occurred during a period when painting and
sculpture advanced with conspicuous success, but it does invite
thoughtful questioning—questioning that reveals ultimately that
this was actually not the case.

In the twelfth century, from its beginning to the attainment of
High Gothic with Chartres, Gothic architecture of the Île de
France was distinctly experimental, seeking new means by which
this marvelous new style might be perfected.[23] The architects of
the cathedral at Laon, for example, still tried to combine the
tribune galleries of the Romanesque cumulative and additive
principle, with the triforium and the newly freed great clerestory
(Plate I). But where the simple cylindrical piers of the nave show
an even flow of the individual bays from west to east, the vaults
treat a double bay as the single unit, by virtue of the use of sexpartite vaults in which three main intersecting ribs are extended
over a pair of normal bays.[24] The sexpartite vaults, in other words,
are still an imperfect solution from the Gothic point of view. The
unvaried sequence of nave piers partly camouflage the difficulty,
but, at the same time, they announce the ambition of achieving
a continuous and unbroken sweep of the whole nave as a spatial
unit. The church at Chars (Seine-et-Oise),[25] (Plate II), like Notre
Dame in Paris, uses a circular rose, unglazed, at the triforium level,
an overt indication of the experimental efforts to find a suitable
treatment of the nave elevation. Like Notre Dame and Laon,

Chars preserves the tribune gallery, which is, from the point of view of Gothic style, an immense and disturbing spatial interval; for the tribune is an inert, dark, and restrictive element in the interior design. That these were crucial problems and of real concern to architects, is revealed not only by the very diversity of such solutions, but also by the consistent efforts made to resolve them. The Cathedral of Bourges is a spectacular instance of the elimination of the tribunes altogether, but it is accomplished by a tour de force.[26] The nave elevation was designed in much the same proportions that it would have had with the tribune gallery, but no tribune was built, and so the nave arcade rises to an inordinate height, as do the adjacent aisles. The calculating ingenuity of the Bourges architect is further visible in his effort to minimize the static effect of the colonettes clustered about the main piers. He has reduced the colonettes to utmost and exceptional slenderness, and carried them consistently on all the piers, from the bases up into the vaults. The solution is not logical, gothically speaking, for the piers do not really tell the truth about the vaults since these are sexpartite. Thus, the vaults span *two* bays, but the piers and the colonettes make it appear that each individual bay has its own complete vault. The general effect of the Bourges interior is spectacular; but although it is charmingly gangling, it is less than elegant.

The classic type for the Gothic interior is virtually present in the Cathedral of Sens (Yonne),[27] where the tribune has not merely been "excised" from an elevation with the old proportions, but excluded in principle; the triforium and clerestory have been brought down into the zone which the tribune occupied in Laon and Notre Dame. The nave elevation is now formed of nave arcade, triforium, and clerestory, related in normal proportions of height; and a combination has been formulated which announces the future tripartite elevation of the classic Gothic cathedrals. As we see it at Sens, the system is still retrospective in one respect, however; namely, in the sexpartite vaults and the double-bay unit. The piers, at least, indicate the vaulting situation quite logically, in that they show an alternation between simple cylindrical piers of columnar design and compound piers of bundled colonettes and shafts, running from the base to the springing of the vaults.

With the High Gothic cathedrals of the thirteenth century, the basic problems were resolved, and the solution, as seen in the naves of Chartres, Reims, Amiens (Plate V), and elsewhere, constitutes a classic Gothic architectural style.[28] These cathedrals employ uniform quadripartite vaulting for every individual bay, finally harmonizing the bays of the arcade level with the vaults, in a genuine and consistent uniformity and continuity. They eliminate the tribune gallery once and for all. Moreover, the stone tracery, which is now employed within the frame of the clerestory zone, not only serves to hold and support the glass of the windows, but functions in the articulation of that zone with the whole elevation of the bay. With the classic elevation established, the architects could turn to refinements within the system. One of the important things which needed attention was that the three parts of the elevation constituted three separate zones which were superimposed above one another but not effectively interwoven. They dealt with this problem by subjecting the tripartite elements to a bipartite relationship in proportion, between the nave arcade as one unit, and the clerestory and triforium as the other.

The process of making sophisticated adjustments within the Gothic architectural clockwork brought still another subtle refinement, that of opening a window in the exterior wall behind the triforium. This innovation was instituted with Pierre de Montereau's design for the nave of Saint-Denis (begun in 1231).[29] The effect of the glazed triforium (Plate III) was to permanently link its aesthetic destiny with that of the clerestory.[30] The idea spread quickly and became standard for both new construction and remodeling. It may be said to have been a pivotal factor in the extraordinary effect of the Cathedral of Beauvais (1247-72, Plate IV). The nave vault at Beauvais is of immense height (about 156 feet), the highest in Gothic building. The slenderness of the piers and the delicacy in the weight balance of the buttressing were achieved with such precarious finesse that the threshold of tolerable strain was passed in 1284, when the vaults collapsed. It was quickly rebuilt with reinforcement, however, and stands as the most spectacular symbol of Gothic architectural ambition, and as a visible expression of the powerful momentum which was driving Gothic further and further.

But it is not in the dazzling feat of Beauvais or in other sensational structures that the real, continuing search of Gothic is to be detected; for even in such works we can see that the architects were aware of still unsolved problems of principle.[31] In the highly developed piers of the Cathedral of Reims, for instance, there persists a deferential allusion to the classical columnar principle in so

far as the piers are accentuated by capitals; their cumulative effect
contains an element of static, metrical regularity. Even in the
brilliant choir of Beauvais, the distinctness of the divisions between
the narrow, successive bays is felt with a certain regularity. The
triforium, an elegant screen of tracery, remains subdivided into
separable units, each with its own gable, and separated from the
next by the wall colonette. These examples are by no means
exhaustive, but they will serve to illustrate some of the principal
elements of High Gothic architecture which the masters of the
Rayonnant period saw as problems and undertook to solve. And
these were not problems of mere detail, although the most that
has been said for the Rayonnant style is that it did make for
changes in secondary detail.[32] They are more than details, and
they are hardly secondary: they represent the visible "creaking
joints" of a yet imperfect system. In the eyes of the new generation
of architects, they were more or less disturbing factors blocking
the road ahead. The final solution of Gothic architecture would
not have been possible before these aesthetic, technical, and structural problems had been solved.

Precise limits for the duration of the Rayonnant have not been
proposed with any serious attempt at an exact definition. Although
it has been assigned to an interval as broad as that between 1250
and 1400,[33] we may take the span from about 1270 to 1370 as the
one which embraces most of its characteristic manifestations.
Already at Saint-Urbain of Troyes (Aube),[34] begun in 1264 and
almost finished by 1290, we see the new direction in its positive
aspect (Plate VI). The choir, completed by 1266, still employs
the triforium, but it is as nearly integral with the window as possible, and it has eliminated any vestige of the column by reducing
the stone of the tracery to a veritable web of stone. The windows
are glazed from buttress to buttress, and the tracery is so slender
that it becomes subordinated to structure and forms a delicate
filament against the light. In the nave, which dates from the second
building campaign which ended in 1290, the triforium has been
eliminated to effect a simple cage of light, which is supported on
the arcades. The capitals of the nave piers have been almost
entirely suppressed, and those which remain seem vestigial references to the old horizontal accents which marked that level. Furthermore, the mouldings of the nave arcades begin to merge with
each other and with the piers. This effect is produced by the deep
grooving of the profiles, but it is also a factor of the reduction of

the capitals. These changes tend toward a pictorial unification of those elements which had, in the past, been articulated in an arithmetic and geometric relationship.

It might be pointed out that Saint-Urbain represents an extension of the principle of the High Gothic small chapel, such as the Sainte-Chapelle of Paris, to a small church.[35] Although this is true, it does not alter the case for the character of the changes which were introduced, or the style in which the older elements were handled at this time. Indeed, it is significant that this period selected the chapel type to be continued and developed. Between the Sainte-Chapelle of Paris and Saint-Urbain of Troyes stands the chapel of the Virgin of Saint-Germer (Oise) of 1259-66,[36] as an intermediate step in a definite progression. Nor is it surprising to find the type further developed in the rest of the thirteenth century and throughout the fourteenth. The idea of the one-cell church lent itself well to a very direct statement of complete spatial unification, and it is this which accounts for the sustained interest in the Sainte-Chapelle type. The Cathedral of Albi (Plate VII), begun in 1282 and completed during the fourteenth century, is the best-known example.[37] It differs in radical essentials from the royal chapel in Paris, however, and the almost unbroken lines of the piers provide one key to the differences. The treatment of light also differs emphatically in spirit, for Albi plays on a sharp contrast between the darker chapels of the lower level and the concentrated lights of the deep clerestory. Kindred in its approach to the single-space-unit principle, is the Jacobin Church at Toulouse, ca. 1260-1305 (Plate VIII), actually a hall-church type, whose supports form a medial subdivision of the whole.[38] That this church belongs to the special architecture of the mendicant orders does not suffice to account for its conscious use of the vaulting ribs as a textural enhancement for the entire upper zone. The sweep of the piers to the very level of the vaults also contributes to the effect of a drive toward total unification of the interior.

The application of the glass house or chapel type to churches represents one of the positive lines of the architectural advance of the fourteenth century in the direction of realizing the ambition to achieve a pictorial effect. In the church of Notre-Dame-des-Menus at Boulogne-Billancourt in Seine (Plate IX), built in a single campaign between 1329 and 1348, we have a small and nearly pure gem of this kind.[39] Here we see how, at every stage, the elements of articulation (which had been accentuated in the High Gothic of the thirteenth century) have become subordinated within a new concept of total unification. An ingenious and highly original extension of the single-cell system was carried out in the very fine Cathedral of Saint-Pierre (formerly the monastic Church of Saint-Bénédict) at Montpellier (Plate X). This church was conceived, planned, and built in one burst of enthusiastic activity, between 1364 and 1367,[40] under the sponsorship of Pope Urban V, whose devotion to Montpellier stemmed from his years spent there as professor of canon law. Detailed correspondence and records remain to tell us that he was extremely pleased with the result. It is rather bare now, but we know that it had paintings, statues, gold and silver furnishings, and other embellishment, which would have provided those textural accents and the tonal warmth now lacking. The progression toward complete and consistent unity is beautifully achieved in the whole, and is felt at every critical structural juncture. The piers are almost unbroken in their flow from the floors into the vaulting ribs; the nave arcades form "picture frames" for the intervening spatial units of the chapels and the rich furnishings that they originally contained.

In the main line of development of the great cathedrals, the vital continuation and transformation are everywhere apparent; but no façade tells the story more brilliantly and completely than that of Strasbourg (Plate XI).[41] Between 1276, when the new façade was begun, and 1365, when the base of the towers had been reached, was constructed one of the finest west fronts of any Gothic cathedral. It was new, however, and different from any before. The stone masses of the tower foundations and buttresses could hardly be eliminated, but they are beautifully transformed, and are expressed in the spatial and textural terms of that pictorial unification by which the Rayonnant began to carry Gothic architecture to its logical conclusion. We have the impression of penetration throughout, and the actual window openings seem no more than larger accents that are incidental to the perforation of the entire façade. Depth is suggested not so much by the actual volumes, but by the succession of spatial screens and the interplay of light among them. In place of the logic of the articulated façade structure of Amiens, Reims, or other High Gothic cathedrals, we have a pictorial concept of screened surface and depth, in graphic, linearized terms. The openings and solids interpenetrate in a lacework, or harpwork, of fine traceries, spun over the entire structure. But the process did not end with the break in the building campaign in 1365, for it was taken up again in 1399, when the north octagon of the tower was begun. It was completed in 1419, and the spire was added between 1420 and 1439.

The interiors of the cathedrals underwent analogous transformations, which are even more remarkable in some ways because they entailed the design and manipulation of complex units of extended space. The Cathedral of Séez (Orne),[42] whose choir, ca. 1270-94 (Plate XII), belongs to an early stage of the Rayonnant, points to one of the solutions found to the problems encountered in achieving pictorial unity. The triforium and clerestory are united as glazed areas, and the nave arcades have been ornamented in a unique way with individual gables. Indeed, the vertical bars of tracery for the triforium originate from the level of these gables, announcing the intention of using the three traditional elevation zones. The whole reads as a controlled progression of light from plane to depth, just as in painting. The clerestory is a simple plane; the triforium, screened by the tracery, develops limited depth; and the main arcades lead to the deeper spatial intervals of the aisles. Together the aisles comprise a framing zone of cubic light compartments, thanks to the bold glazing of the outer walls of the lower story. In a sense, the piers remain old-fashioned, but they are not without novel subtlety, for the use of a single slender shaft, carried from base to vault, reduces to a minimum the divisions between the bays. This allows the upper walls to read with more fluid continuity in a horizontal, as well as a vertical, direction.

It is clear that we are now in a period in which the newly felt possibilities of Gothic architecture are pursued in a vital, creative, and highly original way. But the point may be worth fuller illustration: At Saint-Thibault, in the Côte-d'Or in Burgundy (ca. 1297 to post 1323),[43] we are struck by a remarkable reinstatement of a blind gallery as part of a doubled triforium (Plate XIII). The blind gallery is related to a unified vertical process, a continuous tracery web that is formed with incredible gracility. This web serves as a coloristic accent between the light plane of the clerestory and the screened lighted space of the glazed triforium. The experiment with this idea at Saint-Thibault shows, as clearly as anything could, the calculated intent with which plane and depth, dark and light, structure and texture, were used as the conscious aesthetic means by which the Rayonnant sought to achieve new effects related to new purposes. Such departures are most indicative for a positive interpretation of the more "classical" Rayonnant three-story glass cage, such as Saint-Sulpice-de-Favières in Seine-et-Oise (Plate XIV).[44]

Constructed at about this same time, the Benedictine Abbey Church of Saint-Ouen at Rouen, the choir of which was built between 1318 and 1339 (Plate XV),[45] represents a purer return to the main line of the older French Gothic, but with the addition of such new ideas and elements as we have observed from previous examples. The piers became continuous, all-embracing "moldings," while the upper elements of the nave elevation were subdivided to such an extent that they became virtually linearized. As at Séez, the outer walls of the aisles are meant to be read in relationship to the whole design of the nave. Between the piers, there is total fenestration (Plate XVI), and a subtly refined development from plane to expansive spatial units. From walls of light in the clerestory, we progress to screens of light in the triforium and in the view through the arcade to the outer wall. The vast unity of the nave is framed by a ring of light, composed of the aisles and the ambulatory—the counterpart in depth of the crowning plane of light in the clerestory.

In making my claims for a positive interpretation of the French Rayonnant, I am well aware of those views which give English architecture exclusive priority in the fourteenth century. Enthusiasm for English architecture needs no new endorsements. However, the historical evaluation of it needs correction and amendment along the lines of a total stylistic analysis rather than excerpted citations of individual elements of the style. For instance, it is said that the English Decorated style, *ca.* 1250 to 1330 or 1340, is the catalyst which, in the last quarter of the fourteenth century, brought architecture back to life in France with the beginning of the Flamboyant.[46] (The Rayonnant, it will be recalled, is considered a dying—if not dead—architecture.) I have tried to show that, to the contrary, French architecture vigorously pursued new aims during this period that is presumed to be a void. How does the French Rayonnant, thus revealed, compare with the contemporary English style?

The Decorated is well represented by Exeter Cathedral, the nave of which was built in 1328-42 (Plate XVII), which has been called "perhaps the most harmonious of all church interiors of the Decorated (or Curvilinear) style." [47] The elaborate lierne vault is no doubt splendid, but to the eye accustomed to "orthodox" principle in Gothic architecture, the effect of that vault upon the interior is strangely incongruous. Instead of providing a climax toward which the nave moves in its vertical development, the vault overwhelms the interior. One reason for this is that the ratio of the height to the width is "crushingly low," [48] so that the vaults appear to seal the nave space. Another is the curiously evasive way in which Exeter and other English churches of the time deal with the problem of articulation between the ribbed vaulting system and the main piers.[49] Instead of being linked to each other or developing from and into each other, the wall shafts, which are drawn down from the vault ribs, rest on sculptured corbels that are set just above the abaci of the piers. In effect, this original but disruptive device masks the point of expected juncture of the shafts with the piers in so far as continuity and articulation are concerned. The different color of the piers, their abaci, and the number of the capitals of the colonettes accentuate the horizontal division in the design in a way which further militates against balance and harmony in the vertical development. We have but to think of such Rayonnant naves as that of the contemporary Saint-Ouen at Rouen (Plate XV) to appreciate the difference between the English system and the French, which clearly and cogently integrated these same elements.

The "Bishop's Eye" in the south transept of Lincoln Cathedral (*ca.* 1325) and the great east window of Carlisle (1293-1322) are among the most beautiful expressions of the English Curvilinear style.[50] The system of tracery which they employ anticipates by some fifty years its general use in French Flamboyant. But although they are, in this way, prophetic, their achievement is restricted to those individual parts of the building; the architectural style of the entire edifice is not affected. In the French Rayonnant, however, comparable additions and remodeling were carried out with scrupulous and subtle concern that such changes be at least integrated with the whole of that particular area of the structure. Thus on the interior face of the entrance wall of the north transept of the Cathedral of Meaux (Seine-et-Marne),[51] the added screen of wall tracery is composed in relation to a new triforium, so that the entire wall expresses the newer aesthetic of line, plane, light, and space. The fact that the architectural vocabulary is still that of the Geometric style, which English architects had already outgrown by the turn of the fourteenth century, becomes secondary. At Meaux, as elsewhere in France where similar remodeling was in progress, the composition follows the original principles and logic of the first Gothic; but, at the same time, it advances it, as a whole architectural system, in the new direction. The English architects relished and exalted the vaulting ribs, adding ridge-ribs, multiplying the tiercerons, and exploiting both the spatial and textural possibilities of ribbing with great ingenuity, as in the aisle vaults of Bristol (*ca*. 1298-1332) and in the glorious choir of Gloucester (*ca*. 1331-50).[52] This was obviously not an aspect of church architecture which entranced the French designers, however. The ridge-rib was known in France as early as the twelfth century, and the tiercerons are to be found in the local Angevin style of the thirteenth century.[53] It cannot be an accident, therefore, that these were not adopted more generally, and that the French used the elaborated rib system mainly for domical vaults or in tower vaults. We can only conclude that they were aware of the effect that such ribs had of tending to enclose and delimit space. As we have observed in the English examples, the elaborate ribbed vault created a textured surface whose effect conflicted with the logical relationships within the canonic system of structure, supports, vertical articulation, and continuity in space.

While English architecture of the fourteenth century may, in such respects, have departed emphatically from the fundamental line of Gothic style, it is not to be devalued on that account, nor can anything be detracted from the originality and precocity for which it is adequately recognized. Rather, its deviations—even aberrations—from "true" Gothic provide an important foil against which French architecture of the period may be better understood. To speak of "true" Gothic may seem to prejudge the issue, but Gothic style in architecture must have as its essential condition such principles as we may be able to find in that system which was begun and brought to fruition in France during the twelfth and thirteenth centuries. Whatever else is found in that interval may be shown to have been borrowed from the Île de France. The revaluation of French Rayonnant architecture proposed in this paper would indicate that in the fourteenth century, too, France remained true to the central principles and the main line of the Gothic development. Far from bringing about decline, Rayonnant architects carried Gothic style forward toward its logical conclusion along the lines of a most authentic principle. They completed the solution of those problems left by the thirteenth century and gave to the fifteenth its modern architecture.[54] And this accomplishment did not remain an internal affair, for we can see the diffusion of French Rayonnant beyond national borders in such works as Antwerp Cathedral.[55]

Celles-sur-Belle (Plate XVIII) is a pure continuation of French fourteenth-century style into the fifteenth century; its Flamboyant detail is practically invisible against the chaste perfection of that Rayonnant framework which is at the foundation of its style. The Church of Saint-Séverin in Paris is a more manifest Flamboyant transformation of the fourteenth-century style (Plate XX).[56] The continuous and unified Rayonnant piers have been twisted on the axial point in the ambulatory in an expressive response to the complex spatial situation in the eastern portions of the building. Here, however, is an instance in which the Rayonnant has not quite attained a satisfactory resolution of the aesthetic and technical problem of the Gothic church building. That the problem was seen and tackled, however, is perfectly plain when we look at the ambulatory of the Cathedral of Narbonne, whose eastern portions date from 1272 to 1319 (Plate XIX).[57] Here the attempt to achieve unity and continuity among the irregular bays of the ambulatory has been made by means of a novel treatment of the ribs and their corresponding moldings on the piers; but the "engaged colonettes" contrast awkwardly with the main body of the huge cylindrical piers.[58] At Saint-Séverin, however, the response of the piers to the rib-system in the vaults has been easily and harmoniously resolved. Indeed, this solution not only expresses the complex curving movements of the ambulatory, but enhances it. Here, then, was attained the final step in achieving total pictorial unity and the spatial equivalent in depth of those characteristics of Flamboyant style which had been superficially connected with tracery alone. Those *mouchettes* ("bellows") and *soufflets* ("falchions") of Flamboyant tracery are but the aesthetic keys of a stylistic score which expresses the dramatic, fused continuity in all of the architectural relationships of the whole structure.

The church at Brou, built as late as 1513-32,[59] may serve to remind us that what the fourteenth century achieved in its Rayonnant architecture made possible the final Gothic of the Flamboyant, the style which could and did survive in the North during that very century when painting and sculpture yielded more and more to the Italian Renaissance. Whichever of them we may prefer, it was Flamboyant which thrived as the strong, almost

impervious compeer of the architecture of revived antique principle in Italy. We might do well to speak of Rayonnant as Late
Gothic, and Flamboyant as Last, or Final, Gothic, by way of
expressing more adequately the full scope of the essential continuity which connects the entire development of Gothic architecture in France.

1. *La Divina Commedia, Purgatorio,* XI, 95-96, ed. H. Oelsner, trans.
Thomas Okey (London: J. M. Dent, 1933), p. 133.

2. *I Commentarii,* II, 3-4, ed. J. von Schlosser (Berlin, 1912), I, 35-37.

3. Giorgio Vasari, *Lives of Seventy of the Most Eminent Painters, Sculptors
and Architects,* ed. E. H. Blashfield, E. W. Blashfield, and A. A. Hopkins,
trans. Mrs. Jonathan Foster (New York, 1897), I, 13.

4. See Kenneth Clark, *The Gothic Revival* (London, 1928 [rev. ed., 1950]),
p. 30 n., for the seventeenth-century forerunners.

5. The most comprehensive presentation of the whole development in this
broad sense is to be found in Erwin Panofsky, *Early Netherlandish Painting*
(Cambridge, Mass., 1953), especially in the Introduction and first chapter.
There is no comparable treatment of the sculpture of this period, but an
extensive index to recent literature may be found in D. Roggen, "Prae-
Sluteriaanse, Sluteriaanse, Post-Sluteriaanse Nederlandse Sculptuur," *Gentse
Bijdragen tot de Kunstgeschiedenis,* XVI (1955-56), 181 ff.

6. Cf. John Pope-Hennessy, *Italian Gothic Sculpture* (London, 1955),
pp. 9 ff., 178 ff.

7. Erwin Rosenthal, *Giotto in der mittelalterlichen Geistesentwicklung*
(Augsburg, 1924). Note, especially, the striking comparisons given in the
plates.

8. Cf. Panofsky, *loc. cit.*

9. *Ibid.,* pp. 29 ff.

10. *Ibid.,* p. 63. Panofsky points out that although the Northern artists had
followed Sienese and North Italian inspiration earlier in the century, it was
not until the end of it that they were able to grasp the spirit and style of the
Florentine school.

11. *Ibid.,* pp. 36 ff., and Fig. 23.

12. Panofsky, *op. cit.,* Chap. ii.

13. H. W. Janson, *The Sculpture of Donatello* (Princeton, 1957), Plates
XVIII-XX.

14. Henri David, *Claus Sluter* (Paris, 1951), Plates X, XV.

15. Nikolaus Pevsner, *An Outline of European Architecture* (1st American
ed.; New York, 1948), Plate XLVII.

16. *Ibid.,* p. 60.

17. The architecture of the Midi is the one regional exception. See Raymond Rey, *L'Art gothique du Midi de la France* (Paris, 1934), p. 335: "Le déclin du XIIIᵉ siècle et la première moitié du XIVᵉ furent dans le Midi un printemps architectural." See also Pevsner, *op. cit.*, p. 60: "Only in the *midi* there exists work of European significance." Rey, however, sees in this architecture the link of continuity between Romanesque and the Renaissance: "Le gothique du Midi est le prolongement du roman" (p. 334), and "Si la Renaissance a retrouvé l'antiquité, elle a aussi amplifié et rajeuni le gothique français du Midi en l'étendant à toute l'Europe" (p. 335).

18. John Harvey, *The Gothic World* (London, 1950), Fig. 177.

19. Examples are found in such recent and specialized studies as that by Louise Lefrançois-Pillion, *L'Art du XIVᵉ siècle en France* (Paris, 1954), p. 19: "Le malheur des temps et aussi, sans doute, l'abondance des constructions du siècle précédent, expliquent suffisamment la rareté des chantiers importants ouverts au XIVᵉ siècle."

20. Cf. Robert de Lasteyrie, *L'Architecture religieuse en France à l'époque gothique* (2 vols.; Paris, 1926-27), Vol. I, Chap. iv, and Vol. II, pp. 13-20, still the most satisfactory discussion of the character and development of the plans, elevations, exteriors, details, and so on, of fourteenth-century architecture in France.

21. C. R. Morey, in *Mediaeval Art* (New York, 1942), virtually omits any discussion of fourteenth-century architecture. Jean Bony, in *French Cathedrals* (London, 1951), pp. 12-13, treats the changes brought in with Rayonnant with sympathetic insight, but seems to regard the development as an anticlimax. De Lasteyrie, in *op. cit.*, I, 113, is, at least, well aware of the continuity between fourteenth- and thirteenth-century architecture, and of the character of the changes made in the parts of the structure ("l'art gothique n'avait cessé d'évoluer"). He maintains, furthermore, that the changes made during these two centuries are analogous to those made during the twelfth and thirteenth. However, he does not attach so much importance to the changes in the fourteenth century as to those in the thirteenth. Moreover, he does not view the character of Rayonnant style as a distinct achievement, but as a continuous modification of parts. Indeed, for him the thirteenth and fourteenth centuries represent a single period and style (cf. Vol. II, p. 5 n. 1).

22. *Gothic Architecture in England* (London, 1905), p. 128: "French architecture was practically annihilated. Her thirteenth-century style ceased to be; and died without an heir." Although she states it in less blunt terms, this seems also to be the belief of Lefrançois-Pillion, in *op. cit.*, p. 8, who places painting and sculpture on a par with progressive developments in Europe but finds architecture "celui qui reste le plus tributaire du passé et paraît le moins gros d'avenir."

23. Cf. Erwin Panofsky's brilliant analysis of this development of the High Gothic system, in *Gothic Architecture and Scholasticism* (Latrobe, Pa.: Archabbey of Saint Vincent, 1951), pp. 44 ff. See also De Lasteyrie, *op. cit., passim*.

24. Cf. De Lasteyrie, *op. cit.*, I, 41, 43, for illustrations.

25. *Ibid.*, I, 17; also compare the illustrations on pp. 54, 55 for a similar treatment of the elevation at Notre Dame, which represents an earlier project for the interior.

26. See Bony, *op. cit.*, Plates LXXV, LXXVI; cf. De Lasteyrie, *op. cit.*, I, 93.

27. See Bony, *op. cit.*, Plates LXV, LXVI.

28. See Panofsky, *Gothic Architecture, passim.*

29. *Ibid.*, pp. 78-79. See also Sumner McK. Crosby, *L'Abbaye Royale de Saint-Denis* (Paris, 1953), Plates LVI-LVIII.

30. Arthur Kingsley Porter, in *Mediaeval Architecture* (New Haven, 1912), II, 278, says that this change was achieved at the expense of logic and "marked the first falling-off of Gothic architecture from strictly structural principles." In its retrospective orientation, this approach is typical of the view that High Gothic represents the final solution. The argument of the present paper is that Rayonnant architecture represents a pictorial ambition and achievement. Seen in this light, the glazed triforium is a precocious and logical step in the new direction.

31. Compare this view with the usual position that Beauvais marks the final peak of Gothic architectural development in France. See Pevsner, *op. cit.*: "Rheims, Amiens and Beauvais did nothing more than perfect [the system of Chartres]" (p. 42); and, "Rheims, Amiens and Beauvais are the final achievement of an evolution," and, later, "This balance of high tensions is the classic expression of the Western spirit—as final as the temple of the 5th century B. C. was that of the Greek spirit" (p. 46).

32. "Il n'y aura plus évolution ou progrès que secondaire" (Lefrançois-Pillion, *op. cit.*, p. 18). Joan Evans, in *Art in Mediaeval France* (London, 1948), p. 94, cites as "the only great innovation of this time," the addition of the side chapels along the nave. De Lasteyrie, *op. cit.*, I, 113 and elsewhere, regards the changes as less important than those of the thirteenth century, although he is most alert to the changes and analyzes them in detail.

33. De Lasteyrie, in *op. cit.*, II, 5 n. 1, calls the period from 1140 to 1200 *gothique primitif;* it was followed by a single period from 1200 to 1400 which he calls *gothique.*

34. Porter, in *op. cit.*, II, 322, says: "St. Urbain, perhaps the lightest and most fragile of all Gothic constructions, represents the acme of rayonnant architecture, and were not its dates firmly established might well be assigned to an epoch at least fifty years later."

35. De Lasteyrie, *op. cit.*, I, 113.

36. *Ibid.*, I, 115, Fig. 82.

37. See Rey, *op. cit.*, pp. 99 ff., in which there are illustrations and comments about the original appearance of the interior before the addition of the tribunes.

38. *Ibid.*, pp. 55 ff.

39. Maurice Dumolin and George Outardel, *Les Eglises de France, Paris et la Seine (Répertoire historique et archéologique par département* [Paris, 1936]), pp. 289-90.

40. Raymond Rey, "La Cathédrale de Montpellier et ses origines," in *Congrès archéologique de France, CVIIIᵉ Session, Montpellier* (Paris, 1951), pp. 9-31.

41. Cf. Hans Haug, Robert Will, *et al., La Cathédrale de Strasbourg* (Strasbourg, 1957), Plates XV, XLIV, CIX, etc.; and E. Lefevre-Pontalis, in *Congrès archéologique de France, LXXXIIIᵉ Session, Metz, Strasbourg, et Colmar* (Paris, 1922), pp. 113 ff.

42. De Lasteyrie, *op. cit.,* I, 140-41, etc.

43. Marcel Aubert, "Saint-Thibault," in *Congrès archéologique de France, XCIᵉ Session, Dijon* (Paris, 1929), pp. 252-66.

44. See De Lasteyrie, *op. cit.,* I, 307-8.

45. Cf. André Masson, "Eglise Saint-Ouen," in *Congrès archéologique de France, LXXXIXᵉ Session, Rouen* (Paris, 1927), pp. 102 ff.

46. Cf. Harvey, *op. cit.,* p. 74: "The resulting English Curvilinear Decorated style invaded France, and became by virtue (or vice?) of French logic Flamboyant, when England had abandoned curves for the insular right lines of Perpendicular." Cf. also, Pevsner, *op. cit.,* p. 73. The position is usually supported by evidence that tracery forms in England seem to anticipate the Flamboyant adoption of similar designs in France, but this is not strictly true (cf. Bony, *op cit.,* p. 15). Moreover, the argument implies that Flamboyant *style* derives from architectural detail, and this is inherently unlikely. For reactions against the thesis of English priority, see Max M. Tamir, "The English Origin of the Flamboyant Style," *Gazette des Beaux-Arts,* XXIX (1926), 257 ff., and the conclusion: "It is more plausible to consider the curvilinear style and the flamboyant style as parallel in the application of certain decorative elements and of certain peculiarities of construction" (pp. 267-68).

47. Peter Meyer and Martin Hürlimann, *English Cathedrals* (London, 1950) p. 32.

48. Bond, in *op. cit.,* pp. 53-54, includes Gloucester and Tewkesbury in this class.

49. Cf. *ibid.,* pp. 240-41, which contains lengthy comments on the inadequacy, insecurity, and illogical character of the solutions in many of the English churches.

50. See G. H. Cook, *Portrait of Lincoln Cathedral* (London, 1950), Plates XXV, XXVI; and Bond, *op. cit.,* plate facing p. 128.

51. Cf. De Lasteyrie, *op. cit.,* I, 306, and II, 264. The principles underlying this system of giving a unified treatment to a wall by extending the tracery designs over solid areas is already announced in the designs of Jean de Chelles for the south transept façade of Notre Dame in Paris, begun in 1258.

52. Pevsner, *op. cit.*, Plates XXXV, XXXVII. For the aesthetic of the English elaboration of the ribbed vault, cf. Paul Frankl, "The 'Crazy' Vaults of Lincoln Cathedral," *Art Bulletin,* XXXV (1953), 95-107.

53. Cf. Frankl, *op. cit.*, p. 100. For Angevin Gothic, see De Lasteyrie, *op. cit.*, II, 82 ff., with illustrations.

54. Cf. such interiors as Saint-Satur in Cher (1361-67 ff.) which, but for the tracery, shows the essence of the fifteenth-century solutions (see the illustration in Porter, *op. cit.*, II, 235).

55. See the illustration in Harvey, *op. cit.*, p. 167; cf. pp. 70-71 for other examples.

56. Dumolin and Outardel, *op. cit.*, p. 54 ff.

57. De Lasteyrie, *op. cit.*, I, 110-11.

58. Cf. *ibid.*, pp. 286-87, for a discussion of this development in the treatment of the supports. Unfortunately, De Lasteyrie deals with this kind of experimentation as an interesting curiosity and only in its negative aspect. It can hardly be an accident that the Rayonnant architects found in the tiny pier colonettes of Bourges (1195-1260) a possible means for handling the difficult spatial aesthetic of the ambulatory, not only at Narbonne, but also at the Cathedral of Toulouse. De Lasteyrie speaks of the Narbonne colonettes as "si minces et si déformées qu'on ne peut y voir autre chose que des moulures." We may agree with him that this "n'est pas d'un heureux effet," but the colonettes do provide eloquent testimony to the deliberation with which the Rayonnant pursued the new aims.

59. See the illustration in Harvey, *op. cit.*, p. 166.

A RECONSIDERATION OF THE *MODUS TENENDI PARLIAMENTUM*

GEORGE P. CUTTINO

As a first-year graduate student casting about for background material in connection with a thesis entitled "Some Aspects of the Conduct of English Diplomacy in the Reign of Edward III, 1327-1339," I was introduced to a book by Egon Friedell. The title of it was *A Cultural History of the Modern Age*. Friedell was a retired Austrian actor, turned historian, who committed suicide after the Anschluss. His book, like Henry Adams' *Mont-Saint-Michel and Chartres,* is fascinating, provocative, and provoking— the sort of book a beginning student of the Middle Ages should read once and then try to put away along with other childish things. Friedell was convinced that "modern man" began in the year 1348, the year of the Black Death, and he was almost prepared to name the hour and the day. But like many such imaginative reconstructions of an age, Friedell's interpretation contains a grain of truth. The fourteenth century was one of the great historical crucibles in Western civilization. That is why it has always plagued historians; and that is probably why the volume on the fourteenth century in the Oxford History of England was among the last of that series to appear. It is not because we do not know enough about the fourteenth century. Sir Maurice Powicke remarked that had he waited another ten years he could never have written his volume on thirteenth-century England because of the vastness of the material to hand. We find ourselves in the same position: we know too much about the fourteenth century; we know so much that we despair of making generalizations without immediately having uncomfortable mental reservations.

On the other hand, there is no doubt that when we look at the fourteenth century we find ourselves face to face with ideas that, however deeply they may be rooted in the past or influenced by contemporary events, are essentially new and look toward the future. Marsilius of Padua, for example, as Alan Gewirth has shown us, is, with a bow to the Norman Anonymous, a person

31

with just such ideas. There is, however, another fourteenth-century document that is in some respects even more remarkable than the *Defensor pacis,* and it is this document that I wish to discuss.

I have called this paper "A Reconsideration of the *Modus tenendi parliamentum,*" and this title demands some explanation. The *Modus* is the *Dialogus de scaccario* of parliament, the earliest known treatise we have of that institution. It is extant in twenty-five manuscripts (six are translations) that range in time from the end of the fourteenth to the beginning of the sixteenth century, and it enjoys the distinction of having been exemplified, in its Irish version, under the great seal.[1] But, unfortunately, it has been the stepchild of English parliamentary historians. Coke swallowed it whole, but Prynne, calling it a "modern consarsination [*temp.* Henry VI] by some unskilled Botcher," castigated Coke for his "supertranscendent credulity to believe and affirm." [2] Stubbs followed Prynne, alluding to its "many misstatements" and to its "proved worthlessness,"[3] yet he printed a condensed version of it, based on Hardy's edition of 1846, in his *Select Charters.*[4] Pollard was the first historian of parliament to make use of the *Modus,* and he was taken to task by James Tait for having accepted it without reserve, although he had doubted "if the Modus is more scientific than Tacitus' *Germania.*" [5] Pasquet stated flatly that "the doubtful authority of that document is well known," [6] and Tout, puzzled by it, called it "Lancastrian" and dismissed it in a footnote.[7] The late Maude Clarke's exhaustive work on the *Modus* [8] opened a controversy rather than settled an issue. In an article, "The Interpretation of the Statute of York," the late Gaillard Lapsley remarked, in a manner reminiscent of that historical gadfly, J. H. Round:

> She [Miss Clarke] had convinced herself that the mysterious tract known as the *Modus Tenendi Parliamentum* could safely be treated as contemporary and official evidence as to the nature and organization of parliament and the political views underlying moderate public opinion in 1322. Accordingly she derived from this *ignis fatuus* of parliamentary history the ideal which inspired the Statute of York.[9]

The latest writer on English constitutional history states:

> It has been conjectured, for instance, with some plausibility, that a chancery clerk wrote the *Modus Tenendi Parliamentum* at this time, to constitute what must have been an extremely skilful and understanding manifesto for the Lancastrians in 1321.[10]

Now all this acrimonious discussion arises from three points. The first is the actual date of the *Modus,* which has been assigned by modern writers to the reigns of Edward II, Edward III, and Richard II. The second is the fact that the ideas in the *Modus* do not tally with the interpretation of the nature of parliament as Maitland is supposed to have conceived it and as McIlwain elaborated it.[11] Third, these ideas appear to most historians of parliament as being too advanced for the times and consequently as not being a true reflection of the actual climate of opinion as it has been conceived. Let us look at these points in turn.

The date of the *Modus* has now been established beyond all reasonable doubt. Miss Clarke and the late W. A. Morris, in independent studies, came within a year of each other, the former assigning it to the year 1322 and the latter to 1321.[12] Their arguments were perfectly convincing and should have settled the issue then and there, but Richardson and Sayles thought otherwise and assigned to the English version a later date than the Irish which, all are agreed, belongs to the late fourteenth century.[13] Professor Galbraith has dealt with this view completely and finally, and it can now be stated, without pinpointing the date as precisely as did Miss Clarke and Professor Morris, that it belongs to the period 1316-24.[14] We have to do, then, with a treatise from the reign of Edward II, and we have only to remember Tout's Ford Lectures to know that the place of the reign of Edward II in English constitutional and administrative history was not only large, but even crucial for future developments.[15]

Galbraith has done more than fix the date of the *Modus;* he has, in a most convincing argument, attributed it to a chancery clerk named William Airmyn (alias Ayreminne or Ayermin). As his argument can be buttressed from other sources,[16] we shall have to review the facts of Airmyn's life and career for whatever light they may cast on the ideas expressed in the *Modus.*

The *Dictionary of National Biography* states that he "was descended from an ancient family settled at Osgodby, Lincolnshire," but this is obviously a slip, for Airmyn is in Yorkshire, near Osgodby, Hemingborough, Cliffe, and Barlby, all of which places furnished the loconymics of prominent chancery clerks. He was, to quote the latest scholar who has been concerned with his career, "one of the greatest of the ecclesiastical statesmen of the fourteenth century . . . and one of the most important and influential men in the reign of Edward II. He was one of that large, close-knit group of clerks from the diocese of York which was the dominant influence in the royal administration throughout the reign." [17] Like so many others, he began his career late in the reign of Edward I, probably in the chancery, rather than in the exchequer, as the *Dictionary of National Biography* states. By 1307, he had sufficiently attracted the attention of his superiors, and consequently the royal favor, "to have in the forest of Galtres [co. York] four oaks fit for timber of the king's gift." [18] By the middle of the next reign Bartholomew de Badlesmere, steward of the king's household, in a letter to the cardinal priest of St. Ciriac in Thermis, referred to him as "discretum virum . . . dicti domini regis clericum specialem et cancellarie sue secretarium," and the king himself, writing to the cardinal deacon of St. Adrian, called him "dilectus clericus et secretarius noster confidentissimus" and later extolled his virtues in flowery terms of flattery to Pope John XXII.[19] To William himself he wrote in 1321: "Nous vous sauoms moit bon gre de la diligence et peniblete qe vous mettez en noz busoignes deuers vous. . . ." [20] Two weeks before Airmyn's death, in the following reign, Edward III, "having regard to his manifold services . . . and to the great place he has held for king and realm," granted that after his death the executors of his will should have free administration of his goods, money, jewels, animals, and other things." [21] Perhaps the sincerest compliment paid him came from one of his colleagues, John Walwayn, who as a chancery clerk probably knew him well: "uir prudens et circumspectus et, precipue in hiis que tangunt cancellarium domini regis, efficax et expertus." [22]

His career as king's clerk was more successful than most. "He was," Tout tells us, "the man to whom the foremost place was generally given among the keepers of the great seal, when the custody of the seal was put into the hands of a commission of chancery clerks. Moreover, he was the second chancery clerk to combine the offices of keeper of the rolls of chancery and keeper of the *domus conversorum* in which these rolls ultimately found their home." [23] As such, he was responsible for the transfer of the rolls of parliament to the custody of chancery.[24] He later (in 1322) became keeper of the privy seal and, in the reign of Edward III, treasurer.[25] He died on March 27, 1336, at his house at Charing near London. Sidney Lee, who wrote the account of him for the *Dictionary of National Biography*, remarked at the end: "The old verdict on his career, which stigmatised him as 'crafty, covet-

ous, and treasonable,' seems substantially just." But the most recent scholar who has examined the details of his life has finally,
after more than six hundred years, successfully acquitted him of
these charges.[26]

Two aspects of Airmyn's career need not concern us except for
their implications. He was a notorious pluralist [27] (but then most
king's clerks were) [28] who became bishop of Norwich. As such, he
must have been well versed in canon law, although there is no
proof that he was a doctor of it, as were quite a few of his colleagues in the king's service. He was intimately concerned in the
negotiations with France growing out of the War of Saint-Sardos,
and incurred the king's displeasure for his part in arranging the
terms of the treaty that ended it.[29] The point in this connection
is that any English envoy who had to deal with the tangled feudal
relationship between the duke of Aquitaine and his overlord had
also to know his Roman law, since he was almost inevitably bound
to be pitted against the skilled experts of the Parlement de Paris.[30]

As to Airmyn's economic status there is no doubt. In the thirty-
three years covered by entries on the Close Rolls pertaining to
his monetary transactions, he borrowed only £366-6/8,[31] which he
repaid, and he made 159 loans, the total of which was in excess
of £10,000, of which he was able to collect a little less than half
before his death. His debtors included the king, clerks, merchants,
priors, knights, and citizens of London.[32] This sum, in terms of
modern purchasing power amounts, at a conservative estimate,
to more than $1,000,000. Airmyn held lands in the counties of
Kent, Hertford, Cambridge, Westmoreland, Northampton, York,
Essex, Somerset, and Lincoln, some by temporary grants of issues
from the king, and others in his own right.[33] He was, to say the
least, a wealthy man long before he became bishop of Norwich.
He must have been interested in stable government, and the fact
that Badlesmere thought highly of him suggests that he had cast
his lot with the "middle party," headed by Pembroke, rather than
with the Lancastrians. At any rate, had he lived in a later age
and had he not been a cleric, he would surely have been one of
the landed gentry.

Airmyn's activities in parliament are, of course, of especial interest. He first appears in parliamentary records as proctor of
the Abbot of St. Augustine's, Canterbury, at the Hilary Parliament of 1306 held at Carlisle.[34] He was summoned, among justices and others of the council, to the Lenten and November Par-

liaments at Westminster in 1313.[35] He was present in council at
Northampton on October 22, 1314, in connection with the hearing of a suit between the abbot of Croyland and Thomas Wake.[36]
In the York Michaelmas Parliament of 1318, he received expedited petitions touching the Flemish and Robert Valoines, pre-
centor of York.[37] As keeper of chancery rolls he was present in
council in chancery in 1319 on an order being made upon the
petition of the abbot of Northampton granting that his name be
expunged from the register as a prelate liable to be summoned to
parliament.[38] In October, 1326, he was present in the extraordinary council at Bristol and joined in the election of the duke of
Aquitaine as regent and *custos* of the kingdom.[39] In the new reign,
he was present in the roles of petitioner, commissioner to treat
with the French, trier of petitions from Gascony, Ireland, Wales,
and the Isles, and councillor at the parliaments of 1327, 1328,
1331, 1333.[40] These entries are telling enough evidence of Airmyn's familiarity with parliament, but even more striking is the
fact that we have the first day-by-day journal of proceedings in
parliament from his own hand:

> Memoranda of the parliament of the lord Edward, king of Eng-
> land, son of Edward, king of England, summoned and held at
> Lincoln on the quindene of Saint Hilary in the ninth year of the
> reign of the said king [1316], set down by William Airmyn, clerk
> of the chancery of the aforesaid king, named and especially ap-
> pointed by the same king to this task.[41]

There is nothing like it again until 1330, after which time, with
the exception of two gaps, the practice becomes standard. On the
basis of this account and two other pieces of evidence, Richardson
and Sayles have concluded that "it is probable that he was clerk
of the parliament from 1316 onwards." [42] Surely, few people can
have been in so strategic a position for understanding parliament
or for knowing what people were thinking and saying about
parliament.

Let us pass on to the second point. If we take the argument of
the *Modus* and compare it with Airmyn's actual record of the
Hilary Parliament of 1316, we can consider the thesis that the
former, as I have said, does not tally with the interpretation of
the nature of parliament as Maitland is supposed to have conceived it and as McIlwain elaborated it. Here we have to do with

the question of whether parliament was essentially judicial or political in character, and this is but another way of asking whether it corresponded more to the Parlement de Paris or to the English parliament as we know it in later history.

On this point the *Modus* leaves little doubt. Its primary concern is with representation of the community of the realm and not with law or justice in any narrow legal sense of those words. Justices as such are mentioned in only eight of its twenty-six articles,[43] and serjeants of the king's pleas in only one,[44] and the chancellor, who is not yet a legal officer of the crown, is given preference over the chief justice for the task of making the opening speech, a duty that can be discharged by even a simple clerk.[45] Even in the physical arrangement of parliament, justices are placed below the higher clergy and nobility, the chancellor, and officials of the exchequer.[46] Article XV is even more explicit:

> . . . Nor is any justice in England a justice in parliament, nor do they have *per se* a record in parliament, except to the extent that fresh power has been assigned and given to them in parliament by the king and peers of parliament, as when they have been assigned with other suitors of parliament to hear and determine various petitions and plaints delivered in parliament.

Nor in the difficult cases and judgments considered by parliament is their role, or in fact, that of the chancellor, an important one,[47] "because all peers are judges and justices."[48] Indeed, neither justice nor chancellor is "of parliament."[49] The crucial article is Article XVIII, where the order of deliberating the affairs of parliament is set forth. These are clearly listed in descending order of importance. The first have to do with a state of war, if such exists, and with the royal family; the second, with "common affairs of the kingdom," and the most common are those concerned with the implementation of decisions already reached. In the third place are "individual affairs," by which we must understand "petitions." Obviously, only the last have to do with justice and a court of law as we would think of them. The second are primarily administrative, and the first are beyond doubt matters of state that are essentially political.

If we turn from theory—if, indeed, the *Modus* can be called theoretical—to fact, we find that the latter substantiates the former. Let us look at Airmyn's record of the Lincoln Hilary Parlia-

ment of 1316. In this connection, it may be useful to construct
a table of events in the order of their occurrence.

16 October 1315   Writs of summons are issued for a par-
                                liament to meet at Lincoln on the
quindene of Saint Hilary next [27 January 1316].[50]

28 January 1316   The king opens parliament in a cer-
                                tain chamber in the hospice of the
dean of Lincoln where prelates, earls, and others are gathered.
                        William Inge, one of the justices of
Common Pleas, makes the opening pronouncement to parliament,
stating that the king's reasons for summoning it were "the various
arduous negotiations touching the king himself and his kingdom
and especially his land of Scotland." He asks that these be handled
with dispatch, since the king is concerned over the long distances
some have had to travel and over the scarcity of food. Nevertheless, consideration of these matters is postponed until the arrival
of Thomas earl Lancaster and other magnates, whose counsel the
king desires. Until then, the prelates, earls, and others are to con-
vene daily and consider other matters.
                        John Sandall, the chancellor, and
others are directed to receive procurations and excuses and to
turn over to the king the names of those not coming nor excusing
themselves nor sending proctors so that "he may be able to
command what he ought."
                        It is agreed that petitions be received
and expedited "as it was formerly accustomed to be done at other
parliaments" and that they be received until the morrow of the
Purification B. V. M.

[3 February 1316]   Receivers are named.
                        The chancellor, treasurer, and justices
of the two benches are instructed to reduce to writing all matters
pending before them in pleas that cannot be settled outside parliament, to refer them to parliament so that they may be dealt with
there as they ought to be.

29 January 1316   It is agreed to proceed with petitions
                                until the arrival of the earl of Lancas-
ter and the other magnates. Hearers and expediters are appointed.

31 January 1316   In the king's presence, Humphrey de Bohun, earl Hereford, promises that the king will observe answers already given to petitions of the prelates, will correct insufficient answers, and will deal with those unanswered as it shall seem fitting to the prelates, magnates, and the king's council.

1 February 1316   In the king's chamber the bishops of Norwich, Chichester, Exeter, and Salisbury are sworn of the king's council; and the king names the bishops of Norwich and Exeter, Jean de Bretagne, earl Richmond, and the earl of Pembroke as lieutenants in his absence until the arrival of the earl of Lancaster and the other missing magnates.

12 February 1316   In the hall of the dean of Lincoln, in full parliament, Lancaster and the other absent magnates now being present, the king has the opening pronouncement repeated, "supplicating and enjoining the prelates, magnates, and his other faithful subjects present there that they counsel him on these matters and that they make him suitable aid." It is agreed that the prelates and magnates will deliberate these matters on the following day in the Chapter of the Church.

13 February 1316   The meeting is duly held, and it is agreed, and commanded by the king, that another meeting be held on the morrow at the house of the Brothers of the Order of the Blessed Mary of Mt. Carmel.

14 February 1316   It is agreed that a certain proclamation setting the price of provisions be revoked, and that they be sold at a reasonable price, as had been the custom before. Writs are sent out under the great seal.

                     A certain statute concerning sheriffs and hundreds is agreed upon. This, we know from another source, was done "by information of his prelates, earls, barons, and other great men of the realm . . . and also by the grievous complaint of the people," and by the assent of prelates, earls, barons, and other great estates.[51]

17 February 1316   In the presence of the king and prelates and magnates, the bishop of Norwich, by the king's mandate, reviews the previous items and adds that the king will abide by the Ordinances and also by the peram-

bulations of the forest made in the time of his father, reserving to the king his reasons against such perambulations. Letters and writs are issued about this.

The bishop also announces that he has spoken to Thomas earl Lancaster "certain words on behalf of the king to remove any doubt the earl is said to have had about the lord king; assuring him that the lord king bore him and the other magnates of his kingdom sincere and complete goodwill, and that he held them as his faithful and liege men in especial royal favour." The king wishes him to become chief of his council; and after some deliberation, Thomas agrees to this and is sworn. The earl had his conditions, which need not concern us, except that they were embodied in the form of a bill handed to Airmyn by the bishop of Norwich and Badlesmere, who on the king's behalf ordered him to enroll it verbatim.

20 February 1316   The magnates and the community of the realm grant the king specific military aid for the Scottish war, the details of which are duly set down. The king agrees to issue letters for himself and his heirs that this aid shall not constitute a precedent. By their advice, military service is to begin on 8 July 1316 at Newcastle-on-Tyne.

The citizens, burgesses, and knights of the shire concede an aid of "a fifteenth on moveable goods of citizens, burgesses, and men of cities, boroughs, and royal demesnes." Parliament ends.[52]

Now it may be that the Hilary 1316 Parliament at Lincoln was an extraordinary one. Certainly there were drawn knives, a good deal of profanity, and at least one bloody nose. But those were extraordinary times, and the burden of proof must lie with those who can demonstrate from skeletal records that the meat on the bare bones of parliamentary accounts during this reign was different from that suggested by Airmyn's journal. The conclusion seems to be perfectly obvious: we are dealing only secondarily with a "high court," and most certainly primarily with an institution whose business is above all political, and to a lesser degree, legislative.[53] This is exactly what the *Modus* implies.

We come now to the third and last point, that the basic ideas of the *Modus* are out of kilter with the times.[54] Here we are not primarily concerned with those articles of the *Modus* that attempt to establish a "standing operating procedure" (to borrow military terminology) for all parliaments. They are doubtless the products of bitter experience on the part of an exasperated clerk with an orderly mind. For the most part they embody measures of reform. Parliament, to the author of the *Modus,* was obviously a serious business, perhaps the highest and most serious business of the kingdom. Hence he makes elaborate provisions to ensure the presence of the king (doubtless influenced by Edward II's habit of sleeping late) and of all the component parts of parliament, specifying rather stiff fines for those who do not appear and send no proctors or excuses. It is important that parliament be held in a public place (there is obviously to be no behind-the-scenes skullduggery), that its members speak out and not mumble their words, that it be free of external pressures and disturbances, and that its proceedings be duly recorded and be made available even to a pauper, should any of them concern him. On this last point it may be unkindly remarked that we are possibly dealing with a bureaucrat who, like modern university administrators, is intent on creating more bureaucracy. Finally, parliament is not to be dissolved until all petitions have been answered; indeed, "if the king permit the contrary, he is perjurious." [55] It is clear that to this clerk of chancery, parliament is the central institution of the realm and as such must be encompassed by all necessary safeguards. This fact in itself is testimony to the importance, at least in the official eye, of a practice that had become an institution in little more than half a century. It is remarkable that its importance was recognized by men of that time and that its future was a matter of some concern.

These things are interesting and significant enough, but they do not stand at the center of the argument of the *Modus.* The real core of the *Modus* is to be found in Article XXIII and, secondarily, in Article XXVI. It is the provisions of these articles that have troubled the "philosophers" of parliament—and I use the word "philosophers" deliberately. We shall have to look at these articles in some detail.

Article XXIII is concerned with aids; that is, with unusual grants for war as well as with the customary feudal ones (knighting of the eldest son, marriage of the eldest daughter). These are to be demanded in full parliament; and "full" parliament clearly means clergy, magnates, and commons. All must consent to them. Then, we are told—and this is the crux of the matter—

. . . it is to be understood that two knights, who come to parliament for that shire, have a greater voice in parliament in granting

and denying than a greater earl of England, and in like manner
the proctors of the clergy of one bishopric have a greater voice in
parliament, if all be agreed, than the bishop himself, and this in
all things that ought to be granted, refused or done by parliament:
and this is obvious because the king can hold parliament with the
community of his kingdom, bishops, earls and barons being absent,
provided that they have been summoned to parliament, although
no bishop, earl or baron come at his summons . . . and thus it
is proper that all that ought to be affirmed or annulled, conceded
or denied or done by parliament, ought to be conceded by the
community of parliament, which exists out of the three grades
or kinds of parliament, that is to say out of the proctors of the
clergy, the knights of the shires, citizens and burgesses, who represent the whole community of England, and not out of the magnates because each of these is at parliament for his own person
and for no other.

This equating of the commons with the community of the
realm (and the lower clergy here are essentially "commons of the
clergy") and the granting to them of preponderant importance in
parliament appear to smack of Wallace Notestein's *The Winning
of the Initiative by the House of Commons* [56] and consequently
are anachronistic in the reign of Edward II. Are they really out
of place, or are they the conclusions—or, perhaps, projections—of
an acute observer whose point of view has been shaped by actuality
and by certain ideas that had been exerting considerable influence
in England since the days of Bracton, if not earlier?

It is a sober fact that out of 71 (or possibly 77, depending on
how they are defined) parliaments between 1258 and 1300, representatives of the shires and towns attended on only nine occasions,
and that out of 158 (or possibly 160) parliaments between 1301 and
1485, the commons were present on all but eight occasions, being
invariably present after 1325. The turning point is exactly the
period to which the *Modus* belongs, and it is not too much to assume that its author was perspicacious enough to sense the direction in which the wind was blowing. But of far greater consequence is the fact that Article XXIII of the *Modus* might well be
an excerpt from one of Gaines Post's contributions to *Traditio*.[57]
It is shot through with Romano-canonical principles, and particularly the maxim "Quod omnes similiter tangit, ab omnibus com-
probetur" (C. 5, 59, 5 ¶2—Justinian). Post has explained how this
maxim, which originally "meant literally the consent of all indi-

viduals who each had legally established interests or rights in a
thing that was common equally or in varying degrees to all," [58] became extended so as to make it possible for governments of communities to be effective even while having to get the consent of
all who were touched. In this connection Post remarks—and what
he says is particularly pertinent to Articles XXIII and XXVI of
the *Modus*—

> . . . Since the business touched all, all the members must be sum-
> moned to the meeting, for all must have the right to discuss and
> debate. . . . Further, by responding to the summons, and giving
> to their delegates, full powers to consent, the communities had no
> legal right, after the assembly was held, to pretend that they had
> not been given due process, and hence were not bound by the
> will of the king in his assembly. . . . But if all must be sum-
> moned, it did not follow that the king could do nothing if all
> did not respond and meet in assembly. For the two laws offered
> rules on default to the effect that the court (and the king presided
> over the assembly as the supreme judge presiding over his high
> court) could decide the case or business in the absence of interested
> parties who refused to heed the summons The wilfully absent
> had no legal right later to appeal the sentence or decision.[59]

These tenets were commonplaces even in the thirteenth century.
The author of the *Modus* knew his two laws probably as well as he
knew parliament, and it is not surprising to find him insisting on
the principle of *plena potestas*,[60] or to read in Article XXVI "that
although any of the said five grades [of parliament] after the king
be absent, provided however all have been summoned by reasonable summons, it [parliament] is nonetheless held to be full." [61]
There is in Article XVII even the suggestion of "the subordination of consent, both of individuals and of a majority, to the idea
of the end of society, the common good or welfare and public
utility." [62]

The provisions of Article XXIII, while no less in accord with
Romano-canonical concepts, go a step further. Whatever the
author's feudal and hierarchical leanings—and he could scarcely
escape having them—he clearly affords proof that, again to quote
Post, "by the late thirteenth century the *maior pars* was numerical
rather than *sanior*." [63] The magnates are individuals, while the
representatives of the lower clergy, shires, cities, and boroughs are
something more. They are proctors of corporations, and these cor-

porations add up to "the community of England" by the sheer
weight of numbers. We are not concerned here with popular sovereignty, but we are certainly face to face with the idea that
representation of a larger community seems inherently to command more respect and greater authority than the individual magnate's being present in parliament *per se* and *pro se,* for he represents nobody but himself—an idea that was even familiar to men
of the thirteenth century.[64]

Historians of the Middle Ages can sometimes "come a cropper,"
as the English put it. There is the classic example of the mediaeval
chronicler who stated categorically that all the sheriffs of England
were changed in the course of a single year. No historian believed
him: it was only idle gossip bruited about the scriptorium. But
when the records, that is, the official accounts of the central government, came to light, it became evident that this was no idle
gossip at all, but the plain truth. Is it too much to suggest that
historians have treated the *Modus* in the same fashion? Galbraith
is fond of insisting that a mediaevalist—or for that matter, any
historian—must go to the documents, live with them and absorb
them (by osmosis, if in no other way), if he is not to be "caught
off base." The late Maude Clarke did her work well. She saw the
Modus for what it was, an extraordinary and perhaps a prescient
view of parliament, but one, as I hope that I have demonstrated,
that was not entirely foreign to the intellectual current of the
times. If this means that we must revise our conception of the
early fourteenth century in the light of the *Modus,* then we had
better be about it.

Appendix

THE MANNER OF HOLDING PARLIAMENT [65]

Here is described the manner in which the parliament of the
king of England and of his English was held in the times of king
Edward, son of Etheldred the king; which manner was recited by
the more discrete of the kingdom in the presence of William duke
of Normandy the conqueror and king of England, the same conqueror enjoining this, and by him approved, and used in his days
and also in the days of his successors the kings of England.[66]

I. Summoning of parliament

The summoning of parliament ought to precede the first day of parliament by forty days.[67]

II. Concerning the clergy

To parliament ought to be summoned and come the archbishops, bishops, abbots, priors and other greater clerics, who hold by earldom or barony, by reason of such tenure, and no lesser ones unless their presence and coming be required otherwise than on account of their tenures, either that they be of the council of the king, or their presence be deemed necessary or useful to parliament; and the king is required to furnish them their outlay and expenses in coming to and remaining at parliament; nor ought such minor clerics to be summoned to parliament, but the king used to direct his writs to such also asking that they be present at his parliament.

Item, the king used to issue his summons to archbishops, bishops, and other exempt persons, such as abbots, priors, deans, and other ecclesiastical persons, who have jurisdictions by such exemptions and separate privileges, that they cause to be elected for each deanery and archdeaconry of England by those deaneries and archdeaconries two skilled and suitable proctors of that archdeaconry to come and be present at parliament, to answer, accept, depute, and do exactly what all and singular persons of those deaneries and archdeaconries would do if they and all and singular of them were personally present.

And that such proctors come with their warrants in duplicate, sealed with the seals of their superiors, [to the effect] that they have been elected and sent for such procuration, of which letters one will be surrendered to the clerks of parliament to be enrolled and the other will remain in the hands of the proctors themselves. And thus under these two kinds of summons the whole clergy ought to be summoned to the king's parliament.[68]

III. Concerning the laity

Item, all and singular earls and barons and their peers ought to be summoned and come, that is to say, those who have lands and revenues to the value of a complete earldom, viz., twenty fees of one knight, each fee computed at twenty pounds' worth, which make four hundred pounds' worth in all, or to the value of one complete barony, that is to say, thirteen fees and the third part of one knight's fee, each fee computed at twenty pounds' worth, which make in all four hundred marks; and no lesser laity ought to be summoned or come to parliament, by reason of his tenure, unless their presence be useful or necessary to parliament for other reasons, and then in their case the same practice ought to be followed as has been prescribed for the lesser clerics, who by reason of their tenure are least obliged to come to parliament.[69]

IV. Concerning barons of the Ports

Item, the king used to send his writs to the guardian of the Cinque Ports that he have elected from each Port by the Port itself two suitable and skilled barons to come and be present at his parliament to answer, accept, depute, and do exactly what his baronies would do just as though all those and singular from those baronies were personally present there; and that such barons come with their warrants in duplicate, sealed with the common seals of his Ports, that they have been duly elected attorneys for this purpose and sent on behalf of those baronies, one of which will be surrendered to the clerks of parliament, and the other will remain in the hands of the barons themselves. And when such barons of the Ports, licence having been obtained, had been about to depart from parliament, they then used to have a writ under the great seal to the guardian of the Cinque Ports that he cause such barons to have their reasonable outlay and expenses from the community of that Port, from the first day on which they came to parliament up to the day on which they returned to their own [homes], mention having been made and expressed in that writ, of the stay that they made at parliament, of the day on which they came and on which they were licensed to depart; and mention once used to be made in the writ of how much such barons ought to receive from their communities *per diem,* that is to say, some more and others less, according to the abilities and standings of the persons, nor did there used to be fixed for two barons *per diem* more than twenty shillings, account having been taken of their stays, labours and expenses, nor is it customary for such expenses to be allowed for certain by the court, for any persons thus elected and sent on behalf of the communities unless these persons were honourable and well-behaved in parliament.

V. Concerning knights of the shires

Item, the king used to send his writs to all the sheriffs of England that they cause to be elected each from his county by the county itself two suitable knights, honourable and skilled, to come to his parliament, in the same manner in which it has been said of the barons of the Ports, and about their warrants in the same manner, but for expenses of two knights from one shire it is not the custom for more than one mark *per diem* to be allowed.

VI. Concerning citizens

In the same manner the mayor and sheriffs of London, the mayor and bailiffs or the mayor and citizens of York and of other cities used to be commanded that they themselves elect on behalf of the community of their city two suitable citizens, honourable and skilled, to come and be present at parliament in the same manner in which it has been said about the barons of the Cinque Ports and knights of the shires; and the citizens used to be the peers and equals of the knights of the shires in the expenses coming, remaining, and returning.

VII. Concerning burgesses

Item, in the same manner the bailiffs and good men of the boroughs used to be and ought to be commanded that they themselves from among themselves and on behalf of themselves elect two suitable burgesses, honourable and skilled, to come and be present at the king's parliament in the same manner in which it has been said about the citizens; but the two burgesses used not to receive *per diem* for their expenses more than ten shillings and sometimes not more than half a mark, and this used to be assessed by the court according to the size and authority of the borough and according to the standing of the persons sent.[70]

VIII. Concerning the manner of parliament

Now that the form has first been shown by what right, and how long in advance a parliamentary summons ought to be made to each, and who ought to come by summons and who not; second is to be said who they are who by virtue of their offices ought to come, and are required to be present throughout the entire parliament, without summons; whence it is to be required that the two principal clerks of parliament chosen by the king and his council, and the other secondary clerks about whom and whose offices will be spoken more particularly later, and the chief crier of England with his assistant criers, and the chief usher of England, which two offices, that is to say, the office of crier and usher used to belong to one and the same [person], these two officers are required to be present on the first day; the chancellor of England, the treasurer, the chamberlains and barons of the exchequer, the

justices and all the king's clerks and knights, together with serjeants at king's pleas, who are of the king's council, are required
to be present on the second day, unless they have reasonable
excuses to the effect that they are unable to be present, and then
they ought to send good excuses.

IX. Concerning the opening of parliament

The lord king will sit in the centre of the greater bench, and
he is required to be present at prime on the sixth day of parliament: and the chancellor, treasurer, barons of the exchequer and
justices used to record defaults made in parliament in the order
that follows. On the first day will be called the burgesses and
citizens of all England, on which day if they do not come, the
borough will be amerced at a hundred marks and the city at a
hundred pounds: on the second day will be called the knights of
the shires of all England, on which day if they do not come, the
county from which they are will be amerced at a hundred pounds:
on the third day of parliament will be called the barons of the
Cinque Ports, and afterwards the barons, and then the earls:
whence if the barons of the Cinque Ports do not come that barony
from which they are will be amerced at one hundred marks; in the
same way a baron *per se* will be amerced at a hundred marks and
an earl at a hundred pounds; and it will be done in the same
manner concerning those who are peers to earls and barons, that
is to say, who have lands and rents to the value of one earldom or
one barony, as it has been said before under the title concerning
summoning: on the fourth day will be called the proctors of the
clergy; if they do not come, their bishops will be amerced for each
archdeaconry that will have made default at a hundred marks:
on the fifth day will be called the deans, priors, abbots, bishops and
at length the archbishops, and if they do not come, each archbishop
will be amerced at a hundred pounds, a bishop holding an entire
barony at a hundred marks, and in the same manner concerning
the abbots, priors, and others. On the first day a proclamation
ought to be made, first in the hall or in the monastery, or in some
other public place where parliament is held, and afterwards
publicly in city or town that all those who will have wished to
present petitions and plaints to parliament shall deliver them from
the first day of parliament through the five days next following.[71]

X. Concerning the sermon to parliament

One archbishop, or bishop or one great clerk discrete and eloquent, chosen by the archbishop in whose province parliament

is held, ought to preach on one of those first five days of parliament in full parliament and in the presence of the king, and this when parliament will have been for the most part joined and congregated, and in his sermon in due course enjoin the whole parliament that they with him beseech God, and adore Him for the peace and tranquillity of king and kingdom, as will be said more particularly in the following title concerning the pronouncement to parliament.

XI. Concerning the pronouncement to parliament

After the sermon the chancellor of England or the chief justice of England, that is to say that one who holds pleas *coram rege,* or another suitable, honourable and eloquent justice, or clerk, chosen by the chancellor and chief justice themselves, ought to announce the reasons for parliament, first in general and afterwards in particular; standing: and thus it is to be known that any members of parliament, whoever he may be, will stand while he speaks, the king excepted, so that all of parliament may be able to hear him who speaks, and if he talk obscurely or speak too low, let him talk a second time, and speak more loudly or let another speak for him.

XII. Concerning the speech of the king after the pronouncement

The king after the pronouncement before parliament ought to ask clergy and laity, naming all their ranks, that is to say archbishops, bishops, abbots, priors, archdeacons, proctors and others of the clergy, earls, barons, knights, citizens, burgesses and other lay [persons], that they diligently, studiously and sincerely work towards treating and deliberating the affairs of parliament just as they might understand and perceive this to be great and important first for the will of God and afterwards to his and their dignities and advantages.

XIII. Concerning the absence of the king in parliament

The king is required absolutely to be personally present at parliament, unless he be detained through physical illness and then he can keep to his chamber so that he do not lodge outside the manor, or at least the town, where parliament is held, and then he ought to send for twelve persons from the greater and better [of those] who have been summoned to parliament, that is to say, two bishops, two earls, two barons, two knights of the shire, two citizens and two burgesses, to see his person and to testify to his condition, and in their presence he ought to commit to the archbishop of the place, the seneschal, and his chief justice, that they together and separately begin and continue parliament in his name, express mention having been made in that commission at that time as to the cause of his absence, which ought to be sufficient, and to advise the other nobles and magnates of parliament together with the clear testimony of their said twelve peers; the reason is that there used to be complaint and grumbling in parliament on account of the absence of the king, because it is a damaging and dangerous thing to the whole community of parliament and the kingdom when a king would be absent from parliament, nor ought he nor can he absent himself, except only in the case aforesaid.

XIV. Concerning the places and sessions of parliament

First, as it has been said above, the king will sit in the middle place of the greater bench and on his right side will sit the archbishop of Canterbury, the bishops of London and Winchester and after them in turn the other bishops, abbots, and priors in rows; and on the left side of the king will sit the archbishop of York, the bishops of Durham and Carlisle and after them in turn the earls, barons, and lords; always such a division being observed among the aforesaid grades and their places that no one sit except among his peers, and the seneschal of England is required to oversee this, unless the king wishes to assign another to this. At the right foot of the king will sit the chancellor of England and the chief justice of England and his colleagues, and their clerks who are of parliament; and at his left foot will sit the treasurer, chamberlains and barons of the exchequer, justices of the bench and their clerks who are of parliament.

XV. Concerning the principal clerks of parliament

Item, the two principal clerks of parliament will sit in the midst of the justices, and will enrol all pleas and affairs of parliament.

And it is to be known that these two clerks are not subject to any justices, nor is any justice in England a justice in parliament, nor do they have *per se* a record in parliament, except to the extent that fresh power has been assigned and given to them in parliament by the king and peers of parliament, as when they have been assigned with other suitors of parliament to hear and determine various petitions and plaints delivered in parliament; but these two clerks are immediately subject to the king and his parliament in common unless perhaps one justice or two be assigned to them to examine and emend their enrolments. And when the peers

of parliament have been assigned to hear and examine any petitions especially by themselves, when they themselves are unani-
mous and agreed in rendering their judgments on such petitions,
then they will recite such petitions and the process had concerning
them and render judgement in full parliament, so that these two
clerks primarily enrol all pleas and all judgements on the principal
roll of parliament, and deliver those rolls to the treasurer before
the dismissal of parliament, so that these rolls absolutely be in the
treasury before the recess of parliament, saving nevertheless a
transcript therefrom for these clerks, or a counter-roll if they wish
to have it. Let these two clerks, unless they be in other offices with
the king, and receive fees from him, so that they might live hon-
ourably therefrom, receive from the king *per diem* one mark for
their expenses in equal portions, unless they be at the table of the
lord king; and if they be at the table of the lord king, then they
receive in addition to their table *per diem* half a mark in equal
portions, for the whole parliament.

XVI. Concerning the five clerks of parliament

The lord king will assign five skilled and proven clerks of whom
the first will minister to and serve the bishops, the second the
proctors of the clergy, the third the earls and barons, the fourth
the knights of the shires, the fifth the citizens and burgesses, and
each of these, unless he be with the king and draw from him such a
fee or such wages that he be able to live honestly therefrom, will
draw from the king two shillings *per diem,* unless he be at the
king's table; and if he be at table, then he will draw twelve pence
per diem; these clerks will write the queries of those and the
answers they make to king and parliament, will be present at
their councils wherever they wish to hold them; and when done
with them, will assist the principal clerks in enrolling.

XVII. Concerning difficult cases and judgements

When contention, doubt or a difficult case of peace or war
emerges in the kingdom or outside, let that case be referred and
recited in writings in full parliament, and let it be treated and
argued there among the peers of parliament, and if it be necessary,
let it be enjoined by the king or on behalf of the king, if the king
not be present, to each grade of peers that each grade address itself
to it, and that that case be delivered to its clerk in writings, and
they cause that case to be recited in a certain place in their presence; in such a way that they themselves order and consider among
themselves how better and more justly it could be proceeded in

that case just as they themselves for the person of the king and their own persons, and also for the persons of those whose persons they represent, wish to answer before God, and let them report their answers and advices in writings, and all their answers, counsels and advices hereupon having been heard, let it be proceeded according to better and saner counsel and where at least the greater part of parliament concur. And if through discord between the king and any magnates or perhaps among the magnates themselves, the peace of the kingdom be impaired, or the people or the country be troubled, so that it seem to the king and his council that it be expedient for that affair to be treated and emended by consideration of all the peers of his kingdom or if through war the king and his kingdom be troubled, or if a difficult case emerge before the chancellor of England, or if a difficult judgement might be required to be rendered before the justices, and such as these, and if perhaps in such deliberations all or the greater part are not able to agree, then the earl seneschal, the earl constable, and the earl marshal, or two of them, elect twenty-five persons from all the peers of the kingdom, that is to say two bishops, and three proctors, for the entire clergy, two earls and three barons, five knights of the shires, five citizens and five burgesses, which make twenty-five; and these twenty-five can elect from themselves, if they wish, twelve and condescend to these, and these twelve six and condescend to these, and these six further three and condescend to these, and these three cannot condescend to fewer, unless licence be obtained from the lord king, and if the king consent these three can agree to two, and of these two one can agree to the other and thus at length his ordinance will stand above the whole parliament; and thus having condescended from twenty-five persons down to one single person, unless the greater number are able to agree and ordain, in the end a single person, as it has been said, will ordain for all, who cannot disagree with himself; saving the king and his council that they be able to examine and emend such ordinances after they have been written, if they know how and wish to do this, so that it be done there then in full parliament, and by the consent of parliament, and not behind parliament.[72]

XVIII. Concerning the order of deliberating the affairs of parliament

The affairs for which parliament has been summoned ought to be deliberated according to the calendar of parliament, and according to the order of petitions delivered and filed, no respect had to the persons of any whatsoever, but who first has proposed first be brought up. On the calendar of parliament all the affairs of parliament ought to be called up in this order: first concerning war if there be war, and concerning other affairs touching the persons of king, queen and their children; second concerning the common affairs of the kingdom such as concerning making laws against the defects of original laws, [laws] of judgement and of execution, after judgements rendered, which are the most common affairs; third ought to be called up individual affairs, and this according to the order of petitions filed, as has been said before.

XIX. Concerning the days and hours of parliament

Parliament ought not to be held on Sundays, but on all other days, that day always excepted, and three others, that is to say, All Saints, Souls and the Nativity of St John the Baptist, it can be held; and it daily ought to be begun at the hour of mid-prime, at which hour the king is required to be present, and all the peers of the kingdom. Parliament ought to be held in a public place, and not in private, nor in a secret place; on feast days parliament ought to be begun at the hour of prime on account of divine service.[73]

XX. Concerning the ushers of parliament

The chief usher of parliament will stand within the great house of the monastery, hall or other place where parliament is held, and will guard the house so that no one enter parliament except who owes suit to and has business at parliament, or has been called because of the affair that is being prosecuted in parliament, and it is necessary that this usher have knowledge of the persons who ought to enter in order that entry on no account be refused to anyone who is required to be present at parliament; and this usher can and ought, if it be necessary, to have several ushers under him.

XXI. Concerning the crier of parliament

The crier of parliament will stand outside the house of parliament, and the usher will announce his proclamations; the king used to assign his serjeants-at-arms to stand by the great space outside the house of parliament, to guard the house so that none would make assaults or disturbances around the houses, through which parliament might be impeded, on pain of seizure of their bodies, because by law the house of parliament ought not to be closed, but to be guarded by the ushers and king's serjeants-at-arms.

XXII. Concerning the stations of speakers in parliament

All peers of parliament will sit, and no one will stand except when he speaks, and speak so that anyone in parliament is able to hear him; no one will enter parliament or leave parliament except through one chamber; and whoever speaks to anything that ought to be deliberated by parliament, will stand while speaking; the reason is that they be heard by the peers, because all peers are judges and justices.

XXIII. Concerning aids of the king

The king used not to demand an aid from his kingdom except for immediate war, or making his sons knights, or marrying his daughters, and then such aids ought to be demanded in full parliament, and to be delivered in writings to each grade of peers of parliament, and to be answered in writings; and it is to be known that for such aids to be granted it is necessary that all the peers of parliament consent, and it is to be understood that two knights, who come to parliament for that shire, have a greater voice in parliament in granting and denying than a greater earl of England, and in like manner the proctors of the clergy of one bishopric have a greater voice in parliament, if all be agreed, than the bishop himself, and this in all things that ought to be granted, refused or done by parliament: and this is obvious because the king can hold parliament with the community of his kingdom, bishops, earls and barons being absent, provided that they have been summoned to parliament, although no bishop, earl or baron come at his summons; because formerly there had not been a bishop, or an earl, or a baron, [yet] even then kings held their parliaments, but the contrary is otherwise, granted that the communities, clergy and laity, had been summoned to parliament, just as they ought by law, and on account of some certain reasons they refuse to come, for example if they should pretend that the king did not rule them just as he ought, and should assign specifically in certain articles that he had misruled them, then there would be no parliament at all, although all the archbishops, bishops, earls, barons and all their peers were present with the king; and thus it is proper that all that ought to be affirmed or annulled, conceded or denied or done by parliament, ought to be conceded by the community of parliament, which exists out of the three grades or kinds of parliament, that is to say out of the proctors of the clergy, the knights of the shires, citizens and burgesses, who represent the whole community of England, and not out of the magnates,

because each of these is at parliament for his own person and for
no other.

XXIV. Concerning the dissolution of parliament

Parliament ought not to be dissolved so long as any petition
remains unheard, or, at least, to which no answer has been determined, and if the king permit the contrary, he is perjurious; no
single one of all the peers of parliament can or ought to depart
from parliament, unless licence therefor has been obtained from
the king and all his peers and this in full parliament, and let a
notation of such licence be made on the roll of parliament, and
if anyone of the peers, during parliament, should fall ill, so that
he be not able to come to parliament, then for three days let him
send excusers to parliament, on which day if he should not come,
let two of his peers be sent to him to see and testify to such illness,
and if there be suspicion, let those two peers be sworn that they
speak the truth therein, and if it be discovered that he had malingered, let him be amerced as though for default, and if he had not
malingered, then let him depute as attorney someone sufficient
in their presence to be present at parliament for him, nor can the
healthy be excused if he be of sound mind.

Dissolution of parliament ought to be conducted thus: first
ought to be asked and publicly proclaimed in parliament and
within the pale of parliament, whether there be anyone, who has
delivered a petition to parliament, to whom an answer has not yet
been given; then if no one declares, it is to be supposed that each
is remedied, at least in so far as can be answered by law, and then
first, that is to say, when no one who has exhibited a petition at
that time declares, we shall license our parliament.

XXV. Concerning transcripts of records and processes in
parliament

Clerks of parliament will not refuse anyone a transcript of his
process, but will deliver that to each who has asked for it, and
they will always receive a penny for ten lines, unless perchance
good claim of penury has been made, in which case they will
receive nothing. The rolls of parliament will measure ten inches
in width. Parliament will be held in whatever place of the kingdom might be pleasing to the king.

XXVI. Concerning the grades of peers of parliament

The king is the head, the beginning and end of parliament, and
thus he has no peer in his grade, and thus out of the king alone

is the first grade. The second grade is composed of the archbishops, bishops, abbots, priors, holding by barony. The third
grade is composed of the proctors of the clergy. The fourth grade
is composed of the earls, barons and other magnates and nobles
holding to the value of an earldom and barony, as it has been said
before under the title concerning laity. The fifth grade is composed of knights of the shires. The sixth grade of citizens and
burgesses: and thus parliament is composed of six grades. But
it is to be known that although any of the said five grades after the
king be absent, provided however all have been summoned by
reasonable summons, it is nonetheless held to be full.

1. The basic work on the *Modus* is M. V. Clarke, *Medieval Representation
and Consent* (London, 1936), a book which appears not to have been read
too carefully by its critics.

2. *Ibid.* pp. 74-75.

3. W. Stubbs, *The Constitutional History of England* (Oxford, 1887), II,
209 n. 7; III, 445-46.

4. W. Stubbs, *Select Charters and Other Illustrations of English Constitutional History*, 9th ed., by H. W. C. Davis (Oxford, 1929), pp. 500-506.
Charles Bémont was the first scholar to attempt a systematic survey of manuscripts of the *Modus* ("La Date de la composition du *Modus tenendi parliamentum in Anglia*," in *Mélanges Julien Havet* (Paris, 1895), pp. 465-80).
Sir T. D. Hardy's *Modus Tenendi Parliamentum* (London, 1846) was based
on a single manuscript. The best texts are those of Miss Clarke, *op. cit.*,
pp. 373-92, and I have translated her text of the English version as an appendix to this paper.

5. A. F. Pollard, *The Evolution of Parliament* (2nd ed.; London, 1934),
pp. 432-35.

6. D. Pasquet, *An Essay on the Origins of the House of Commons*, trans.
R. G. D. Laffan (Cambridge, 1925), p. 166 n. 2.

7. T. F. Tout, *Chapters in the Administrative History of Mediaeval England* (Manchester, 1928), III, 138 n. 2.

8. *Supra*, n. 1.

9. G. T. Lapsley, *Crown, Community and Parliament in the Later Middle
Ages: Studies in English Constitutional History*, ed. H. M. Cam and G. Bar-
raclough (Oxford, 1951), p. 156; reprinted from *English Historical Review*,
LVI (1941), 22-49, 411-46.

10. B. Wilkinson, *Constitutional History of Medieval England, 1216-1399*
(London, 1952), II, 106.

11. Sir Maurice Powicke remarks in a letter that "it is now 'unhappily' the
fashion to say that McIlwain's book rescued Maitland's great introduction
to the Memoranda de Parliamento of 1305 from undeserved obscurity. Mait-

land set himself a definite job—to show how the petitions to the king in council in parliament reveal the relation between various aspects of the administration, and he did this and more very clearly and brilliantly; but, in doing it, I do not think that he committed himself to a view of parliament as a court of justice and that alone."

12. Clarke, *op. cit.;* W. A. Morris, "The Date of the 'Modus Tenendi Parliamentum,'" *English Historical Review,* XLIX (1934), 407-22.

13. H. G. Richardson and G. O. Sayles, *The Irish Parliament in the Middle Ages* (Philadelphia, 1952), p. 137.

14. V. H. Galbraith, "The *Modus Tenendi Parliamentum,*" *Journal of the Warburg and Courtauld Institutes,* XVI (1953), 81-99.

15. T. F. Tout, *The Place of the Reign of Edward II in English History* (2nd ed., revised by Hilda Johnstone; Manchester, 1936).

16. Quite apart from the circumstantial evidence provided below, there is the remarkable coincidence afforded by a comparison of the record of the Hilary Parliament of 1316 at Lincoln (*Rotuli parliamentorum* [London, 1783], I, 350-55), compiled by Airmyn, and the provisions of Article IX of the *Modus*. On the other hand, it must be made clear that the attribution of the authorship of the *Modus* to Airmyn rests on circumstantial evidence alone, and Professor Galbraith remarks that "such evidence, while it may hang a man, is not enough to prove that he wrote a book" (*op. cit.,* p. 92). Professor Wilkinson hinted, but barely hinted, at the name of another chancery clerk, William Thunnerk, as the possible author (*op. cit.,* II, 106 n. 45).

17. J. L. Grassi, "William Airmyn and the Bishopric of Norwich," *English Historical Review,* LXX (1955), 551-52.

18. *Calendar of Close Rolls (1302-7),* p. 508.

19. N. Denholm-Young, ed., *The Liber Epistolaris of Richard de Bury,* Roxburghe Club (Oxford, 1950), Nos. 203 (p. 94), 205 (p. 95), 233 (pp. 105-6).

20. Public Record Office, Ancient Correspondence, XXXVI, No. 209, quoted in J. C. Davies, *The Baronial Opposition to Edward II* (Cambridge, 1918), Appendix No. 112 (p. 591), where the reading is *pemblece* instead of *peniblete*. See also *Calendar of Chancery Warrants (1244-1326),* pp. 453, 469.

21. *Calendar of Patent Rolls (1334-38),* p. 239.

22. N. Denholm-Young, ed., *Vita Edwardi Secundi,* Medieval Texts, eds. V. H. Galbraith and R. A. B. Mynors (London, 1957), p. 141.

23. Tout, *op. cit.,* pp. 165-66.

24. Galbraith, *op. cit.,* p. 91.

25. In 1334, he was also appointed to inquire into the causes of disputes between scholars at Oxford and their *familiares* and servants and to restore order there. *Calendar of Patent Rolls (1334-8)* (hereinafter referred to as *C.P.R.*), p. 66.

26. Grassi, *op. cit.,* pp. 550-61.

27. See, for example, *Calendar of Papal Registers (1305-42)*, pp. 98, 141, 239.

28. G. P. Cuttino, "King's Clerks and the Community of the Realm," *Speculum*, XXIX (1954), 395-409.

29. P. Chaplais, *The War of Saint-Sardos*, Camden Third Series, LXXXVII (London, 1954), 198, 199-201, 227, 243, 251, 267, 268, 277 n. 1.

30. See G. P. Cuttino, *English Diplomatic Administration, 1259-1339* (Oxford, 1940).

31. This does not include a loan of 180 marks, duly repaid, which he made together with John Hotham, bishop of Ely, and acknowledged on March 2, 1319 *(C.C.R. (1318-23)*, p. 127) and another of £1000, duly repaid, made together with John Stratford, bishop of Winchester, William Clinton, Geoffrey le Scrope, and Richard de Bury, borrowed from Richard Melton, archbishop of York and acknowledged on February 19, 1333 (*C.C.R. [1333-7]*, p. 89).

32. The exact figures are £10,944-12/3/4 lent and £5421-2/9 collected. The precise page references can easily be got by consulting the indexes to the volumes between 1296 and 1337, in addition to *C.P.R.* (1334-8), p. 46. One delivery to the king of wheat and corn from one of his holdings amounted to £134-18/-(*C.C.R. [1313-8]*, p. 338).

33. *C.C.R. (1307-13)*, pp. 122, 209, 459; *ibid. (1313-8)*, pp. 324, 562; *ibid. (1318-23)*, pp. 554, 628; *ibid (1323-7)*, p. 330; *ibid. (1327-30)*, pp. 26, 65; *ibid. (1333-7)*, pp. 28, 37, 106, 195, 221, 423, 468; *C.P.R. (1307-13)*, p. 517; *ibid. (1313-7)*, p. 32; *ibid. (1321-4)*, p. 245; *ibid. (1324-7)*, p. 135; *ibid. (1327-30)*, pp. 196, 241; *ibid. (1330-4)*, pp. 186, 517; *ibid. (1334-8)*, pp. 21, 122, 127, 155; *Rotulorum originalium abbrevatio*, I, 232, 233, 252; *Calendar of Charter Rolls (1327-41)*, pp. 233, 234. He bought forty acres of meadow in Butterwick (Lincs.) in 1317 (*C.C.R. [1313-8]*, p. 584); *Calendar of Inquisitions Post Mortem*, VII, Nos. 107, 300.

34. *Rot. parl.*, I, 190.

35. Sir F. Palgrave, ed., *Parliamentary Writs and Writs of Military Summons* (London, 1827-34), II, 82 (No. 26), 102 (No. 24).

36. *Parl. Writs*, II, 136 (No. 34).

37. H. G. Richardson and G. O. Sayles, eds., *Rotuli parliamentorum Anglie hactenus inediti, MCCLXXIX-MCCCLXXIII (Camden Third Series*, Vol. LI [London, 1935]), p. 76. He also had in his keeping, as late as December, a petition delivered at this parliament by Auger de Podenx (*C.C.W. [1244-1326]*, p. 495).

38. *Parl. Writs*, II, 199-200 (Nos. 49, 50).

39. *Ibid.*, II, 349 (No. 4).

40. *Ibid.*, II, 350 (No. 6); *Rot. parl. ined.*, p. 164; *Rot. parl.*, II, 28, 409, 61, 68, 69.

41. *Rot. parl.*, I, 350 *et seq.*

42. H. G. Richardson and G. O. Sayles, "The King's Ministers in Parliament, 1272-1377," *English Historical Review*, XLVII (1932), 195, citing

H. Cole, ed., *Documents Illustrative of English History,* Record Commission (London, 1844), p. 12; and *Parl. Writs,* II, 252 (No. 59).

43. Arts. VIII, IX, XI, XIII, XIV, XV, XVII, XXII.

44. Art. VIII.

45. Art. XI.

46. Art. XIV.

47. Art. XVII.

48. Art. XXII.

49. Art. XXVI.

50. *Parl. Writs,* II, ii, 152-4.

51. *Statutes of the Realm,* I, 174-75.

52. A detailed account of this parliament, but one containing one important misreading of the rolls, may be found in Davies, *op. cit.,* pp. 408-24. The above summary is from Airmyn's record.

53. There were only thirty-seven petitions in the Hilary Parliament. A good deal of theorizing about the nature of parliament has been based on the rolls and pertinent petitions, but no one has yet undertaken the rather formidable task of examining other records, clearly dated at the times and places of parliaments, for what light they may throw on the vast amount of business transacted in parliaments and never recorded in the official records.

54. It is tempting to compare the ideas expressed in the *Modus* with those implied in the Statute of York in 1322, but such comparison would go well beyond the limits of this paper. See G. L. Haskins, *The Statute of York and the Interest of the Commons* (Cambridge, Mass., 1935); Lapsley, *op. cit.;* and Gaines Post, "The Two Laws and the Statute of York," *Speculum,* XXIX (1954), 417-32.

55. Arts. IX, XI, XIII, XV, XVI, XIX, XXI, XXII, XXIV, XXV.

56. London, 1925.

57. I have drawn heavily on Post's articles for what follows regarding the concepts of Roman and canon law as they seem to be implied in the *Modus*. The two most important articles are "Plena Potestas and Consent in Medieval Assemblies," *Traditio,* I (1943), 355-408, and "A Romano-canonical Maxim, 'Quod omnes tangit,' in Bracton," *ibid.,* IV (1946), 197-251. These are highly technical. For the non-specialist, Post has summarized his findings in an admirably lucid article, "A Roman Legal Theory of Consent, *Quod omnes tangit,* In Medieval Representation," *Wisconsin Law Review,* Vol. 1950, pp. 66-78. Quotations are from this.

58. Post, *op. cit.,* p. 71.

59. Post, *op. cit.,* pp. 72, 75, 76.

60. Arts. IV-VII.

61. We need not be bothered by the six "grades" of parliament, as was Stubbs. The question of "estates" was fluid until well on in the century.

Mr. J. E. A. Jolliffe has pointed out that the "estates" of 1381 correspond to the "grades" of the *Modus*. *The Constitutional History of Medieval England* (3rd ed.; London, 1954), pp. 434-35.

62. Post, *op. cit.*, p. 71. Cf. *supra*, p. 14, where the king makes reservations about perambulations of the forest, as reported in Airmyn's account of the Hilary Parliament of 1316.

63. Post, *op. cit.*, p. 72.

64. G. L. Haskins, *The Growth of English Representative Government* (Philadelphia, 1948), Chap. ii.

65. Translated from the text of Miss Clarke. I have deliberately made it as literal as possible in order that it may accurately reflect the language of the original. The notes to the various articles are based on Miss Clarke's observations.

66. This is, needless to say, a figment of the author's imagination and obviously written for effect in order to give his treatise the sanction of long usage.

67. This is the time specified in Magna Carta for summons to the Great Council, and also for university summons in the thirteenth century.

68. Having two proctors from each archdeaconry was the practice in the larger dioceses of the north and also, in an irregular way, in the province of Canterbury.

69. "These figures . . . derive ultimately from Magna Carta (cl. 2), where the relief paid for a knight's fee is fixed at 100 shillings and that for an earldom or barony at £100. This ratio carried with it the implication that twenty fees made up an earldom or barony and, when the baron's relief was reduced to 100 marks at the end of the thirteenth century, it was natural to conclude that a barony consisted of thirteen and a third fees."—Clarke, *op. cit.*, p. 197.

70. "The *Modus* rates seem to be worked out to a schedule, without any relation either to official orders or to actual practice."—Clarke, *op. cit.*, p. 201.

71. Edward II was a late riser.
The formal opening on the sixth day does not correspond to recorded practice. It may be a reform suggested by the delay in the Hilary Parliament of 1316 at Lincoln.
There is no record of the collection of fines.

72. "The idea of a committee of estates was . . . fully developed by the magnates, for themselves, in the first half of the reign [of Edward II]; in the final struggle it was suddenly extended to include the commons. . . . Here it is enough to emphasize the likeness between Chapter XVII and the procedure at the deposition [of Edward II]. . . . In short, the chapter . . . bears all the marks of a theory of government untested by experience."—Clarke, *op. cit.*, p. 193.

73. Parliament normally met within legal terms until the reign of Edward III.

FRENCH LITERATURE IN THE FOURTEENTH CENTURY

GRACE FRANK

The literature of the fourteenth century, like that of every other era, cannot be summed up in generalizations. Literary fashions wax and wane, political and social conditions in various places and at various times influence writers in different ways, and above all, we have, as in every century, individual authors whose temperaments and circumstances predispose them to write in a particular manner. Also, one may add, in Kittredge's words, "genius comes only by the grace of God."

It is an easy generalization to say, as has been said, that in the fourteenth century Italy had Dante, Petrarch, and Boccaccio, England had Chaucer, while France had only Froissart. But it must be remembered that during much of this century France suffered the ravages of war and the brutalities of invasion. Petrarch, who traveled through France after the treaty of Brétigny, vividly describes the wreckage that he saw, the evidences of arson and pillage, murder and rape.

Moreover, during the Hundred Years War, with its intermittent battles, many of the French aristocracy, if they were not killed, lived abroad as captives or hostages. This was the class that by tradition had supported literature in France. Before the invention of printing, writers necessarily wrote for the ears of auditors rather than for the eyes of readers; the courts of the nobility provided valuable audiences, and professional men of letters were largely dependent for their livelihood on aristocratic patrons. All the great authors of the fourteenth century whose names we know, whether they came from France, Italy, or England, lived on influential patronage of one sort or another. Nor need this be too much deplored, since the age of the despots in Italy is one of the times when human genius flowered. Then too, the chance to frequent the courts of the mighty permitted men like Chaucer, Petrarch, and Froissart to travel widely, and to fertilize not only their own talents but those of one another. However, it is only fair to recall

61

that in France at this time literature could be fostered in relatively few courts. The presence of foreign troops on French soil and the absence of important patrons may therefore help to explain why France, which in the preceding centuries had fathered the epic, the troubadour lyric, and the chivalric romance, had so little to offer between 1300 and 1400.

This was also a time when in France, for whatever reasons, the ideas and ideals that had inspired earlier writers showed signs of cracking. Old beliefs and loyalties had lost their potency. The Church itself was divided, with a dissolute papal court in southern France at the beginning of the century and two popes at the end of it, one in Avignon and the other in Rome. The unquestioning faith of the twelfth and thirteenth centuries had been replaced in some instances by criticism and cynicism. To be sure, even in the earlier period, certain unorthodox sects—like the Waldensians, for example—had begun to assume the right to hold private opinions on sacred subjects. But they were reformers rather than cynics. In the time we are considering, faith itself had cooled.

Chivalric notions, too, which in the beginning had worn religious trappings and aroused mystical devotion, now seemed unrealistic. The French military class, which for so long had spent its energies on defending Christianity from the infidels, could not even defend its own land from the English invaders. The *Lancelot* in prose might be the bedside companion of noble lords and ladies, but its spirit had evaporated when Froissart could equate the cruel and bloody warriors of his own day with Knights of the Round Table. The chroniclers profess to write in honor of chivalry, but the society they picture bears little relation to the illusion they cherish. King Arthur and the Emperor Charlemagne might still be golden idols, but their clay feet were beginning to show.

Another ideal of the early Middle Ages had been the unity of Christendom as a continuation of the Roman Empire. Petrarch for a time had seen in Cola di Rienzi a reincarnation of the ancient heroes of Rome, but he had always regarded the German Emperors as usurpers, and after the fall of Rienzi, he began to dream only of Italian unity and not of a universal empire. Froissart's sympathies were not engaged by any country, but by a social class: his allegiance was to the aristocracy of any land that welcomed him. He admired courage and was fascinated by the feudal society around him. He did not realize that the soul had left the body of chivalry and that the noble soldiers he knew were hardly counterparts of Perceval, Lancelot, and Galahad. In any case, the idea of patriotism was foreign to him, and he was not scandalized by those who changed sides during contemporary battles. Indeed he himself revised his early work on the *Chronicles* when he left his English protectors and wrote for French patrons.

But there is another, happier side to the picture. Although the fourteenth century witnessed a decline in the influence of the Church and the old ideals of chivalry, and although it abandoned the notion of a universal state approximating the Roman Empire, it began to experience the stimulating spirit of the rising towns, of their trade associations, and of the new class of citizens that was emerging. Learning and culture were no longer exclusively in the hands of the clergy. The independent judgments of the laity were becoming increasingly important. It is significant that although writers of the time might take minor orders and accept the patronage of the nobility, nevertheless Chaucer, Petrarch, Boccaccio, and Froissart can all be grouped together as citizen authors. Their thoughts betray a mundane rather than a cloistered orientation, and at least two of them, Chaucer and Boccaccio, exhibit an interested awareness of the common man and his problems.

In fourteenth-century France this tendency is best represented by the drama. But before we consider that, let us examine the more aristocratic writings of the time, writings by professional men of letters, whatever their origins, men whose names are known to us, who wrote primarily for the nobility and who, for the most part, would probably have had little to do with the anonymous persons who wrote for the theater of the citizenry.

It is needless to stress the fact that France in the twelfth and thirteenth centuries had created an amazingly fertile literature. Its continuing influence was felt from Iceland to Sicily, from Germany to Spain. French epics and lyrics, short lays and long courtly romances were widely translated and imitated. So successful and prolific was this literature that, like the English poetry of the romantic period, it laid deadening hands on the future of the land that gave it birth. Imitation stifled creation. As a consequence, despite new experiences and a new social structure, most professional French writers of the fourteenth century still clung to old conventions of matter and technique instead of venturing upon original ideas.

I should like to speak briefly at this point of only three of the more famous professional French writers of the time: Guillaume de Machaut, Jean Froissart, and Eustache Deschamps.

Guillaume de Machaut, who lived from about 1300 to about 1377, an author greatly honored in his own day, was a musician as well as a poet, a composer who followed the troubadour custom of writing melodies for his own verses; and his music contributed to his fame. Unfortunately, he lacked the literary talent to rejuvenate the old courtly lyric. The troubadours and trouvères had at least sought for an endless originality of form and expression, if not always of theme. Machaut, with little new to say, further hobbled his work by employing such fixed types of verse as the *ballade* and *rondeau*. His contemporaries erroneously credited him with inventing these rigid forms. Actually, he did not, but he made them popular and his followers eagerly adopted them. However, three stanzas on the same rhymes with a refrain repeating half of them do not make a poet. Like other writers of his kind, Machaut tended to lean upon tired phrases and to observe rules instead of creating them. His lyrics sometimes have facility and charm, but they lack the bite of novelty and sincerity.

Machaut wrote long narrative poems as well as short lyrics, and following the pattern made popular by the authors of the *Roman de la Rose*, he often used the framework of the dream and populated his landscapes with allegorical figures. Typical of many such works is the adventure of a poet who falls asleep on a day in spring and finds himself in a garden where he meets such abstract characters as Reason, Fortune, Nature, Faith, and so on. He is instructed by these symbolical persons and argues with them—usually about love.

For example, in one such poem, *Le Jugement du roi de Bohême*, Machaut represents himself as seeing a knight and a lady wandering in a garden. They are both exceedingly sad: the lady's lover has died and the knight has been betrayed by his mistress. They argue as to which has suffered most. Our poet overhears the discussion and suggests that they turn to his patron, the King of Bohemia, for an opinion. They proceed to the royal residence where the king renders a decision in favor of the betrayed knight for reasons which you can guess. Although the poem introduces many allegorical figures and continues the type of *judicium amoris* made famous in the twelfth century in the circles of Eleanor of Aquitaine and her daughters, Machaut's introduction of himself and the king and the location of the judgment in the king's own castle give the poem a certain realistic fillip.

In another debate about a lover's problems, *Le Jugement du roi de Navarre,* Machaut makes himself the protagonist and defends himself against the charge of having been remiss toward his lady. A further touch of actuality occurs in the Prologue where the poet mentions various events of 1348 and 1349: the peasants' uprisings, the persecution of the Jews, the religious activities of the Flagellants, and the disastrous effects of the Black Death. He is like Boccaccio in setting frivolous scenes against dark events; but with Boccaccio background and foreground interact to add depth to the picture, whereas Machaut's prologue—though it gives a sense of verisimilitude to the poem—has little functional connection with what follows. The poem, in fact, is essentially another casuistic discussion about love, with an unattractive pack of quarrelsome women furnishing a slight trace of humor by their castigations of the author.

In the course of his longer pieces Machaut manages to insert a large number of stories or "examples." These are taken from the Bible, the bestiaries, from Greco-Roman literature, from mediaeval sources of many kinds, and even from contemporary tales, perhaps of the author's own invention. Such examples were intended to embellish, entertain, and instruct. They range from the stories of Dido and Aeneas, Jason and Medea, Piramus and Thisbe, through references to Lancelot and Tristan, to anecdotes of Machaut's own day that begin with some topical phrase like "It happened recently that a clerk of Orléans . . . " or "Not long ago a great lady came to Paris with her daughter . . . ." These incidental tales give one a good idea of the literary lore acceptable to courtly circles in the mid-fourteenth century as well as of certain manners and customs of the time.

One of Machaut's most influential works was his *Voir Dit,* which was written when the author was over sixty. The narrative proceeds by way of letters, with inserted poems, that supposedly passed between Machaut and a young woman who professed to be in love with him, sight unseen. How much of this epistolary romance was real, how much fiction, it is hard to say. Most scholars assume that there is a considerable amount of truth in it, and that the aging poet really had an affair with a young woman of some social prominence, an affair, however, in which her ambition to be the mistress and inspiration of a famous author was more deeply impli-

cated than her heart. Yet the *Voir Dit* can still be read with pleas-
ure: the psychological ramifications of the liaison—the doubts,
hopes, plans for meeting, the quarrels and reconciliations of the
lovers, the warming and cooling and rewarming of their feelings
—give the romance an abiding substance.

Machaut's professional status as a man of letters is apparent
from the praise of his contemporaries, but above all from the
eminence and generosity of his protectors. These included such
men as John of Luxemburg, king of Bohemia, Charles, king of
Navarre, and eventually the Dauphin of France, who became
Charles V. Though the poet is referred to in documents as
"master" and though he had pursued theological studies (he
became a canon), he earned his living by means of his pen.
Through his writings he attracted the favor of the great nobles
who gave him preferments of various kinds. He acted as secretary
and almoner of King John and enjoyed the prebends of several
canonries bestowed upon him by his benefactors. With these
highly placed men he lived on intimate terms, and traveled widely
in their train. Naturally his writings conformed to the tastes of
those who employed him and whom he so frequently eulogized.
They are graceful trifles for the most part, full of pretty ornamental devices, but wanting in any real grandeur of theme. One
might say that Machaut (unlike Chaucer) repaid his considerable
debt to the *Roman de la Rose* in debased coinage.

Froissart, too, represents the professional man of letters of his
age. He wrote his *Chronicles,* he says, to praise the exploits of
famous men. Born about 1337 in Valenciennes, he went to London as a young man, and by 1361 had presented to Queen Philippa
of England (who, like himself, was from the province of Hainaut)
a poem that he had composed about the battle of Poitiers. He
was graciously received and spent five years in the brilliant English
court at a time when London was full of eminent French captives
and hostages who were being generously treated by their captors.
From both the French and English who had participated in the
Hundred Years War, Froissart learned much about the persons
and battles involved. A good reporter and a vivacious narrator, he
tried to reproduce faithfully what he learned from his sources,
and in the various editions of his *Chronicles* he only indirectly
reflects his own personality, mirroring more accurately the opinions of others, especially the prejudices of his patrons.

Froissart was primarily a historian and should be judged as such. But he also wrote lays, *ballades,* and long narrative poems, all of which betray the influence of Machaut. In some of his early light verses and in a longer narrative poem, *L'Espinette amoureuse,* he gives us fresh and charming reminiscences of his youth when, he says, he listened to the tales of minstrels and learned that all joy comes from love and arms. He was not yet fourteen when he met the lady who occupied his thoughts for ten years before finally rejecting him. Later he vows that this experience helped make a man of him. At any rate, the poem reveals that Froissart, like Machaut, can be personal within the rigid confines of the conventional poetry of his time. But his sentiments seldom ring true and hardly rise above the superficial. He reflects the well-being and contentment of a man who never suffered deeply. In fact, according to Gaston Paris, even in narrating scenes of horror, Froissart exhibits "an almost joyous serenity." Paris also suggests that the effect of impartiality sometimes achieved by the *Chronicles* is merely the result of the author's insensitiveness.

After the death of Queen Philippa, Froissart went back to Valenciennes and finished the first book of the *Chronicles* for the queen's nephew, Robert of Namur. Soon, however, he acquired two French patrons, Guy de Blois, who gave him a fat living, and Wenceslas, Duke of Luxemburg and Brabant. It was for Wenceslas that he wrote his romance, *Méliador,* in which he intercalated some of the duke's own lyrics. *Méliador* is probably Froissart's most ambitious literary production, but it is pretty poor stuff. An involved story of about thirty thousand lines, it tells of the rival adventures of various knights in wooing a princess and of how the best of these knights, *Méliador,* won her. King Arthur's court is involved, and the romance has been variously described as a pale reflection of the *Lancelot* in prose and as the kind of tale that drove Don Quixote out of his mind.

In any case, Froissart's works, like those of Machaut, indicate that although chivalry and feudalism were dying, the feudal lords remained, and that although these lords may no longer have believed sincerely in the old ideals of the epic, the courtly lyric, and the courtly romance, their retainers paid lip service at least to certain traditions of the earlier literature. Many of the French nobility, it would seem, whatever their scepticism, must have indulged in wishful thinking and hoped to ape the exploits of the Arthurian heroes. Unfortunately, they lived in an age when knighthood was no longer in flower, but in decay.

A poet of a different stamp is Eustache Deschamps, who lived from about 1346 to about 1406 or 1407. Unlike Machaut and Froissart, Deschamps gives the impression of having been an unhappy man throughout most of his life. To be sure, he was a devoted follower of Machaut; and, as a student of law and later among convivial companions or pleasantly housed in royal palaces, he may have enjoyed gay hours, creature comforts, good food, and the society of complacent women. But if one follows him through the ten large volumes of his works, the overwhelming impression is of complaints: complaints about the evils of the time, the war, the epidemics, the behavior of kings and prelates, the envy, greed, ambition, luxury, ingratitude, and dissoluteness of the world about him, the burdens of the poor, the unhealthy condition of a Church racked by schisms—all these mingled with complaints about his own ill health, unpaid wages, and his patrons' neglect and unfulfilled promises.

Who was this dour, embittered poet? After finishing his law studies at the University of Orléans, he entered the service of one important protector after another, serving two kings, Charles V and VI, and various princes and dukes, often simultaneously. His benefactors recognized his legal training by employing him as their bailiff and administrator in different posts, but they also used him in more intimate capacities, such as equerry and *maître d'hôtel*. At times they made him gifts of houses and money. But Deschamps seems everlastingly dissatisfied. The promised gifts do not arrive, the houses are in ruins or subject to lawsuits. He constantly speaks of his need for more funds. He seems also to have suffered inordinately from the cold and from some aggravated form of arthritis.

Sick, tired, old before his time, mocked at by the young, he consoles himself by castigating the vices and disorders of the time. Thus, in a way, his verses are an epitome of fourteenth-century disillusionment. In one poem he writes:

> I hate my days and my sad life
> And curse the hour when I was born.
> I present myself humbly to Death . . .
>   I see myself a part of every ill.

"I see myself a part of every ill" is his refrain here; another refrain in a somewhat similar poem reads, "The world is growing old; it cannot last."

If Deschamps did not so often let his own petty concerns intrude upon his moral indictments, one could more readily admire the man and his achievements. Even so, one does welcome a new and serious note in him. His satirical verses sometimes seem almost modern. A clerk or scholar himself, he advises kings and nobles to do more studying and learning. (His only criticism of scholars is that they talk too much and perform too little.) As a magistrate, he deplores the inequalities in the administration of justice. More than once he inveighs against the crushing taxation of the poor. And he speaks out freely against the royal court as a place where the humble are oppressed by the powerful and where in order to live in peace one must be blind, deaf, and dumb.

However, he is not always consistent, and apparently the ups and downs of his own fortunes influenced his principles. Even in lighter matters he can be capricious. Despite his happy marriage and a poem written for his daughter advising her to be a good wife like her mother, he follows the fashion of his time in attacking both women and matrimony. He accuses women of flirting and chattering too much, of being extravagant, fickle, provoking, bad-tempered, and quarrelsome. Marriage is slavery, he says: it results in grief and poverty and brings on the sufferings of jealousy and betrayal. Better free love than marriage, better a mistress than a wife. At one point he observes that it is dishonorable for a man to marry a rich, old wife, but he cynically advises that very course, since, after the death of the rich, old wife, her husband will be free to use her money and marry a younger woman more to his taste.

Apparently, Deschamps was untroubled by the inconsistency between his realistic diatribes against women and the many lyrics in the old troubadour tradition that he wrote for his noble patronesses. These are filled with courtly phrases, conventional protestations of undying devotion, references to the need for secrecy and to the slanders of would-be rivals, delicate demands for tokens of affection, and implications that heartbreak will result if the poet is denied his lady's grace.

As an author, Deschamps was prodigiously fertile: his works include some fifteen hundred pieces. He obviously composed with great facility; in fact, one feels in him a compulsive writer. His most usual verse form was the *ballade,* but he also wrote many *chansons royaux, rondeaux, virelais,* and other types of poems, as well as three prose works and twelve works in Latin. He is often banal, but he effectively varies his rhythms, sometimes uses new and unusual words, and under stress of strong emotion, he can be eloquent.

What one misses in Deschamps is poetic grandeur. To be sure, he was courageous in attacking great issues and in giving good, though unpleasant, counsel to his patrons; he was loyal in defending those he admired against vilification, compassionate toward the sufferings of the poor, patriotic in assessing the desperate situation of France and in urging powerful men to act. He nevertheless alienates his audience by the constant intrusion into important themes of peevish grumbling about personal grievances. Small difficulties and great evils are jumbled together, so that subjects essentially momentous are made to seem trivial. Then too, the light structure of his favorite verse forms, the *ballade* and *rondeau,* give inadequate support to the weight of his indignation. Yet Deschamps, for all his faults, exhibits a sense of responsibility, lacking in men like Machaut and Froissart.

Before turning to the drama, it may be well to pause for a moment to stress a few salient facts about the more professional French literature of the fourteenth century that we have been sampling. During this time, the life of the old epics and romances was being artificially prolonged by dull imitations or prose replacements. The content of the troubadour lyrics was little changed, but their exciting rhythms and vocabulary succumbed to the stereotypes of the *rondeau, ballade, virelai,* and *chanson royale.* External characteristics of the *Roman de la Rose* were copied without being given any vital human significance. There was a new note of realism in some of the poetry and an increasing use of allegory—that mediaeval substitute for psychology—but the few innovations did little to revivify the literature of the age. The patina of the past remained, a kind of rust that failed to cover a rotting core. Men like Machaut, Froissart, and even Deschamps appear for the most part to lack literary depth. They treat their main theme, love, as little more than an insignificant game, and they conceal their hollowness with prolix and pedantic learning.

But it is only fair to say of these three poets that, like their early French predecessors, they exercised much influence both at home and abroad. Chaucer, for example, in his so-called French period was indebted to all three of them. Indeed Chaucer has been called "a French love-poet writing . . . in the English language," and, "the culminating artist of the French tradition." As for François Villon, his debt to Deschamps is discernible in many poems, the debtor in this case improving so vastly on his creditor that he could be a great poet even within the confining form of the *ballade*.

When we turn to the French drama of the fourteenth century, we leave the courts of the aristocracy and descend into the market place. That is, all of the plays of the time which survive today, with one exception, seem to have been written for popular consumption. And, unlike the works of the professional men of letters, they are anonymous. Some of them were products of guilds. All of them, even those most religious in their subject matter, exhibit an earthiness quite foreign to the literature we have been considering.

I should like to examine first a collection of forty miracle plays known as the *Miracles de Nostre Dame*. In each of these plays the Blessed Virgin Mary saves an erring mortal from the consequences of his sin. The sins include every variety known to the modern screen. But hesitation on the part of the sinner before committing the crime, true repentance afterward, and sincere appeals to Our Lady enable him to achieve grace. The plots vary widely and can be traced to many different sources. Yet underlying them all is a certain uniformity. In every play the Blessed Virgin appears in person, accompanied by saints and angels who sing songs in her honor. And the ending is always the happy one of salvation. One of the most famous of these dramas has formed the basis of several modern versions, among them Maeterlinck's *Soeur Béatrice* and Max Reinhardt's successful spectacle *The Miracle*. This is the story of the young nun who is seduced by a lover and leaves her convent, but whose place, because of her reluctance to depart, her great piety, and her eventual repentance, is filled throughout her absence by the Blessed Virgin herself.

It has long been surmised that this collection of plays owes its origin to some guild, and recently it has been proved that the guild in question was that of the Parisian goldsmiths. From records of societies like theirs and from the two manuscripts in which the collection is preserved, we may deduce that one of the *Miracles* was performed each year as part of the festivities in honor of Our Lady, the guild's patron saint.

The songs interpolated in the plays are *rondeaux* and accompanying the plays in the manuscripts are separate poems *(serventoys)* in praise of the Virgin that resemble courtly lyrics in form and diction. Obviously, the tone of the *serventoys* is very different from that of the plays; like the songs in *rondeau* form, it testifies to the extent of the influence exerted by literary traditions. It has been suggested that when members of the guild assembled to witness the plays, possibly at the banquets usual on such occasions, they also held poetical contests, awarding prizes to the best of the poems that had been submitted.

The plays, as we have said, embrace a great diversity of plots, and like the tales of Chaucer and Boccaccio, they bring into action people of every class of society. Some are about saints, but men and women from the highest to the lowest ranks of Church and State make their appearance. They range from popes and cardinals to hermits, priests, and nuns; from emperors, empresses, kings, and queens to heralds, bailiffs, sergeants, and executioners. Included also, among others, are students, minstrels, children, fools, beggars, pilgrims, midwives, innkeepers, and many types of servants. Because the plays are for the most part derivative in theme and their plots are borrowed from older stories, one must be cautious in interpreting them as portrayals of fourteenth-century life. Nevertheless, contemporaneous conditions are evident in the denial of confession and extreme unction to condemned criminals, in the assignment of important roles to hermits and, occasionally, less honorable ones to monks and nuns, and in the remark of a charlatan to his fellow thief that the English have stolen all his loot.

Although the authors of these plays may have had learning of a sort—the intercalated poems and the prose sermons preceding many of the *Miracles* betray the hands of clerks—nevertheless the atmosphere of the collection emanates from the milieu for which it was composed. Women in the *Miracles* are not goddesses on pedestals, but true daughters of Eve. The attitude toward love and marriage is that of the citizenry, not that of courtly society. No coy dalliance here with other men's wives! Fidelity is a virtue; men and women who break their marital vows expect to be punished. In general, the plays abjure allegory and substitute realism. Merchants go off on business trips and drive hard bargains. We witness a woman in childbirth, another about to be burned, still another on the point of being raped. Nuns and monks yield to mundane passions, and persons of the most exalted station succumb to the same temptations that doubtless plagued the titillated spectators.

Indeed realism goes so far in the *Miracles* that God, the Blessed Virgin, the archangels, angels, and saints address the erring mortals whom they admonish with the easy familiarity of equals. As Petit de Julleville says, "Nothing is more natural in these plays than the supernatural."

The authors, however, were close observers of human nature. A canon, unwillingly lured into marriage by his relatives, leaves his bride on their wedding night, but not without experiencing fleshly yearnings as he views her naked in bed. In another play, the brother of the Emperor of Rome is entrusted with the care of the Empress during her husband's absence, but himself falls in love with her. In a long monologue he analyzes both his overwhelming desire and his feelings of guilt at betraying his brother; he sways alternately between "I will" and "I won't," and he uses every possible sophistry to persuade himself that he must have the woman he loves although he knows he must not.

Of course, the plays vary in merit, but the best of them have a continuing dramatic impact, and several have been performed successfully in our own time. Many of the plots are intricate and are developed with suspense; the characters have actuality and their problems evoke the universal emotions of pity, fear, and horror. It should also be remembered that music served to heighten the feelings that were aroused. And naturally the religious theme, namely that faith in the Blessed Virgin and prayers for her intercession can save the worst of sinners, must have assuaged the hearts of many a guilty mediaeval spectator.

The religious element in the *Miracles de Nostre Dame* is sometimes submerged by the excitingly mundane plots. With the earliest French Passion play, however, the so-called *Palatine Passion* of the fourteenth century, the religious matter and purpose become more obvious. Indeed, in two versions of the narrative poem on which the play is based, that purpose emerges clearly, for the prologue of the poem scolds those who would rather hear about Roland and Oliver than about Christ's sufferings on the cross.

The *Palatine Passion* is a meager thing when compared with its great successors, and, unlike the *Miracles* of the Parisian goldsmiths, it seems to have been written for a provincial audience. But in its brief compass of just under two thousand lines, some thirty-seven characters appear, besides an unknown number of anonymous angels, Jews, and souls in limbo. And the action extends from preparations for the Last Supper through all the well-known incidents before and after the Crucifixion, and ends with the three Marys at the tomb, the angelic announcement to them of the Resurrection, and their subsequent telling of the news to St. Peter.

The Passion play in its many manifestations was designed to rival other forms of diversion as well as to dramatize biblical history and enliven the teachings of the Church. A comparison of the *Palatine Passion* with its liturgical and biblical sources and with its more pretentious descendants shows a generous measure of originality in some scenes, and their crude realism and humor indicate a desire to entertain as well as to instruct. For example, when Judas receives his thirty pieces of silver for betraying his master, he proceeds to count them one by one and then exclaims that he has been cheated: there are only twenty-eight. And the playwright is at some pains to indicate that the nails used in the Crucifixion were inexpertly forged by the wicked wife of the smith after the smith himself had refused to use his professional skill for such an evil purpose. Indeed, our dramatist seems to delight in scenes of cruelty as he dwells at length on the torturing and beating of Jesus. He is also very fond of devils, and one of the best scenes takes place during the Harrowing of Hell. Another lively episode in the play gives us a picturesque harangue by the spice merchant from whom the three Marys, on their way to the tomb, try to buy unguents with which to anoint Jesus. The merchant claims to be a physician from the great mediaeval medical center of Salerno, and he vaunts his wares like a circus barker. He offers the Marys not only the ointment they desire, but herbs to make the old young, to enable lovers to embrace their sweethearts without being seen, and still others guaranteed to raise the dead.

Another play of the fourteenth century also reflects the taste of the populace. This is *Le Jour du Jugement*, which, though it lacks the realism and humor of the *Palatine Passion*, must have been very impressive, for it links the story of Antichrist with the Day of Judgment and introduces a vast multitude of biblical and apocryphal figures, as well as some that are fabrications of the playwright. In the play, we see devils instructing Antichrist on how to imitate Christ so that he too, by their magic, can heal the blind and sick, succor the oppressed, and resurrect the dead. Of course, punishment of this usurper is not long delayed. He is doomed, but not alone. A long procession of the damned pass before us: an abbess and bishop who have sinned together, a king, bailiff, provost, lawyer, an adulterous queen, an erring prioress, a usurer, his wife, servant, and even his small child. Here is a cast of characters reminiscent of those in the miracle plays. And the author displays his proletarian sympathies by damning any persons who have been unkind to the poor and all, even children and servants, who have lived on the fruits of usury. At the end of the play, in a grandiose final scene, apostles and saints aid in the task of separating the saved from the damned: the blessed are gently led away to paradise while angels pour out vials of wrath on the wicked and devils brutally drive them to hell.

This dynamic treatment of the Last Judgment must have been a sensational, animated version of the scene so often depicted by mediaeval artists. Nearly a hundred characters took part in the play, and despite its relative brevity—it occupies less than three thousand lines—it gave the people a pageant of vast proportions with surprising theatrical effects in its contrasting movements and costumes. Just as the *Palatine Passion* was a forerunner of the magnificent and sumptuous Passion plays of later periods, so the piece about Antichrist and the Last Judgment, with its enormous range of characters, its complicated and suspenseful plot, was a precursor of the grandiose dramatic spectacles of the following centuries. Indeed the most famous and beautiful of all the French religious plays of the fifteenth century, the *Passion* by Arnoul Greban, owes much in technique and even in language to these unpretentious antecedents.

The last French play to which I would call your attention is a play about the patient Griselda, known as *L'Estoire de Griseldis*. It was written at the very end of the century, in 1395, and, unlike the plays we have been considering, it is not a play of the market place or the guilds, but a dramatic work probably performed at court. Before this time we know of mimed *entremés,* or interludes, produced during royal banquets, and we hear of mimed spectacles given in connection with the processional entries of royal guests, but no other play like the *Griseldis* has come down to us.

The theme was first developed by Boccaccio in the *Decameron.* Petrarch retold Boccaccio's Italian story in Latin, and in this form it had wide currency. From Petrarch (and a French translation) Chaucer took his English version for the Clerk's contribution to the *Canterbury Tales*. From Petrarch, too, the story was twice translated into French prose, once by Philippe de Mézières, whose translation forms the basis for *L'Estoire de Griseldis*. Indeed, it has been plausibly suggested that Philippe himself, a much traveled diplomat, a royal counselor of Charles V, and a tutor of Charles VI, wrote the play and that its first performance had something to do with preparations for the marriage of Isabelle of France and Richard of England, a project dear to Philippe, who hoped thereby to establish a durable peace between the two countries.

The theme of all the versions of the Griselda story deriving from Petrarch is the same: the almost unearthly patience of Griselda in the face of her husband's testing of her. Our dramatist adds colorful hunting scenes to his source and emphasizes the pageantry of courtly life. He also uses Griselda's humble status as an excuse to introduce shepherds who seem especially eager to express contentment with their lot and to exalt the advantages of their simple, pastoral life. At times, there is a humorous twist to their comments, a playful treatment which suggests the aristocratic attitude of the stylized *pastourelle* rather than any tendency to sympathize with the hardships of the lower classes.

Despite the fact that this is the first serious French play with a non-religious theme and that it was destined for a noble rather than a bourgeois audience, it is not too different from the plays we have been considering. The human beings it portrays are not unlike those in the miracle plays or even some of those in the Passion plays; and Griselda's virtue has a little of the superhuman quality that pervades the heroes and heroines of the saint plays. But here for the first time, outside the realm of farce and comedy, divine intervention is missing. Both the subject matter and the treatment of it are worldly. The motivation is mundane rather than religious. The play has sometimes been likened to a morality play since it dramatizes an abstraction—constancy. Yet its characters are real people, not allegorical figures, and the virtue of wifely submission bears little relation to the virtues canonized by the moralities. Here then, at the end of the century, is the drama, secularized and destined for an aristocratic audience. It has given us something new.

In conclusion, let me forget for a moment my reluctance to generalize. Glancing back at the French literature of the fourteenth century, we have found that it falls into two categories. One was largely the work of professional men of letters and was designed for the aristocracy: it seems essentially static and offered little that was original. The other, more nearly reflecting the rising influence of townsfolk and guilds, is best mirrored in the drama; and the drama, for all its defects, had a forward movement, a potentially dynamic vitality.

Of course, one should not be too rigid about this division; a king and his court might—and did—enjoy the Passion plays, whereas his subjects, given an opportunity to hear them, undoubtedly would have delighted in certain works by Machaut, Froissart, and Deschamps. There is a democracy about all literature that tends to break through barriers. But, speaking generally, for the fourteenth century, the division is recognizable.

As for what in art and literature is derivative, what evolutionary, and what original, one can only judge in retrospect. Surveying the literature of France between 1300 and 1400, we find little outside the drama that seems freshly inspired. And yet it is only necessary to mention Chaucer, Petrarch, Boccaccio, and Villon to realize how the alchemy of genius turned dross into gold and how what was best in the works of this era could survive and be used in happier times and places. Regarding the drama, its universal appeal in the fifteenth, sixteenth, and seventeenth centuries to courtiers and groundlings alike needs hardly to be emphasized. Yet it is worth remembering that many a flowering in the garden that we call the Renaissance can be traced back directly to small seedlings nurtured during the late mediaeval period.

THE COLLEGE SYSTEM IN THE FOURTEENTH-CENTURY UNIVERSITIES [1]

ASTRIK L. GABRIEL

The Fourteenth and Twentieth Centuries: A Problem of Bricks and Brains

When we examine the history of education and educational facilities in Western civilization, we find that the fourteenth century is strikingly similar to our own, particularly with regard to the problems created by the increased demand for learning. The problems are the same: the need for financial assistance to help create the frames and agencies of intellectual life such as colleges and universities, and for restoring the dignity of the teaching profession by forming an elite to carry on the noble tradition of the preceding century. Just as there is a wishful tendency today to increase the respect and financial independence of the teacher, so the fourteenth century tried to establish, and later succeeded in establishing, a hereditary aristocracy of the teaching profession.

> If you sleep amid the clerics, ye shall be as the wings of a dove covered with silver, . . . wings . . . which bring divine things to men, transcend the skies, and reach the prince of heaven! [2]

The fourteenth century brought to a climax the efforts of the preceding century by enforcing an uncontested respect for the dignity of the teacher, in making him equal to the knight and noble citizen of mediaeval communities (*nobiles viri et primarii cives*).[3] And, like our own, the fourteenth century became more and more conscious that the misunderstandings of a divided world could be greatly reduced by promoting the efficacy of instruction in the oriental languages. The Council of Vienna, imposing the financial burden on prelates and colleges, ordered, in 1312, that the universities of Paris, Oxford, Bologna, and Salamanca offer courses conducted by two regent-masters in Hebrew, Greek, and the Aramaic languages.[4] Both Roger Bacon [5] and Ramon Lull lamented the paucity of true scholars in Arabic, Hebrew, and Greek,

79

and both men proposed the same solution—the foundation and endowment of colleges by princes and ecclesiastical authorities.[6]

However, the most impressive similarity between our century and the fourteenth is the feverish endeavor to establish sufficiently endowed colleges to alleviate the shortage of learned men.

The Formation of God-loving and Patriotic Scholars

The founders of the fourteenth-century colleges were inspired by an ardent desire to restore the fame and purity of studies, in part by strengthening discipline and in part by improving social conditions among the students of the great centers of learning. In Paris, this inspiration took the form of a nostalgic remembrance of the great traditions of learning that were prevalent there in the thirteenth century, a longing for "this praise-worthy learning of the University of Paris (*doctrina laudabilis Parisiensis*)." [7] The main purpose of the founding of colleges was to produce good scholars (*bonos scolares*), who would bring peace and unity to countries torn by wars, dissensions, and injustice, and to have good students possessing a perfect balance between piety and learning. At Oxford and Paris, the founders wished to form clerics who would be mirrors of justice, militant judges of equality, and a glory to their countries—as Robert of Eglesfield expressed it in the statutes of Queen's College (1340).[8] The introductory paragraphs of the college statutes of Oxford, Cambridge, and Paris express the desire of producing God- and country-loving scholars—in a word, upright citizens (*ad augmentum cultus divini, reique publicae commodum*) [9] by whom countries and republics would be stabilized (*regnum et respublica stabilitur*),[10] wise and learned scholars who would bring starlike glory to their Church and to their country (*stellarum gloria*).[11] The founder of the College of Boncour (1353) wished to form and mold in his college such scholars as would enlighten and advise kingdoms for the benefit of all.[12] According to the founder of the College of Tours (1333), this end would be achieved by lucid and salutary teaching (*perlucida et salutaria documenta*), given in honor of God, who is the Lord of all sciences.[13]

The statutes of almost every college point to the great dignity of being a scholar. Definite efforts were made to take away the privileged position of the knighthood and give it to the scholar. The educational ideas of the college founders were taken over by men such as Pierre Dubois, who dreamed of training a special type of spiritual and political missionary for the Orient. He even wanted to convert the confiscated priories of the Knights Templar into schools, and in this desire, he reveals the main endeavor of the century: to stabilize the aristocratic nature of the teaching profession.[14] In the newly founded colleges the intellectual elite became segregated from the crowd of ordinary scholars, and one more step was made toward realizing the idea of an aristocracy of learning, which was not afraid to assert that the virtue of wisdom, which is the acquisition of learning, assures a supremacy of the non-noble over the noble.[15]

The Proper Order of Learning

The educators of the fourteenth century noticed in time the signs of disintegration in the once solid and valuable system of learning. They saw that the school practices (*actus scholastici*) of the universities had lost their vitality and significance. They realized also that the foundation of all sciences, a thorough training in grammar, had been limited to a hasty teaching of the rudiments, with the emphasis put more and more on such lucrative studies as civil and canon law. They detected that "some students in other sciences, through default of good teaching and sufficient learning in grammar, often fall into the danger of failing where they had set before themselves the desire of success." [16] This message of William Wykeham, the founder of the still existing New College in Oxford (who besides this illustrious center established a college for grammar students in Winchester in 1382),[17] would be good advice today to certain proponents of education in the sciences, to those who expect discoveries from technically trained scientists who have not been taught the proper method of logical thinking. The founders of the fourteenth-century colleges tried to re-instate the proper order of learning, starting with the learning of grammar, which in their language meant the study of classics. Wykeham was right in saying: "By the knowledge of grammar justice is cultivated and the prosperity of the estate of humanity is increased." [18] Learning the texts of civil law did not always teach how to remain just, but the patient learning of quotations from the classics prepared future lawyers to understand the inner nature of justice. It was for the same reason that the always practical-minded Pierre Dubois insisted so much on the proper way to teach grammar. The founders of the colleges wished to promote the study of the liberal arts, not merely the kinds of knowledge that were useful. They took liberal arts to mean, in Aristotle's words, those arts "that provide enjoyment." [19]

Practical Considerations in the Foundation of Colleges

Besides this zealous endeavor to train an elite who, for the love of wisdom and knowledge, would become exiles [20] in order to dispel the darkness of ignorance and the fog of error (as the preamble to the charter of foundation of the University of Grenoble expressed it),[21] the founders took other not less important practical purposes under consideration. They wished, for example, to alleviate the shortage of teachers (*ex deffectu docentium*) [22] caused by the lack of competent masters, and to fill in the ranks of clerics that had been decimated by the ravaging plagues and the miseries of war in 1359 (*morsu pestilencie sublata multitudine*).[23]

Another practical consideration seemed to arise, particularly in France, from the fact that the founding prelates noticed the growing anticlericalism of the brilliant class of lawyers and counselors—the civil servants—whose career in the Church was blocked by the lack, during their student years, of sufficient benefices and supporting prebends.[24] The fourteenth-century founders were, therefore, very anxious to establish as many *bursae* (scholarships) as possible in canon and civil law, in order to train for civil service clerics who would be equally devoted to the King and Pope, to the State and Church, to *ecclesia* and *respublica*.

Number of Colleges

The dynamism of the fourteenth century could not be better illustrated than by statistics comparing the number of colleges founded in the thirteenth, fourteenth, and fifteenth centuries.[25] In France, 20 colleges were founded in the thirteenth century, 54 in the fourteenth (Paris, 37; [26] Montpellier, 4; [27] Angers, 1; [28] Toulouse, 9; [29] Avignon, 1; [30] and Cahors, 2 [31]), and 12 in the fifteenth. In England, the figures are 4 for the thirteenth, 12 for the fourteenth (Oxford, 5; [32] Cambridge, 7; [33]), and 9 for the fifteenth. In Italy, 1 was established in the thirteenth, 10 in the fourteenth (Bologna, 4; [34] Padua, 5; [35] and Perugia, 1 [36]), and 5 in the fifteenth. Salamanca [37] and Lerida [38] each founded one college in the fourteenth century. In Germany, the first universities were founded only in the second half of the fourteenth century. In the fourteenth century, Prague had 4; [39] Vienna, 1; [40] Heidelberg, 3; [41] Erfurt, 1 [42]—a total of 9 against the 7 of the fifteenth century. Taking everything into consideration, we may say that 87 colleges sprang from the fertile soil of the fourteenth-century universities, against the 58 colleges founded during the thirteenth and fifteenth centuries.

Among the thirty-seven colleges founded in Paris during the fourteenth century, the most important were Navarre (1304), the center of the forward scientific movement of the century; Lemoine (1302 [see Plate XXI]); Montaigu (1387, 1392), the controversial house of strict discipline [43] and of string beans (Maison des Haricots); [44] Narbonne (1317), which gave Pope Clement VI to the Universal Church; [45] Du Plessis (1321, 1322); De la Marche (1362, 1374); Dormans-Beauvais (1370), the alma mater of Boileau, author of *L'Art poétique;* [46] Fortet (1394), where the Très Sainte Ligue was founded.[47] Of the four colleges founded in Montpellier, the colleges of Saint-Ruf (1364) and Des Douze-Médicins (1369) gained fame. Saint-Martial was the best known of the nine colleges established at Toulouse. Several colleges were also instituted in Angers, Cahors, and Avignon. Of the five fourteenth-century colleges in Oxford we still admire Exeter, the college of Michael de Tregury, the first rector of the University of Caen; [48] Oriel; Queen's; and the New College (Plate XXII), the alma mater of Archbishops Chichele and Cranley. First among Cambridge's seven comes King's Hall (before 1316), immortalized in Chaucer's "The Reeve's Tale" as

> . . . a greet collegge
> Men clepen the Soler Halle at Cantebregge.[49]

Then come Michael House; University College; Pembroke (Plate XXIII), where preference was given to students of French birth; Gonville; Trinity Hall; and Corpus Christi, one of the treasures of Cambridge, with its Old Court still reflecting the splendor of the original foundation.[50]

In Prague, the Carolinum gained fame; there Emperor Charles IV most patiently listened to a four-hour disputation.[51] In Vienna, the Collegium Ducale was a well-endowed faculty house.[52] Among the Italian colleges founded in Perugia, Padua, and Bologna is the magnificent College of Spain in Bologna,[53] the unimpaired dignity of whose mediaeval architecture ranks it with the harmonious buildings of Oxford and Cambridge.

Growth in a Century of Depression

The surprising growth of the colleges cannot be attributed to favorable economic, social, and political conditions. The fourteenth century was rather a century of depression in which there were monetary and commercial crises. Periodical dearth (*caritia*), wars, epidemics, hunger, and famine decimated the population. A stagnant commerce, the decadence of the drapery industry in Flanders, the Jacquerie in France (1357), and the insurrection in England (1381) were not encouraging factors.[54] Between 1348 and 1374, when Gonville, Trinity Hall, and Corpus Christi colleges were founded at Cambridge, England suffered a 40 per cent decrease in its population. But the unpropitious economic factors did not halt the optimism and the ardor of the founders. Nor were the founders of French colleges discouraged by such national disasters as the battles of Crécy (1346), Calais (1347), and Poitiers (1356). Some fifteen colleges were founded after Crécy.

The most impelling motives for growth were to be discovered in the founders' spirit of charity and in their sincere desire for the improvement of studies. John of Hubant, priest and president of the Camera Inquestarum in Paris, requested that the candidates for his college be of good and poor families; [55] Etienne Vidé's stipulation for the College of Boissy (1358) is even more touching: he wanted "needy students, children of poor and low people . . . as we and our fathers were." [56]

The Founders

From the point of view of their social background, the founders can be divided into prelates, university-trained ecclesiastics (many of whom were outstanding civil servants), members of the royal families, the lay aristocracy, and a very small group of lay people.

Among the prelates we find Popes Innocent VI (Saint-Martial, Toulouse, 1359),[57] Urban V (Des Douze-Médecins, 1369); [58] Cardinals Egidio Albornoz (College of Spain, 1367),[59] Jean Lemoine (Lemoine, 1302),[60] Jean de Dormans (Dormans, 1370),[61] Talleyrand de Périgord (Périgord, 1363),[62] Audoin-Aubert, Bishop of Ostia (Maguelone, 1363),[63] Pierre de Monteruc (Sainte-Catherine or Pampeluna [Pamplona], 1379, 1382),[64] and Angelico Grimouard, Bishop of Avignon (Saint-Ruf, 1364); [65] and archbishops and bishops who were the founders of the colleges of Aicelins-Montaigu (1314),[66] Narbonne (1317),[67] Bayeux (1309),[68] the College of De Rodez (1371),[69] the College of Oviedo (1386),[70] Exeter (1314, 1316),[71] and New College (1379).[72] In addition there are many cathedral chanters, canons, university-trained priests and civil service men, physicians, and professors of law.[73]

Lay initiative came from members of the royal families: Jeanne de Navarre, wife of Philip the Fair and Countess of Champagne (Navarre, 1304); [74] Jeanne de Bourgogne (Bourgogne, 1331); [75] Elizabeth de Burk, Countess of Clare (University or Clare Hall, 1326); [76] and Marie de Valence, Countess of Pembroke (Pembroke, 1347).[77]

The absence of the rich burgher and bourgeois classes is striking. There is one exception: the founding of Corpus Christi College in Cambridge (1352) by the religious guild of Corpus Christi and the Blessed Mary,[78] a foundation made through the efforts of Henry Duke of Lancaster, whom Froissart called "a valiant lord, wise and imaginative." [79]

The participation of burghers, usually averse to the scholastic population of their town, was just an isolated case in Cambridge. The reconciliation of town and gown, of burghers and clerics, was not lasting. In 1381, the first generation of the descendants of the burghers who founded Corpus Christi forgot all about the truce between scholars and townspeople. They attacked the college, and "breaking upon the House and doors, they traitorously carried away the Charters, Writings, and Muniments, with Jewels and other Goods of the same College." [80] An old woman by the name of Margaret Steere gathered the ashes of the old writings and scattered them in the air, saying, "away with the skill of the clerks, away with it." [81]

Some of the foundations were of a co-operative nature, such as that of the Collège des Lombards (1334), which was founded by a French prelate, a burgher of Modena, a pharmacist, and a canon of Paris—all of whom were of Italian origin.[82]

Besides the founders, a great number of ecclesiastics and university scholars contributed to the support of students and *bursae.* Aubert de Guignicourt (1300-1360) made several donations to help the studies of a fixed number of students who were sent from Soissons to the College of Laon in Paris.[83] Barthélemy de Bruges, professor of medicine at Montpellier and a famous alumnus of Paris, gave large donations to the Sorbonne, Saint-Nicholas-du-Louvre, and Bourgogne.[84]

But the great love for studies and the burning charity of the founders made them forget sometimes that enthusiasm alone is not sufficient for solid and lasting foundations. Jean Gerson came out against these short-sighted founders. In his treatise *How to Make a Will* he warned prospective founders that an insufficiently endowed college (*ex talibus modicis . . . fundationibus*) would be exposed to miseries and was doomed to failure. It was better to establish a great college with solid foundations, because that assured it a greater chance for survival (*melius enim reguntur, continuantur et permanent*).[85]

The general intention of the founders is best expressed by Girard Cardinal Montaigu (College of Laon, 1314), who wished his students to live freely, peacefully, and quietly (*libere, pacifice et quiete*),[86] a very good directive for those who wish to see their students grow up free men (*libere*) in orderly and disciplined surroundings (*pacifice*), in the silence of comfortable and inspiring institutions (*quiete*).

Fellowship and the Antipluralist Legislation

It is well known that university studies in the mediaeval centers of learning were in large measure made possible by the then existing benefice system. Inaccurate information on absenteeism and the pluralism of benefices tends to cause us to underestimate the immense good that resulted from the right of patronage and of appointment benefices. Bishop Simon of Ghent allowed the leave of 308 beneficiaries in seventeen and one-half years, and Bishop Walter Reynolds of Worcester 156 in five years, in order to encourage them to study in universities.[87] Since these benefices were not always substantial and certainly not sufficient, some incumbents tried to receive several benefices at the same time, and the result was pluralism. The Church took stern measures against this procedure, an action which naturally displeased those who wanted to continue their studies in such costly places as Paris and Bologna.

This antipluralist legislation resembled somewhat the present policy of our great foundations, which check thoroughly to see whether the applicants have received other grants or fellowships. Both agencies, the mediaeval Church and the modern foundation,

ILLUSTRATIONS

PLATE I.—Laon, Cathedral, choir. (Used by permission of Clarence Ward.)

PLATE II.—Chars, Parish Church, interior of nave looking toward choir. (The Fogg Museum of Art, Collection of A. Kingsley Porter, photograph negative. Used by permission of the Museum.)

PLATE III.—Saint Denis, Abbey Church, interior. (Photograph by the author.)

PLATE IV.—Beauvais, Cathedral, detail of choir. (Photograph by the author.)

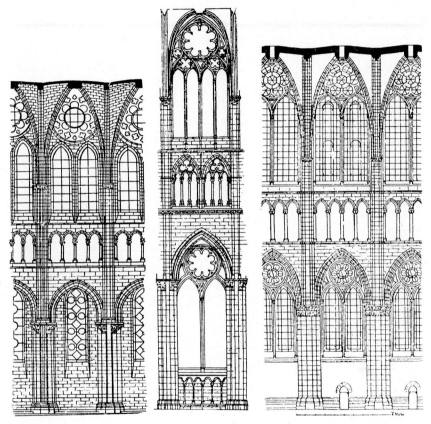

PLATE V.—Chartres, Amiens, and Reims, Cathedrals, nave elevations. (From Rudolf Adamy, *Architektonik des Gothischen Stils* [Hanover, 1887(?)], pp. 137, 141, and 143.)

PLATE VI.—Saint-Urbain of Troyes, choir. (From *Vitraux des églises de France*, with an Introduction by Louis Grodecki [Paris: Editions du Chêne, 1947], Plate VI. Used by permission of the publisher.)

PLATE VII.—Albi, Cathedral, interior. (Used by permission of Les Editions d'Art "Yvon," Paris, France.)

PLATE VIII.—Toulouse, Church of the Jacobins, interior. (Used by permission of Editions Labouche Frères, Toulouse, France.)

PLATE IX.—Boulogne-Billancourt, Notre-Dame-des-Menus, interior. (From Maurice Dumolin and George Outardel, *Paris et la Seine* [*Les Eglises de France* (Paris: Letouzey et Ané, 1936)], p. 290. Used by permission of the publisher.)

PLATE X.—Montpellier, Cathedral, interior. (Used by permission of Bildarchiv Foto-Marburg, Marburg/Lahn, Germany.)

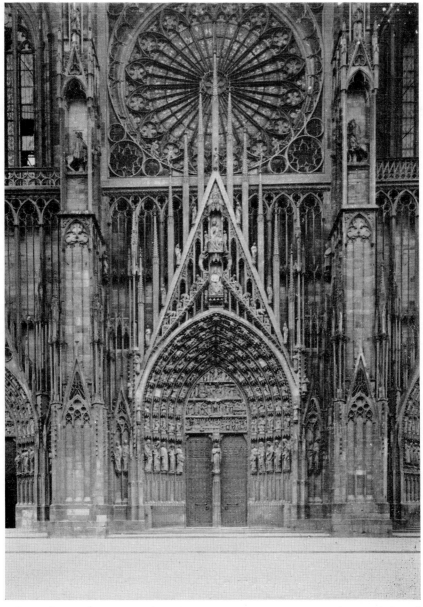

PLATE XI.—Strasbourg, Cathedral, detail of west façade. (Used by permission of Bildarchiv Foto Marburg, Marburg/Lahn, Germany.)

PLATE XII.—Séez, Cathedral, choir. (Used by permission of Michel Dumeige, Librairie "Notre-Dame," Séez [Orne], France.)

PLATE XIII.—Saint-Thibault, Priory Church, detail of choir wall. (From Marcel Aubert, "Saint-Thibault," in *Congrès archéologique de France, XCIᵉ Session, Guide archéologique du Congrès du Dijon* [Paris, 1929], XCI, 254. Used by permission of the author.)

PLATE XIV.—Saint-Sulpice-de-Favières, Church, choir. (The Fogg Museum of Art, Collection of A. Kingsley Porter, photograph negative. Used by permission of the Museum.)

PLATE XV.—Rouen, Abbey Church of Saint-Ouen, interior of nave looking toward choir. (Used by permission of Clarence Ward.)

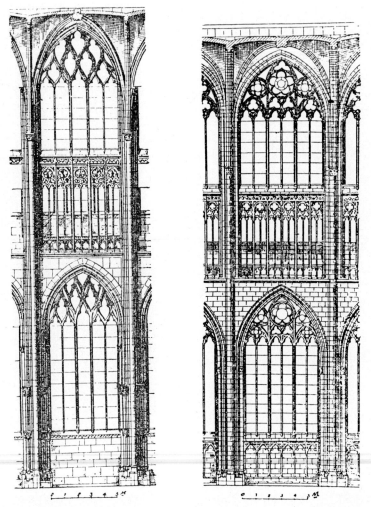

PLATE XVI.—Rouen, Abbey Church of Saint-Ouen, elevations of nave and choir. (From Robert de Lasteyrie, *L'Architecture religieuse en France à l'époque gothique* [Paris: A. & J. Picard & Cie, 1927], II, 22, Fig. 606. Used by permission of the publisher.)

PLATE XVII.—Exeter, Cathedral, interior looking east. (Photo by F. Frith & Co.
Ltd., the Postcard People, Reigate, England. Used by permission of the publisher.)

PLATE XVIII.—Celles-sur-Belle, Church, interior. (Used by permission of Artaud Père & Fils, Editeurs, Nantes, France.)

PLATE XIX.—Narbonne, Cathedral Saint-Just, ambulatory. (Used by permission of Edition Studio Henry, Narbonne, France.)

PLATE XX.—Paris, Eglise Saint-Séverin, ambulatory. (Used by permission of Father Francis Connan, Eglise Saint-Séverin, Paris, and P. Le Moult, Charenton [Seine], France.)

COLLEGE DU CARDINAL LE MOINE ☆

Cour du College du Cardinal le moine.

PLATE XXI.—Courtyard of the College of Lemoine. (Bibliothèque Nationale, Paris, Département des Estampes, Va 256. d.)

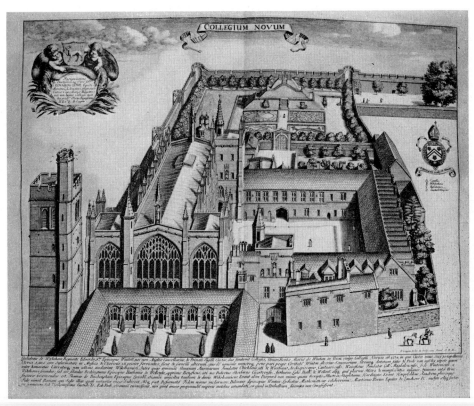

PLATE XXII.—New College, Oxford. (From A. Wood, *Historia et antiquitates Universitatis Oxoniensis* [Oxford, 1674], Bk. II, p. 126, Plate XIX.)

PEMBROKE COLLEGE.

PLATE XXII.—Pembroke College. (From *Cantabrigia depicta* [Cambridge, 1809], facing p. 33.)

PLATE XXIV.—Pierre d'Ailly, Grand Master of the College of Navarre. (Cambrai, France, MS 954, fol. 1.)

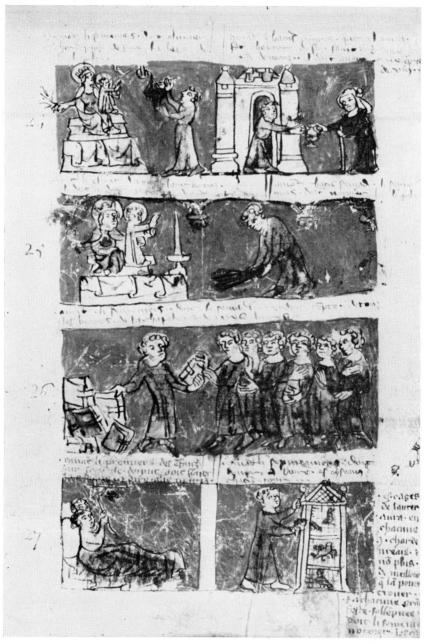

PLATE XXV.—Inspection of the books in the library of Ave Maria College. (Archives Nationales, Paris, MS 406, fol. 10ᵛ, miniature 26.)

agree on a policy of antipluralism. But as the value of certain fellowships decreases, we may find ourselves agreeing with Bishop Walter Cantilupe who, in 1237, said: "I myself, before I was called to my present dignity [of bishop], determined in my mind that if I had to lose one benefice under such a decree [of antipluralism], I would give them all up." [88]

The founders of mediaeval colleges tolerated a small number of benefices, but very intelligently determined the maximum amount any incumbent might receive. In most regulations covering admission, the value of the fellowships was carefully determined along with the maximum number of benefices one might have. Transgression immediately disqualified the fellow from receiving any further revenues he had enjoyed in the college. For instance, in the College of Saint-Michel or Chanac (established after 1343 or 1348), if a theologian received more than forty Paris pounds, a decretist more than thirty Tours pounds, or an artist more than twenty-five Tours pounds, in any form of yearly benefice or patrimony (*sive de beneficio, sive de patrimonio*),[89] he had to give up his place to a poorer and more deserving scholar. In the College of Lemoine all students in arts were excluded when they had more than three silver marks of yearly revenue, the theologians when they had more than four.[90]

Thus by limiting the amount of revenue which could be enjoyed by a scholar, the founders offered an alternative to the antipluralist legislation. By their restrictions they tried to regain those civil servants who, because of lack of benefices, were unable to serve the Church. They assured the education of a well-disciplined elite, who would be able to resist the temptation of fat benefices and would be well enough trained so as to escape the accusation of the often repeated pun against those *"qui nesciunt declinare prebenda"*—who do not know how to decline the word *prebenda* and do not know how to *decline* the prebend. Another great merit of the "benefices" given as fellowships was that they could not be diverted by the Crown or by any political or ecclesiastical power.

Toward the middle of the fourteenth century the universities realized the importance of supporting their scholars and graduates in their applications and petitions for vacant benefices. The universities began to send *rotuli* (lists of applicants) to the Pope.[91] A Cambridge roll of *ca.* 1390 speaks of men "hidden under a bushel" because they could not face the competition of those backed by

powerful persons. The university wished these persons to be promoted according to their merits, or as the university put it,
"erected upon the candlestick of promotion." Yet a look at the
rotuli may convince us that the universities often placed the ranking officers or senior graduates (*pociores in gradu*) at the head of
their lists. At Cambridge, the list was headed by the chancelors
(*olim cancellarii*); [92] at Paris, usually by the acting proctors.

   This "formidable list of seniors" discouraged the beginning
scholars and made their chances very slim. The multiplication
of college "benefices" in the forms of *bursae* opened the way for
the continuation of studies to those who were barred by the holders
of important degrees listed on the *rotulus*. The founders supplied
the lacking revenues to those who were left outside the doors, so
to speak, while others backed by Church or Crown enjoyed "the
delights of the marriage" with the benefices.[93]

Buridan, a Well-paid Professor!

   Taking as an example John Buridan, the head of the Terminist
Movement in Paris, we are surprised to learn that this century-
creating (*saeculum Buridani*) light of the University of Paris was
not supported in his early years by any benefice. Fortunately, however, he was received into the College of Lemoine, in 1308, and
there he conducted his experiments. After he had become rector
in 1329, and his fame was assured, the tide of benefices turned in
his favor. In 1329, he had a benefice in the diocese of Arras; in
1330, John XXII gave him sixty pounds with cure or forty without; in 1342, Clement VI made him canon of Arras; and in 1349,
he received from the same pope a benefice of fifty Tours pounds [94]
and the University of Paris obtained for him from the bishop of
Paris the chaplaincy of Saint André-des-Arts.[95] This latter prebend
was certainly a very desirable sign of appreciation when translated
into material goods because it meant for Buridan the revenues of
52 arpent of good soil, 8 arpent of garden, 8 arpent of woods, 1½
arpent of meadows, 12 *solidi* and 7 *denarii, census minutus,* 10
servants, both male and female, and the use of animals. What professor today would be backed by his cherished alma mater to the
extent of receiving such abundant revenues? In 1349, Buridan
headed the list of the best-provided masters (*sufficientiam modicum habentes*).[96] The University of Paris, like a true *alma mater,*
did everything to provide with sufficient means the man who came

so close to the notion of the *impeto* in Galileo, and to the quantity of movement of Descartes.[97]

Internal Structure of the Colleges

The organization of the fourteenth-century colleges followed the pattern which was established in the preceding century and which was designed by such men as Robert of Sorbon,[98] who died in 1276, Raoul of Harcourt (d. 1307),[99] and Walter Merton (d. 1277).[100] The social structure of the colleges differed from the hospices of the thirteenth century and from the pedagogies of the fifteenth. A hospice was a house rented by a group of students;[101] a hall was an endowed house. A *paedagogium*[102] was a kind of *pensionnat*, where students were directed in their studies by a master or *paedagogus*. A college, on the other hand, was an autonomous or semi-autonomous community of men, invested with certain rights and privileges, living in an endowed building, and engaged in learning under the government of a duly elected or appointed head, who governed according to certain rules or regulations called statutes, which had been approved either by the founder, his executors, or other ecclesiastical powers.

The colleges of the fourteenth century certainly differed from the eighteenth-century idea of the student-hospice, which was ironically defined in a *dissertatio* written in 1787, as a house "where several students elect a head in order to drink and sing under his direction (*ut sub praesidio eius cantent ac bibant*)."[103] The newly founded colleges were religious or secular, just as they had been in the thirteenth century. The secular colleges were either founded for diocesan subjects or were open to any competent applicant. Some were reserved for foreign students. In Paris, colleges were erected for Danish, Swedish, Italian, Scottish, and German students; in Bologna, some were for Spanish and some for French students; and in Prague, some were for Lithuanian students. (The latter, projected in 1397, become effective in 1411.)

The title bestowed upon the heads of the colleges varied: they were called president (*praeses*), provost (*prepositus*), prior, warden (*custos*), grand-maître, or master (*magister*). In the French colleges the academic rank of the head of the college was of greater importance than in the English institutions. At Montpellier, in the Collège des Douze-Médecins, the principal, if he was a *magister*, could have a servant; if he was not a *magister*, he had no servant and was seated after the masters.[104] The English colleges, on the other hand, gave all kinds of privileges to their heads, such as private servants and even separate houses.

Business matters were left to the bursar or treasurer or proctor (*bursarius, receptor,* or *procurator*), whose duty it was to keep the colleges out of financial crises. Some founders thought that it would be better to place the management of money in the hands of the chaplains, who were *ex professo* more conscientious.

One or several chaplains were appointed to direct divine services. It was their duty to attract the students through the beauties of liturgical ceremonies, processions, and Gregorian chants, and to teach them a variety of colorful prayers from magnificently illustrated Books of Hours. Since students did not have time to recite the whole office of the day, it was abbreviated into small units, usually the Hours of the Blessed Virgin, the Holy Spirit, or the Dead.[105] The colleges of the fourteenth century played an important role in the propagation of these Books of Hours, which, because of their popularity in these colleges, became the prayer books of the laity. The founders sometimes specified that the meeting of religious obligations should not interfere with lectures and disputations in schools.[106] The chaplains, those pious promoters of intense liturgical life, left controversies to the well-qualified theologians and philosophers, who were more familiar with the atmosphere of university disputations.

Provisions for the Fellows

The students (*bursarii*) were supported by *bursae,* which were certain amounts of money given to cover weekly expenses.[107] In the first half of the fourteenth century the average *bursa* for grammar students was around three sous.[108] At the end of the century the College of Fortet gave 5 sol. a week,[109] about the equivalent of the amount spent for the binding of a book.[110] Some colleges were more generous than others.[111] Students of the philosophy faculty were the most meagerly provided for; graduate students and students of theology, law, and medicine were more richly supported. In the College of Navarre, a grammarian's *bursa* was 4 sol., and a theologian received 8 sol.[112] In the College of Maître-Gervais, Paris, a student in arts was allowed 3 sol.; one in medicine, 5 sol. for 12 weeks and 6 sol. for 40 weeks; and one in theology, 6 sol.[113] In Oriel College at Oxford, a fellow received 12 pence; [114]

in Queen's College, he received 18 pence (1 sol., 6 sous), at a time when it cost 16 pence to hire a horse for a six-day visit to London.[115] The principals and superior masters usually received more generous treatment than the graduate fellows. Certain college statutes specified yearly revenue instead of weekly allowances. In the College of Pélegry at Cahors (1365), a grammar student received 12 Tours pounds a year, which, if broken down into weekly allowances, would be the usual amount enjoyed by other grammar students.[116] The generous provision of several German colleges can be explained by the fact that these colleges were a kind of institute for advanced studies attended mostly by teaching fellows, whose duties included directing schools, teaching, and disputing (*regere, legere et disputare*).

The *bursae* were paid from endowments, bequests, and other revenues provided by the founders and benefactors from houses that were purchased, rents on various holdings, or benefices restricted to college communities. We are not surprised to find that the founders were very anxious to protect members of their colleges—the master, the fellows, the scholars, and their successors—from any loss of established revenues. Therefore, they were anxious to state very precisely that they

> maye have houlde, levye, perceive, take and enjoye all and singular Mannours, Landes, Tenementys, Possessions, Pencions, Porcions, Tythes, Rightes, Titles, Interests, Commons, Liberties, Franchises, Jurisdictions, Preheminences, Rentys, Revercions, Remaynders, Services, and all other Hereditamntys.[117]

In France, special provisions were made for the expenses to be audited and controlled, usually by the governors; in the English colleges, this task fell to the provost, the treasurer, and specially appointed fellows.[118]

Scholarships and Endowments

The number of scholarships and, consequently, the total number of fellows, cannot be definitely established. Their number depended upon the increase or decrease of the revenues of their respective colleges. In France, the College of Lemoine (1302) started with an ambitious plan of having 100, but reduced the number to 6 to 8, and finally retained 14 scholars.[119] In the College of Bayeux (1309), the original number was 12, but was later raised to 16.[120]

The College of Autun (1341) began with 15 fellows, but later admitted 18. The College of Cornouaille had 5 at first (1321); but later, in 1380, 10 fellows were admitted.[121] Generally speaking, we may say that the average number of students in a college in France was between 6 and 16; in England, between 12 and 20. In Queen's College, Oxford, there were 12 fellows in memory of the 12 apostles.[122] The College of Navarre with 70 students,[123] Du Plessis with 40,[124] and Lisieux [125] and Dormans-Beauvais [126] with 24 each, lead in France. The most influential scholastic establishment in England was New College [127] with an impressive 70 scholars; [128] in Italy, it was the Collegium Gregorianum (1371) [129] with 40. Although I repeat with reservation the following figures given by Thurot because of the fluctuation in the number of fellowships, they are a good indication of the dynamism of the fourteenth century: During the thirteenth century, 64 fellowships were founded in France; in the fifteenth, only 24; but the fourteenth century witnessed the creation of 505.[130]

This would be an impressive number even today if we take into consideration the fact that a mediaeval fellowship provided for food and lodging with "butler service" and that summer and winter garments, shoes, sweaters (*blanchetum*), and tunics were bought from college funds whenever the revenues allow it. The statutes also prescribed that the old clothes and shoes be given to poorer students or to other worthy persons. However, the fellows were warned that the old clothes they gave away not be worthless and entirely worn out, because such donations would deprive the Christian act of charity of its real meaning and importance.[131]

Family-like Atmosphere

The colleges often tried to achieve the flexibility of family life. The fellows belonged to different faculties and to different age groups. Advanced theologians and callow grammarians, twenty-four-year-old jurists and seventeen-year-old artists, lived together in the same college, though in separate houses under separate masters. But they all came together for chapel services.

The family-like atmosphere of the fourteenth-century colleges helped to develop a successful pattern of behavior. The friendliness of the older fellows never reached the cult of informality, and the younger never attempted to force an intimacy arising from conscious "teenolatry." The older scholars set an edifying example

as grown-ups, and they could not be asked the accusing question
that they might face in our time, "How can we grow up wisely
when we do not see grown-ups around us?" The older fellows were
taught intellectual humility, for they were told that their most difficult task was not to expound the *Sentences* to advanced theologians
but to write understandably for the use of small children; indeed,
the mediaeval educators devoted considerable time to composing
sermons for children as young as eight years, and they never under-
estimated their intellectual level. William of Tournai and Hum-
bertus Romanus gathered together the sermons they had given to
small schoolboys; [132] and, following in their footsteps, Pierre
d'Ailly, the glory of the College of Navarre, a statesman and cardinal, found time, in 1387, to write some rules and regulations for
eight-year-old college boys living in Ave Maria College. [133]

It is no wonder that the philosophy of education practiced in
those "mixed" colleges produced such treatises as those written by
Gerson, a graduate of the same College of Navarre. He, the great
chancellor of the University of Paris, composed a treatise, *Doctrina
pro pueris ecclesiae Parisiensis,*[134] in which he did not forget to
insist on such small items as the necessity of installing a vigil lamp
in the small children's dormitory, both as a symbol of their devotion and to give illumination when the "natural necessities" required them to get up during the night (*propter necessitates natu-
rales, quas leviter patiuntur pueri*).[135] In his *ABC des simples
gens,*[136] Gerson wrote for the *petiz enffans, filz et filles,* and warned
prelates that since the reformation of the Church must start with
the right teaching of small children (*ecclesiae siquidem reformatio
[sicut quidam ait] debet inchoari a parvulis*),[137] the reform of colleges must begin with the reform of elementary schools.

Besides the regular fellows, certain fourteenth-century colleges—
Narbonne,[138] Cornouaille,[139] Oriel,[140] and so on—following the example set by the Sorbonne, also admitted guests (*hospes* or *socius
commensalis*), who were called "commoners" in the English colleges. One of the most illustrious guests in Oriel College at Oxford was Thomas of Arundel, afterward archbishop of Canterbury.
These rich commoners helped to defray the expenses of the colleges, and the fellows were warned not to hurt these guests because they brought not only honor but cold cash to the college
(*domus lucretur et honoretur per tales*).[141]

Service Facilities

The aristocratic features of the teaching profession in England are best illustrated by the service facilities made available to the scholars within the colleges. In France, the fellows usually had one servant for the group; but in England, their comfort was assured by an array of attendants. Exeter had servants, a cook, a barber, and a washerwoman; [142] and Queen's impressive list of helpers included a steward, a cook, a scullion, a baker, a brewer, a miller, a barber, a gardener, a washerwoman, night watchmen, and servants.[143] Who in Paris would not have envied the comfort of the fellows of New College, Oxford, where the masters had special servants to carry their books to the nearby university schools?

Autonomy

There was a noticeable difference between the English and French college systems in the fourteenth century. In England, the colleges had greater autonomy and an almost complete independence from the university; in Paris, the university had statutory rights over certain colleges, and the aid of the university was sought in disciplinary cases.[144] The executors of the College of Boissy asked for the protection of the university.[145] The university voiced its opinion even in business management; in 1370, for instance, the university permitted the College of Maître-Gervais to absorb the College of Maître-Clément.[146]

At Paris, the principal master was more of an intellectual leader than at Oxford. Besides entering upon state business (*rem publicam gubernare*),[147] he had to teach, preside at the disputes, and direct other academic activities. At Oxford, the all-out teaching responsibility of the Paris masters was delegated to young fellows, a practice which gave birth to the tutorial system. At Paris, some of the headmasters remained "poor intellectuals," while in England they lived in much greater comfort. At Cambridge, in Peterhouse, it was considered unbecoming for a master to go afoot (*non deceat . . . ire pedes*).[148]

The English fellows had greater voice in the administration of the colleges than had the scholars at Paris. The English colleges were self-governing communities, but in France the governors, officers of the university, interfered with the inner administration of the colleges. In Exeter and Oriel, the head was elected by the fellows, and in New College even the youngest fellow was granted the right to vote in the election of the warden.[149] In France, only the colleges whose memberships were made up almost entirely of those from the higher faculties enjoyed such rights (for example, in the election of the grand master at Navarre and at the Collège des Douze-Médecins in Montpellier), though in the Colleges of Cornouaille [150] and Boissy [151] the fellows—including, apparently, the three grammar students—had the right to elect their master. In Heidelberg, in the College of Artists, the provost was elected by the majority of the fellows.[152]

An interesting form of autonomy was practiced in the German colleges. At Heidelberg, for example, in the Contubernium Dionysianum, the admission of the new fellows into the community depended not only upon the principal (*rectores bursarum*) but also on student representatives (*rector scolarium sive bachantrie*); [153] and at the Collegium Ducale in Vienna, the admission of new members was dependent upon the consent of the community.[154]

The fourteenth-century university in France could not acquire complete control of the colleges, but in the fifteenth century total control was given to the *reformatores* who were elected annually [155] and who visited every college in their official capacity as delegates of the university. In other respects, the internal administration of the colleges was autonomous. True democracy reigned among the fellows in England, where any kind of rivalry was prohibited— for example, "comparisons of family to family, nobility to nobility or ignobility (*comparationesque generis ad genus, nobilitatis ad nobilitatem vel ad ignobilitatem)*" [156] were not allowed. The fellows and their superiors followed the lesson learned from the Greeks: by no means does democracy stand for weakness and disorder.

Famous Masters

The fame and reputation of mediaeval colleges grew and were maintained by the famous masters who lived within their walls, and who "lisoient por Dieu, [et] tenoient escoles loiax." [157] The Sorbonne rose to unparalleled fame in the thirteenth century because of its talented masters, who had been recruited from all over Europe, and because of the strenuous financial negotiations of its founder, Robert de Sorbon, who personally signed more than

141 [158] contracts which were paid in cash (*pecunia numerata solutis nummis*). The royal foundation of Navarre obtained the same material advantages, by reason of which it was destined to become the most auspicious rival of the Sorbonne.

It was mainly a group of Sorbonnists, Navarrists, and Mertonians who produced the new ideas of the fourteenth century. The glorious period of Navarre started with the teaching of Buridan, and continued with Nicholas d'Oresme,[159] a celebrated political economist and a truly universal mind, who translated the *Politics* and *Ethics* of Aristotle, discoursed on the *Nature and Mutation of Money,* and also directed the college in his capacity as grand master (1356). His successor to this dignified post was Petrus Alliacus, or Pierre d'Ailly (Plate XXIV), who, in his treatises on geographical cosmography, clearly stated that if one traveled west rather than east, the distance between Spain and the Indies was much shorter.[160] His *Imago mundi* [161] (printed *ca.* 1483, by Johannes de Paderborn) was personally commented on by no less a man than Christopher Columbus.

However, the new fellows of Navarre could not becloud the reputation of the masters of such old institutions as the Sorbonne and Merton. Albertus of Saxony, the first rector of the University of Vienna and author of new theories on weight, Henry of Langenstein, Marsilius de Inghen, and others deeply interested in statics, kinetics, and astronomy belonged to the community of the Sorbonne.[162] Mertonians prided themselves on such scientists as Thomas Bradwardine, the *doctor profundus* (in Merton College from 1323 to 1335) who wrote on dynamics, mathematics, and theology, and on the fact that their school had produced Walter Burley, John Maudit, William Heytesbury, and John Dumbleton.[163]

The colleges opened their doors wide to the scientific experimentations of the century. Buridan, the early teacher of the theory of *motus* and the law of inertia,[164] made observations concerning the effect of thunder on the spire of the chapel of the college of Lemoine, where he lived before 1308.[165] His motto was *ego vidi,* "I have seen it," [166] which little by little replaced the *auctoritates* of the preceding century.

The exchange of ideas and discoveries between colleges was very rapid: in 1391, the College of Dormans-Beauvais in Paris already had the *Sophismata* of the Mertonian William Heytesbury and the logical works of Galfridus Climeton.[167]

Natural Sciences

The salutary effect of the June 5, 1366, reform of the University of Paris, prescribing the study of astronomy and "mathematical works,"[168] spread to the colleges. In the College of Maître-Gervais, founded in 1370 by the favored physician of Charles V, the king established two scholarships for two masters (*scholares regis*) who would give courses in mathematics—one in the college, the other in the faculty of arts.[169]

Because the teaching of mathematics consisted of seminar-type instruction,[170] the colleges were the most suitable places for giving extracurricular courses. In the College of Brescia in Bologna, a master was paid to give lectures on metaphysics and physics with the stipulation that not only the scholars but anybody who cared to listen, the poor students in particular, would be admitted (*et quibuscumque aliis audire volentibus, et maxime pauperibus congregatis*).[171]

However, the promoters of the natural sciences did not forget the importance of the liberal arts. Master Gervais was as much interested in the salvation of the soul as in the healing of the body. For him the liberal arts opened the way to understanding the mysteries of theology and the secrets of medicine (*viam prebent intelligencie et doctrine*).[172] Though love for natural science flourished most of all at Navarre, such Navarrists as Gerson and Pierre d'Ailly knew the classics better than some of their humanist successors; and Nicholas Clamanges felt more aversion for the old scholasticism than did the Renaissance.[173]

The Idea of the Magister

The idea of the *magister* in the fourteenth century was considerably different from that of the preceding centuries. The twelfth- and thirteenth-century stories about outstanding masters resembled the *exempla* told in the pulpit for the edification of students. When a pretty queen of France cast her eyes on Gilbert de la Porrée and desired the company of this philosopher, he did not hesitate a minute but was ready with the answer: "No."[174] But when the story was told by the anecdote-loving students, Buridan emerged not as an exemplary professor but as the clever, shrewd thinker who outwits the queen in everything.[175]

Buridan's reputation as a logic-loving master caused an amusing anecdote to grow up in connection with his friendship with Pope

Clement VI. In their youth, the pope, then Pierre Roger, and Buridan had a quarrel. In the heat of discussion, young Buridan hit Roger, who was then *bursarius* of the College of Narbonne. When Roger became pope in 1342, and received the *rotulus* of the University of Paris, he noticed Buridan's name on it and summoned him to Avignon to reprimand him. "Why did you hit the Pope?" he asked. The author of the *Summulae logicae* was ready with his answer: "Pater, papam percussi, sed non percussi Papam; id est hominem tunc non papam, sed nunc." For penance the pope jokingly ordered him to teach always in Paris and to have the "presence and absence" of his benefices, making a pun on the word *absentia:* in one sense Buridan could stay in Paris and enjoy his benefices even if they were far away (*absentia*); in the other sense the benefices could be taken away from him (*absentia*).[176]

Exempla did not hurt the reputation of thirteenth-century masters, but the anecdotes which grew up around the fourteenth-century masters overshadowed their merits. Thus Buridan today is much better known for his imagined amatory adventures and for his donkey, which, as Gilson has pointed out, "has not yet been found anywhere in his writings," [177] than for his theories on *impetus*. But everybody repeats with Villon:

> Semblablement, ou est la royne
> Qui commanda que Buridan
> Fust geté en ung sac en Saine?
> Mais ou sont les neiges d'antan? [178]

> Where is the queen with soul so hard
> That Buridan, sackbound, should steer
> A course down the Seine in wet discard?
> Where are the snows of yesteryear? [179]

The fame of the masters of the thirteenth century led to imitation; the fame of those of the fourteenth, to admiration.

The Pedagogical Value of College Debates

The fourteenth century witnessed the introduction into the daily routine of college life of the various types of scholastic disputations. Sometimes these discussions (*collationes*) were private and were reserved for the fellows of the college only; sometimes they were public and attracted a considerable gathering. At the Sorbonne, even outsiders were allowed to express their opinions.[180]

The university writings can be divided into treatises, commentaries, and questions. When questions were disputed, they were called *disputatae;* if they were not disputed, they were called *institutae.* When put into order, they became *quaestiones collectae ordinatae.*[181] The system of disputation differed from college to college, according to the faculty to which the fellows belonged. The topic was usually assigned ahead of time by the head or principal. The most common form of disputation among the artists and grammarians was the *sophismata.* The *sophisma* consisted of the presentation of a statement which was taken as a basis for discussion and was followed by questions.[182] The exercise was aimed at refuting the pseudo proofs of the opponent's *"sophista."*

Sophismata and other disputations reserved for grammarians were held in Boncour [183] and in Queen's College.[184] Almost every college [185] obliged the fellows to be present, under the supervision of a master, at the weekly disputations.

> That in scole is greet altercacioun
> In this mateere, and greet disputisoun.[186]

In certain colleges the statutes required that everybody—both young and old fellows, grammarians and advanced scholars—be present (*omnes intersint*).[187]

Topics were chosen from logic, moral philosophy, metaphysics, mathematics, and other subjects connected with the fellows' studies. Sometimes they covered political, economic, and other types of current problems. When they were *publicae,* such disputations drew great gatherings into the college. The various opinions pronounced during these disputations were collected by the attending scholars. Hence the meaning of such notes as *ista questio collecta est de diversis disputationibus quibus in diversis locis interfui.*[188]

Problems that did not fit into the regular teaching programs were also discussed in the colleges during these disputations. A number of the questions disputed by Buridan in Paris were discussed in a small *bursa* at the University of Prague during his lifetime.[189]

The great significance of the college disputation is that it permitted the fellows to debate any topic in their chapel or college hall free from the control of the faculties of art or theology. The technique of the new disputes, the *sophismata,* gave an uncontrolled freedom to the defendant. Because of the particular nature of the *sophismata,* the orthodoxy of the disputant could not be questioned. The *demonstratio* of the thirteenth-century *quaestio disputata* was replaced in these fourteenth-century disputations by the *persuasio,* in which the opponents would adopt an opinion, not because they considered it true, but only for the sake of discussion—that is, they were *collationis gratia* or *gratia exercitii.*[190] These disputes or *collationes* were not, however, merely for practice, for they provided a testing ground for the most personal opinions of those involved in them. Through them the masters tried to feel out the reaction of the public. Sometimes, under the camouflage of the *sophisma,* the masters announced their own true convictions. Ockham pointed to the real nature of these disputations when he said: "Videmus catholicos de fide absque periculo iustae calumniae ad exercitium disputare,"[191] When Nicholas d'Autrecourt was under fire because of his unorthodox views, he calmly answered that he had pronounced these theses as material for disputation without stating anything pertinaciously ("Hec omnia dixi disputative et causa collationis nichil asserendo pertinaciter").[192]

Thus the colleges, simply by insisting on the practice of *sophismata* and other college disputations, became very good agents for the propagation of philosophical pessimism (nominalism, for example), and introduced a new way (*via moderna*) of approaching the delicate problems of orthodoxy. These disputations were the training ground for those university masters who later in public appearances at ecumenical councils such as that at Constance attracted a great audience (*habet magnam audientiam*).[193]

The great pedagogical value of the disputations lay in the opportunity they gave to the younger students to sometimes have as opponents the great philosophers and theologians of their colleges. At Queen's, small boys (*parvuli*)[194] were opposed by their masters, who were, probably, fellows studying at the faculties of theology or canon law. Here again, the great principal of mediaeval teaching prevailed: never underestimate the intelligence of the young. The fellows were encouraged to exchange their opinions by mutual conferences and meetings (*per collaciones et communicaciones mutuas*).[195] Such exchanges sometimes resulted in the formulation of an opinion that was accepted by the entire college. In the Collegium Majus at Leipzig a fellow could not engage in public disputation at the university on any topic that had not been accepted by the major part of his college.[196]

The fourteenth-century disputations were not, therefore, the "mere discussions" impugned by the Renaissance; they provided an opportunity to project daring ideas and were a most effective method of learning how to get along without teachers, which must, after all, be the final educational achievement of any teaching.

Statutes and Discipline

College statutes were aimed at establishing regularity. Written by the founders, their executors, or other ecclesiastical authorities, they were intended to regulate the spiritual and material welfare of the colleges. They were composed not only for the safeguarding of privileges, but for the enforcement of discipline, with the aim of producing scholars who would be useful to their Church and country. The founders cannot be accused of favoring spirituality, for the purpose of the statutes was to promote the well-being of both the soul and body (*animarum et corporum saluti perfectius et toti rei publice commodum provenire*).[197]

The fourteenth-century regulations are generally elaborate and detailed; frequently they were the work of overcautious jurists. Often they were based on those of the Sorbonne [198] and Merton.[199] Statutes of several colleges reveal a predilection for extreme minuteness. Some, for example, mention that when soup is given to the poor, three slices of bacon should be put in it.[200] Queen's College's statutes think of the *soin de beauté* of the fellows. The shampooing of heads was not entrusted to the washerwomen but was left to the care of the barber.[201] The authors of mediaeval statutes were not afraid to suppose that rules might be broken, adding, however, *quod Deus avertat*—whereas most of our modern academic regulations ignore the frailty of human nature, apparently from fear of the "public-relation–minded" administration.

The statute book was kept in great honor. Sometimes, with a crucifix painted at the beginning, it served as an "oath book." [202] Some were illustrated, such as that of Ave Maria College, where the duties of the students were depicted in thirty-three miniatures on ten pages.[203] The statutes were the supreme control of behavior, the most important deed invoked and utilized in law suits involving the properties and self-administration of the college. Even today, when the fellows of Oxford colleges sit down to a meeting, "there is nothing and nobody to control them, apart from their own Statutes and—to the joy of all foreigners, particularly Americans, who cannot believe that this is true—the Minister of Agriculture and Fisheries and Food." [204]

The mediaeval statutes were inspired by legal sagacity, foresight, and knowledge of human nature. They were written by men who had learned that "ill manners occasion good laws, as the handsome children of ugly parents." [205]

In that golden age of colleges, when the ink used by the miniaturist was still fresh on the statute book, discipline was quite satisfactory. The fourteenth century is free from the turbulent, undisciplined crowds of the fifteenth-century *paedagogia,* the disturbing processions, the loitering in the streets, and the pushing of the *pet au diable* before the doorway of peaceful citizens. Most violations of fourteenth-century discipline were minor and stemmed from human frailty. A study of Merton College in about 1338-39 reveals misconduct such as quarrels among the fellows, noisiness, possession of pet animals, and lack of charity (*non est caritas inter socios*).[206] Some of the colleges allowed the students to have animals or birds as pets or to keep one mascot, but others, such as Queen's [207] and Marmoutier,[208] were against "giving the bread of man to dogs." [209] Hunting with hawks, birds of prey, or hounds was frowned upon, because it was considered unfitting that poor students, living on alms, pursue sports of the rich.[210] The College of Boncour was very strict in its prohibition against keeping horses,[211] but a drawing representing New College shows fellows amusing themselves with a tilting match on horseback.[212]

Besides outdoor sports, such as pitch and toss,[213] *au crocet,* and *pila,* the ancestor of golf, card playing in moderation was allowed, usually as a means of cheering up the sick.[214] At Heidelberg [215] and at the College of Narbonne,[216] playing cards or checkers for a quart or pint of wine (*pro mensura vini, pro pinta vini*) was allowed, but the players dared not make too much noise or spend too much time on the game.

Orderliness in the fourteenth-century colleges demanded that there be no loitering in the corridors after dinner. After grace, only the passing of the loving cup (*potus caritatis*)[217] was allowed, a venerable custom that still exists in the passing of port wine after dinner in some Oxford colleges. All the colleges abhorred noise and loudness. The College of Artists in Heidelberg complained against clamorous singing and pounding and against masters who received their students at ungodly hours.[218] New College in Oxford forbade "wrestlings, dances, jigs, songs, shoutings, tumults, or inordinate noises, effusions of water, beer, or other liquor, or tumultuous games." [219] It would be far from the truth, however, to attribute to these colleges the austerity later deplored by Erasmus and Rabelais, who declared that at the well-regulated College of Montaigu in the time of Giles Aycelin, archbishop of Rouen (1314), the dogs were better treated than the students. The bitter words of Erasmus against the College of Montaigu are often repeated, but very few stop to think that the courses and studies must have been excellent, for that college gave such persons to the world of learning as Erasmus himself (1496), Ignatius of Loyola, and Calvin.[220]

Most of the students were devoted to God, well disciplined according to the etymology of the words—*bene disciplinatus est Deo dedicatus;* [221] a well-disciplined man is a God-loving man.

In the statutes founders sought to assure adequate nourishment for their subjects. Wine was moderately but sufficiently served in the French colleges, and at Leipzig the principal was requested to distribute enough beer (*de cerevisia competente*) to the community to avoid excessive drinking elsewhere, probably in taverns (*ne quis habeat excusationem de singularitate bibendi*).[222] It seems that even the English fondness for substantial breakfasts required curbing, for in 1340, at Queen's, the statutes forbade serving sumptuous and excessively delicious "déjeuners" (*gentacula pretiosa, deliciis excessiva*).[223]

The custom of wearing uniform academic dress was supported by the colleges. The universities required everyone to dress simply as was becoming to scholars devoted to studies.[224] The colleges went further and prescribed a community dress, although the English and French colleges seldom prescribed the color of the livery. In England, at Queen's College, the fellows wore red robes, in remembrance of the robe and blood of Our Lord,[225] and the students were not allowed to wear red or green hose or peaked shoes, "striped, variegated, or parti-coloured clothes, or any not befitting their clerical order." [226] At the College of Navarre, the livery was to be black; [227] at Dormans-Beauvais, blue or velvet; [228] and the *capets* of the College of Montaigu wore gray capes.[229]

Women were discouraged from visiting the premises of most colleges. Parisian colleges were more gallant in that they admitted women of good reputation than was the College of Spain in

Bologna where women were called the "head of sin, arms of the devil [*caput peccati, arma diaboli*], expulsion from Paradise, . . . with whom any dealings must be avoided." [230]

College Architecture

The fourteenth century brought new ideas in college architecture. The oldest colleges in Oxford were laid out on a loose, scattered plan in which the many buildings—hall, kitchen, chambers, chapel, and so on—were separate; but in the fourteenth century the quadrangle was introduced, and it became the marvel of many English colleges, among them New College, where it is contemporary (1380-86) with the founding of the college. However, the progress made toward the establishment of a quadrangle plan was, according to W. A. Pantin, "gradually achieved rather than planned as a whole." [231] It was the genius of Bishop William Wykeham of Oxford which conceived this ideal plan for a college building.[232]

The English colleges also had large bedrooms and living rooms that were used by several persons, a practice that made small individual study rooms necessary. In realizing this need, the planners showed a real knowledge of human behavior, since, as Pantin has said, it is easier to sleep together than to work together.

If the seventeenth- and eighteenth-century plans of Navarre, Lisieux, and Du Plessis [233] which we possess today reflect their mediaeval disposition, then the French seem to have maintained the old, scattered form of college building, although the quadrangle plan prevailed in the colleges of Montaigu, D'Harcourt, Sorbonne, and in the colleges of religious orders. Among the latter is the college of the Bernardins, the beautiful refectory of which still stands, the longest Gothic hall in Paris today.[234]

The builders of the fourteenth-century colleges wanted them admired more from the inside than from without and therefore cared little for such luxuries as the elaborate gates of later centuries.[235]

The Chapel

The liturgical life of the mediaeval colleges centered around the chapel. At Oxford, the chapel of New College, with its screen gates and rich stained-glass windows, challenged the great chapel of old Merton.[236] The fourteenth century witnessed the rebuilding of the Sorbonne chapel in 1344, and its consecration in 1347, on the feast of Saint Ursula, who since has become the patron saint of the Sorbonnists.[237] The chapel of Dormans-Beauvais is one of the rare survivals among Paris college chapels.[238]

Some chapels adapted themselves to the age of the students; at Ave Maria College, the boys were allowed to have live birds in their chapel. A miniature in its statutes depicts goldfinches as a reminder to the boys that the Divine Child played with birds.[239]

The Library: "A Holy and August Place"

Student life in mediaeval colleges was carefully divided between liturgical and intellectual activities, and the libraries of the colleges contained the books that were needed both for the recitation of the Divine Office and for scholastic purposes. Merton, Dormans, and Fortet [240] are worth mentioning among the newly founded colleges with great collections of books.

The rules and regulations for the proper use of the library were usually established by the founders. Inspired by the old device *les bons livres font les bons clercs*,[241] mediaeval churchmen were very generous in providing college libraries with the necessary books. The founders themselves frequently gave good example by donating their own books to the college. There were frequent donations to already existing colleges: for example, those of Stephen of Gravesend, bishop of London (d. 1338), Simon de Bredon, canon of Chichester (d. 1372), and William Rede, bishop of Chichester (d. 1385), to Merton; that of Bishop Walter Skirlaw (d. 1406) of Durham to New College; [242] and those of Pierre Limoges, canon of Evreux, Nicholas de Bar-le-Duc (donated 1310), and Gilles d'Oudenarde (donated 1343) to the Sorbonne. Among the famous authors who gave their own publications to the Sorbonne were Thomas of Ireland, who gave his *Manipulus florum*, and Durand de Saint-Pourçain, who in 1344 presented his own commentaries on the *Sentences* of Peter Lombard.[243]

Detailed regulations concerning libraries in French colleges were given in the statutes of Lemoine, Bayeux, Narbonne, Carnou-aille, Ave Maria, Boncour, Dormans-Beauvais, and Fortet.[244] Among the fourteenth-century regulations for libraries was a requirement that an inventory be drawn up at a definite time of the year in the presence of the administrative officers.[245] At the College of Ave Maria, the *ostensio* (Plate XXV), an accounting of

all the books in the library, took place every Saturday.²⁴⁶ At
Trinity Hall, Cambridge, books had to be shown *realiter, visi-
biliter et distincte.*²⁴⁷

Several college libraries in the first half of the fourteenth century loaned books to students on the principle that the lending
of books was a deed of mercy *(commodare inter praecipua miseri-
cordiae opera computetur).*²⁴⁸ And fourteenth-century librarians
were very liberal in lending books to the teaching staff. Each
master usually had his own key to the library, and if anyone lost
his, he had to change the lock and provide new keys at his own
expense.²⁴⁹ Aware that professors like to pile up books in their
immediate surroundings (despite the vicinity of the library), the
College of Dormans-Beauvais permitted the keeping of books *en la
chaiere du maistre.*²⁵⁰ When books were missing from the libraries,
not all colleges were so severe as the College of Bernardins in the
fifteenth century, whose statutes (1493) decreed that wine be
denied to the librarian as long as any book was absent without
good reason.²⁵¹

The books were kept in *cistae,* or chests. The reference books
were chained, as can still be seen in Merton College. Sir Maurice
Powicke has correctly pointed out that only a part of the books
were kept in the libraries, while the rest were distributed among
the fellows. The reason was that in this way the best copy—we
might say "the critical edition"—could be retained in a safe and
easily accessible place.²⁵²

A sort of reverence toward the library, "a holy and august place
(sacer et augustus locus)," was requested. At the Sorbonne no
member of the society of fellows could enter the library except in
academic gown and bonnet *(nemo e Societate non togatus pilea-
tusque bibliothecam ingreditur).*²⁵³

Conclusion

The fourteenth century is characterized by an abundance of
educational endowments. This bridge-century was a period of
consolidation in which the educational facilities of the previous
centuries were being expanded and made available to a great
number of young people. The century achieved a happy equilib-
rium of moral and intellectual education. Most of the regular
university courses were still given outside of the colleges, but by
holding the disputations and offering some extracurricular courses

within the college walls, the fourteenth century prepared the way for the fifteenth, when almost all the courses were given inside the colleges.

The moral integrity of the college administration set an encouraging example in a period of strong competition for benefices. In this century no power—king, pope, bishop, ecclesiastical or lay authority—ever attempted to press its own candidates for college fellowships.

The growth of the colleges was made possible by the generosity of university-trained donors and benefactors, whose unlimited confidence in the learned men who ran the colleges made donors willing to entrust to them the business administration of the great foundations. It was believed that if the scholars were intelligent enough to teach the youth, they were farsighted enough to run the colleges' business affairs.

The heads of colleges were not only administrators but teachers; they did not believe in administration for the sake of administration. Alain, in his *Propos,* said that every administration is perfect but inhuman: "L'Administration est semblable à une raison mécanique. Tout y est sans reproche, et tout y est inhumain." [254]

The founders of fourteenth-century colleges laid down some principles for the foundation of a successful college: (1) a solid financial basis; (2) freedom of inquiry; (3) tradition, based upon the statutes, as the basic governing power; (4) an intellectual environment supported by a well-equipped library (*sacer et augustus locus*); (5) good fellowship without hypocrisy; (6) respect for individuality; and (7) admittance of fellows without discrimination and, if possible, on an international basis.

In the joyful and obedient observance of the college statutes, the founders, governors, principals, and fellows—everyone—aimed at one end, so that, in the words of William Wykeham, Bishop of Winchester,

there may be one heart and one mind, and that by their good lives, pleasing to God, their hearts set on fire by the rays of the divine love may more quickly and fervently be united in the warmth of brotherly love and sweetness of mutual charity, that so, through the clemency of God [their colleges] . . . endowed and supported by men of so many sciences and faculties, may more firmly, securely, peacefully and strongly persist and for ever endure in the beauty of peace.[255]

1. The source material on the mediaeval colleges of Paris is in great part unpublished. The statutes have been partly published by Bulaeus, Félibien and Lobineau, Feret, Bouquet, Chapotin, and Busquet. The most important manuscript collection and archive material is in the Archives Nationales, (Séries MM, H and S) Arsenal, Archives of the University of Paris: Reg. 102(96); Carton 17(28); 18(30); 19(24); 20(25); 21(27); 22(29); Sainte-Geneviève; Bibliothèque Nationale. Microfilms of the most significant materials on the Parisian colleges are in the Mediaeval Institute of the University of Notre Dame, Indiana.

I am very grateful to G. Calmette, conservateur en chef de la Bibliothèque de l'Université de Paris (Sorbonne); Mlles. J. Vielliard and E. Pellegrin and Mme. A. Vernet at the Institut d'Histoire des Textes; Mlle. Y. Lanhers at the Archives Nationales; Mlles. M. Th. d'Alverny and L. Concasty, and Mmes. Laurain-Portemer, J. Rambaud-Buhot, and S. Bloch at the Bibliothèque Nationale; and Francis Lazenby of the Mediaeval Institute of the University of Notre Dame, for their gracious assistance in procuring the microfilm reproductions of the material on the mediaeval colleges. I wish to thank especially Joseph N. Garvin, C.S.C., for his valuable advice. The generous support of my research by Wallace V. and Trudy Bedolfe, of Toronto, Canada, is gratefully remembered. The kind interest of Francis B. Parise and Frank Bergman, Jr., in my publications is also appreciated.

2. L. Thorndike, *University Records and Life in the Middle Ages (Records of Civilization*, No. 38 [New York, 1949]), pp. 202, 206. The Latin text of this passage is on pp. 409, 411.

3. C. A. Foroloviensis and C. Malagola Ravennas (eds.), *Mauri Sarti et Mauri Fattorini "De claris Archigymnasii Bononiensis professoribus a saeculo XI usque ad saeculum XIV"* (Bologna, 1888-96), I, 14; G. Zaccagnini, *La vita dei maestri e degli scolari nello Studio di Bologna nei secoli XIII e XIV* (Geneva, 1926), p. 18; and J. Le Goff, *Les intellectuels au Moyen Âge (Le temps qui court,* No. 3 [Paris, 1957]), p. 144.

4. H. Denifle and Ae. Chatelain, *Chartularium Universitatis Parisiensis* (Paris, 1891), II, 155, No. 695: "In Parisiensi, Oxoniensi, Bononiensi, et Salamantino studiis, providimus erigendas, statuentes ut in quolibet locorum ipsorum teneantur viri catholici sufficientem habentes hebraice, grece, arabice et chaldaice linguarum notitiam."

5. *Opus Tertium (Rerum Britannicarum Medii Aevi scriptores, Rolls Series,* No. 15 [London, 1859]), I, Chap. x, 33.

6. In 1298 and 1299, Lull was at the University of Paris urging the masters to ask the king to found at Paris a studium of Arabic, Tartar, and Greek (Denifle and Chatelain, *op. cit.,* II, 83, No. 611). We have a letter written by Lull to Philip the Fair (1285-1314) at about the same time, asking him to erect and support a college or colleges where "religious or other men of good moral, filled with heavenly grace for this task . . . might learn the idioms of the infidels."—E. Martène and U. Durand, *Thesaurus novus anecdotorum* (Paris, 1717), I, 1315-16.

7. Statutes of the College of Laon (1313), in M. Félibien and G. Lobineau, *Histoire de la ville de Paris* (Paris, 1725) II, Part I [IV], 325a. (Certain copies were bound in seven volumes, others in five. In order to help readers using the seven-volume edition, I have bracketed the number of the volume.)

8. "Sicque per hanc sancta dulcescit devotio, Christiana excrescit religio, et honesta fidelium lucescit communio. Haec est prima regula veritatis, qua firma sunt consilia; prima forma aequitatis, qua justa sunt judicia; prima norma sanctitatis, qua munitur e[cc]lesia."—Statutes of Queen's College (1341), in *Statutes of the Colleges of Oxford with Royal Patents of Foundation Injunction of Visitors* (London, 1853), I, 5. Abbreviated hereinafter as *Oxford Statutes.*

9. Statutes of Clare Hall (1359), in *Documents Relating to the University and Colleges of Cambridge* (London, 1852), II, 121. Abbreviated hereinafter as *Cambridge Colleges.*

10. Statutes of the College of Bayeux (1308), in Félibien and Lobineau, *op. cit.,* II, Part III [VII], 616.

11. Statutes of the College of Du Plessis (1322), in *ibid.,* II, Part I [IV], 373a.

12. "Par enfans bien apprenant et ayant de quoy apprendre, soient faits sages hommes par lesquels le pays là où ils demeurent, soit enluminé, conseillé, et conforté."—*Ibid.,* II, Part I [IV], 444-45.

13. "Per sua perlucida et salutaria documenta ecclesias, clerumque et populum catholicum illustrantes . . . ad honorem Dei qui scientiarum Dominus est, ipsarumque caput et auctor, et in quo solo perfecta sapienta reperitur."—*Ibid.,* II, Part I [IV], 409a.

14. Charles V. Langlois (ed.), *De recuperatione Terre Sancte: Traité de-politique générale par Pierre Dubois* ("Collection de textes pour servir à l'étude et à l'enseignement de l'histoire" [Paris, 1891]), Chap. lx, pp. 49-50; translated by Walter I. Brandt as *Pierre Dubois: The Recovery of the Holy Land* ("Records of Civilization: Sources and Studies," No. 51 [New York; 1956]), p. 117.

15. "Valet scientie quesita possessio super omnem thesaurum, que quidem erigit de pulvere pauperem, ignobilem clara fama nobilitat et [ig]nobilibus nobilem morum elegantia superponit."—From a sermon of Mino da Colle to his students in G. Zaccagnini, "Lettere ed orazioni di grammatici dei secc. XIII e XIV," in *Archivum Romanicum,* VII (1923), 521-22.

16. Foundation-deed of Winchester College (October 20, 1382), in A. F. Leach, *Educational Charters and Documents 598-1909* (Cambridge, 1911), p. 321.

17. A. F. Leach, *A History of Winchester College* ("English Public Schools" [New York, 1899]), p. 64.

18. "Per litterarum scienciam iusticia colitur et prosperitas humane condicionis augetur."—*Ibid.,* p. 65; Leach, *Educational Charters,* p. 321.

19. Aristotle, *Rhetoric,* I, 5; translated by W. R. Roberts as *Rhetorica (The Works of Aristotle,* ed. W. D. Ross, Vol. XI [Oxford, 1924]).

20. "Hii sunt viri studiosi, disciplinis scolasticis insistentes, qui, amore scientie facti quodammodo exules et de divitibus pauperes."—*Cartulaire de l'Université de Montpellier* (1181-1400), (Montpellier, 1890), I, 296, No. 65.

21. "Ignorantie tenebre profugantur et, errorum funditus eliminata caligine."—M. Fournier, *Les statuts et privilèges des universités françaises depuis leur fondation jusqu'en 1789* (Paris, 1891), II, 723, No. 1546.

22. Statutes of the College of Maître-Gervais (1378), in P. Feret, *La Faculté de théologie de Paris et ses docteurs les plus célèbres* (Paris, 1896), III, 633.

23. *Cambridge Colleges,* II, 121. "Through the want of clergy caused by pestilence, wars, and other miseries of the world, we have seen grievously wounded."—Leach, *A History of Winchester College,* p. 70.

24. W. A. Pantin, *The English Church in the Fourteenth Century* (Cambridge, 1955), p. 44.

25. List of colleges in H. Rashdall, F. M. Powicke, and A. B. Emden, *The Universities of Europe in the Middle Ages* (Oxford, 1936-42), I, 536-39.

26. It is very difficult to establish the exact date of the foundation of a college, because the foundation may depend either upon the date of execution of the will of the founder or upon the date of approval by ecclesiastical authorities. When in doubt, I give both possible dates.

Lemoine (1302)
Navarre (1304)
Bayeux (1309)
Laon de Presles (1314)
Aicelins (1314)—Montaigu (1387, 1392)
Narbonne (1317)
Linköping (fourteenth century). Rashdall *et al., op. cit.,* I, 537, gives 1317.
Cornouaille (1321)
Du Plessis (1321, 1322)
Maclous (before 1323)
Des Ecossais (1323, 1326)
Tréguier (1325)
Marmoutier (1329)
Tours (1330)
Des Lombards (1330, 1334)
Bourgogne (1330, 1331)
Skara (first half of the fourteenth century, though the house was bought in 1292 [Paris, Archives Nationales, M. 73, No. 5]). A. L. Gabriel, *Skara House at the Mediaeval University of Paris. History, Topography, and Chartulary* ("Texts and Studies in the History of Mediaeval Education," No. VIII [Notre Dame, Indiana, 1960]).
Lisieux (1336)
Ave Maria (1336)
Autun (1341)
Tou or De Tulleio (1342, 1387)
Mignon (1343)

Saint-Michel or Chanac (1343, 1348)
Des Allemands (before 1348)
Trois-Evêques or De Cambrai (1348)
Maître-Clément (1349)
Tournai (about 1350)
Boncour (1353, 1357)
Justice (1354, 1358)
[Hostel for the Canons of Saint Jean-des-Vignes-de-Soissons (1335)]
Boissi (1358, 1359)
De la Marche (1362, 1374)
Vendôme (before 1367)
Dormans-Beauvais (1370)
Maître-Gervais (1370)
Dainville (1380)
Fortet (1394)

27. Brescia-Pezenas (1360)
    Saint-Ruf (1364)
    Saint-Benoît (1368)
    Mende (Des-Douze-Médecins), (1369)

28. Fougères (1361)

29. Montlezun or Montlauzon (1319)
    Saint-Raymond (as a *hospitale* in 1233; before 1329). Fournier, *op. cit.,*
       I, 510, No. 558.
    Verdale (1337)
    Béranger (before 1341)
    Narbonne (1341)
    Saint-Martial (1359)
    Périgord (about 1363, 1375)
    Maguelone (1363, 1374)
    Sainte-Catherine (Pampeluna), (1379, 1382). Cf. C. E. Smith, *The Uni-
       versity of Toulouse in the Middle Ages* (Milwaukee, Wisconsin,
       1958), pp. 110-20, 167-75, 214-15.

30. Saint-Martial (1379)

31. Pélegry (1365, 1368). Rashdall *et al., op. cit.,* II, 183, incorrectly gives
       1358.
    De Rodez (1371). H. Denifle, *Die Entstehung der Universitäten* (Ber-
       lin, 1885), p. 365.

32. Exeter (1314, 1316)
    Oriel (1324)
    Queen's (1341)
    Canterbury (1361)
    New College (1379)

33. King's Hall (before 1316)
    Michael House (1324)
    University or Clare Hall (1326)
    Pembroke (1347)

Gonville (1349)
Trinity Hall (1350)
Corpus Christi (1352)

34. Brescia (1362)
    Reggio (1362)
    Spain (1367)
    Gregorianum (1371). Rashdall *et al., op. cit.,* I, 203, 198 n. 2; cf.
    C. Malagola, *Statuti delle università e dei collegi dello Studio Bolognese* (Bologna, 1888), p. xiii.

35. Collegium Tornacense (1363)
    Collegium Jacobi-de-Arquado (1390)
    Ravenna or Pratense (1394)
    Scholares Auximani (1397)
    Ridium (1398). Cf. Rashdall *et al., op. cit.,* II, 19.

36. Gregorianum (1362)

37. Oviedo (1386). Cf. Rashdall *et al., op. cit.,* II, 89.

38. Saint Mary's College, later Assumpta (1372). Denifle, *op. cit.,* p. 505.

39. Carolinum or Collegium Magnum (1366)
    Collegium Jacobi or Domus pauperum (1379)
    Collegium Jerusalem or Lithvanorum, projected in 1379 (1411)
    Collegium Caesareum Wenceslai (1381, 1399). Cf. Rashdall *et al., op. cit.,* II, 220-21; and B. Balbino, *Epitome historica rerum Bohemicarum* (Prague, 1677), pp. 425-29.

40. Collegium Ducale (1384). Cf. J. Aschbach, *Geschichte der Wiener Universität* (Vienna, 1865), I, 44 n. 1.

41. Collegium Jacobitum (1389)
    Collegium Artistarum (1390-91), also called Collegium den Meistern and Domo xii Magistrorum
    Conturbernium Dionysianum (1396). Cf. Rashdall *et al., op. cit.,* II, 252-53. J. F. Hautz, *Geschichte der Universität Heidelberg* (Mannheim, 1862), I, 183-202, thinks that a separate Collegium in der Bursch was the foundation of Conrad of Geylnhausen and the Collegium Artistarum was a different foundation. However, cf. E. Winkelmann, *Urkundenbuch der Universitaet Heidelberg* (Heidelberg, 1886), I, 50, line 7; 51, line 17.

42. Collegium majus. T. C. H. Weissenborn, *Acten der Erfurter Universitaet* ("Geschichtsquellen der Provinz Sachsen," No. 8 [Halle, 1884]), II, 7-8; G. Kaufmann, *Die Geschichte der Deutschen Universitäten* (Stuttgart, 1896), II, 35.

43. Nothing could be more incorrect than to attribute the austerity and filth that Erasmus found in the College of Montaigu during the sixteenth century to the well-regulated institutions of the fourteenth. See Erasmus, *Colloquia Familiaria et Encomium Moriae* (Leipzig, 1886), II, 45-46; *The Epistles of Erasmus,* ed. Fr. Morgan Nichols (New York, 1901), I, 108;

in this article; and M. Godet, "Le Collège de Montaigu," *Revue des études Rabelaisiennes,* VII (1909), 285-305.

44. J. Hillairet, *Evocation du vieux Paris* (Paris, [1952]), I, 515.

45. C. E. Bulaeus, *Historia Universitatis Parisiensis* (Paris, 1668), IV, 182; P. F. [Paul Fournier], "Pierre Roger (Clement VI)," *Histoire littéraire de la France,* XXXVII (1938), 210; cf. 209-38.

46. M. D. Chapotin, *Le Collège de Dormans-Beauvais et la Chapelle Saint Jean-l'Evangéliste* (Paris, 1870), pp. 294-97.

47. Hillairet, *op. cit.,* I, 514.

48. A. de Bourmont, *La fondation de l'Université de Caen et son organisation au XVe siècle* (Caen, 1883), p. 79.

49. *The Canterbury Tales,* in F. N. Robinson (ed.), *The Works of Geoffrey Chaucer* (2d ed.; Boston, 1957), I (A), 56, lines 3989-90.

50. H. P. Stokes, *Corpus Christi (University of Cambridge College Histories* [London, 1898]), Plate IV, facing p. 96.

51. J. F. Hammerschmid, *Prodromus gloriae Pragenae continens Urbium Pragenarum Fundationes, Pragensium a fide Christi suscepta* (Prague, [1723]), p. 531; cf. Balbino, *op. cit.,* p. 359.

52. The building is depicted in the lower margin of a miniature in Guillelmus Durandus, *Rationale divinorum officiorum,* written at the end of the fourteenth century or at the beginning of the fifteenth (Codex Vindob. 2765, fol. 1^r). Dr. F. Gall, archivist of the University of Vienna, kindly called my attention to it.

53. G. Giordani, *Cenni storici dell'almo real Collegio di S. Clemente degli Spagnuoli* (Bologna, 1855); A. Sorbelli, *Storia della Università di Bologna* ("Università degli Studi di Bologna" [Bologna, 1944]), I, 226, 227, 236; G. B. Comelli, *Piante e vedute della città di Bologna* (Bologna, 1914), view of 1636 facing p. 46, designed by Floriano dal Buono; No. 21 is the College of Spain. A critical edition of the fourteenth-century statutes of the Spanish College at Bologna, with an English translation, will be published soon by Berthe Marti.

54. Marguerite Boulet, "Le commerce médiéval européen," in Jacques Lacour-Gayet, *Histoire du commerce* (Paris, s. d.), II, Book II, 308, 347.

55. "Bene natos ex bonis parentibus, maxime honeratis liberis, viuentibus ex suo labore."—Astrik L. Gabriel, *Student Life in Ave Maria College, Mediaeval Paris* ("Publications in Mediaeval Studies," No. 14 [Notre Dame, Indiana, 1955]), 352, Statute No. 92.

56. "Non sint nobiles sed de humili plebe et pauperes sicut nos et predecessores nostri fuimus."—C. E. Bulaeus, *op. cit.,* IV, 354.

57. M. Fournier, *op. cit.,* I, 571, No. 617.

58. *Cartulaire de l'Université de Montpellier,* I, 551; Fournier, *op. cit.,* II, 130, No. 1010.

59. *Statuta almi et perinsignis Collegii Maioris Sancti Clementis Hispanorum Bononie conditi* (Bologna [ex typograpia Haeredis Benatii], 1648), pp. 1-2.

60. Félibien and Lobineau, *op. cit.*, II, Part III [VII], 607-10.

61. Chapotin, *op. cit.*, p. 35.

62. Fournier, *op. cit.*, I, p. 594, No. 642; p. 604, No. 660; p. 627, No. 694.

63. *Ibid.*, I, 601, No. 659.

64. *Ibid.*, I, 667, No. 707.

65. *Ibid.*, II, 104, No. 992.

66. Founded by Giles Aycelin, archbishop of Rouen. The college was restored in 1388, by Peter Cardinal Aycelin de Montaigu (Jaillot, *Recherches critiques sur la ville de Paris* [Paris, 1782], IV, 221).

67. Founded by Bernard de Farges, archbishop of Navarre (Jaillot, *op. cit.*, V, 76-77).

68. Founded by Guillaume Bonnet, bishop of Bayeux (P. Petelle, "Collèges bayeusains à Paris," *Société des Sciences, Arts et Belles-Lettres de Bayeux*, XVIII [1936], 7, 17).

69. Founded by Bernard of Rodez, archbishop of Naples (Fournier, *op. cit.*, II, 561, No. 1441).

70. Founded by Guterius, bishop of Oviedo (Rashdall *et al.*, *op. cit.*, II, 89).

71. Founded by Walter of Stapeldon, bishop of Exeter (W. K. Stride, *Exeter College* [*University of Oxford College Histories* (London, 1900)], p. 1).

72. Founded by William of Wykeham (H. Rashdall and R. S. Rait, *New College* [*University of Oxford College Histories* (London, 1901)], p. 1; A. H. Smith, *New College Oxford and Its Buildings* [London, 1952], pp. 1-12).

73. Arnold of Verdale, professor of canon and civil law and later bishop of Maguelone, founded the college of Verdale in Toulouse in 1337 (Fournier, *op. cit.*, I, 539, No. 593).

74. Feret, *op. cit.*, III, 11.

75. Jaillot, *op. cit.*, V, 55-57.

76. Elizabeth de Burgo Domina de Clare (*Cambridge Colleges*, II, 121).

77. Lady Mary of Saint Paul, widow of Aymer de Valence, Earl of Pembroke (*Cambridge Colleges*, II, 190).

78. *Masters' History of the College of Corpus Christi and the Blessed Virgin Mary* (Cambridge and London, 1831), p. 20.

79. Pantin, *op. cit.*, p. 231.

80. Stokes, *op. cit.*, p. 29.

81. *Ibid.*, p. 30.

82. Félibien and Lobineau, *op. cit.*, II, Part I [IV], 427; Feret, *op. cit.*, III, 47.

83. F. Pegues, "Aubert de Guignicourt Fourteenth Century Patron of Learning," *Mediaevalia et Humanistica*, IX (1955), 71-75.

84. C. L. [Charles-Victor Langlois], "Barthélemi de Bruges, maître ès arts et en médecine," *Histoire littéraire de la France*, XXXVII (1938), 245.

85. J. Gerson, "Considerationes pro volentibus condere testamentum," *Opera omnia*, ed. Ellies du Pin (Antwerp, 1706), III, 759; A. Lafontaine, *De Johanne Gersonio puerorum adolescentiumque institutore* (La Chapelle-Montligeon, 1902), p. 40.

86. Jules Viard (ed.), *Documents parisiens du règne de Philippe VI de Valois* (1328-50), (Paris, 1900), II, 99.

87. K. Edwards, "Bishops and Learning in the Reign of Edward II," *The Church Quarterly Review*, CXXXVIII (1944), 79.

88. "Proposui in animo meo, quod si unicum amitterem beneficium talis pretextu constitutionis, omnia amitterem."—*Matthaei Parisiensis monachi Sancti Albani, Chronica majora*, ed. H. R. Luard (*Rerum Britannicarum Medii Aevi Scriptores, Rolls Series*, No. 57 [London, 1876]), III, 418. Cf. Pantin, *op. cit.*, p. 39.

89. Feret, *op. cit.*, III, 606, No. 28.

90. Félibien and Lobineau, *op. cit.*, II, Part III [VII], 608b.

91. M. Toulouse, *La nation anglaise-allemande de l'Université de Paris* (Paris, 1939), pp. 66-72; D. E. R. Watt, "University Clerks and Rolls of Petitions for Benefices," *Speculum*, XXXIV (1959), 213-29.

92. E. F. Jacob, "Petitions for Benefices from English Universities during the Great Schism," *Transactions of the Royal Historical Society*, Fourth Series, XXVII (1945), 48-49.

93. *Ibid.*, p. 48.

94. E. F[aral], "Jean Buridan maître ès arts de l'Université de Paris," *Histoire littéraire de la France*, XXXVIII (1949), 476.

95. Deed of Fulco, bishop of Paris, dated August 5, 1348 (Denifle and Chatelain, *op. cit.*, II, 621-22, No. 1156).

96. *Ibid.*, p. 645, No. 1165.

97. E. Gilson, *History of Christian Philosophy in the Middle Ages* (New York, s.d.), pp. 516, 795.

98. Astrik L. Gabriel, "Robert de Sorbonne," *Revue de l'Université d'Ottawa*, XXIII (1953), 473-574.

99. H. L. Bouquet, *L'Ancien Collège d'Harcourt et le Lycée Saint-Louis* (Paris, 1891), pp. 52 ff., 59.

100. B. W. Henderson, *Merton College (University of Oxford College Histories* [London, 1899]), pp. 1-34.

101. Charles H. Haskins, *Studies in Mediaeval Culture* (New York, s.d.), p. 21; Charles Jourdain, "La taxe des logements dans l'Université de Paris," *Excursions historiques et philosophiques à travers le Moyen-Âge* (Paris, 1888), pp. 249-63.

102. First mentioned in 1392 (Bulaeus, *op. cit.*, IV, 674).

103. Martial Schluck, *Dissertatio de norma actionum studiosorum seu von dem Burschen-comment* (Nuremberg, 1787), p. 10.

104. Statutes of 1380: "Rector, si magister fuerit, obtineat primum locum. Si . . . non . . . post magistrum vel magistros."—*Cartulaire de l'Université de Montpellier*, I, p. 614, No. 169, Statutes No. vii.

105. V. Leroquais, *Les livres d'heures manuscrits de la Bibliothèque Nationale* (Paris, 1927), I, viii, x.

106. J. B. Mullinger, *The University of Cambridge* (Cambridge, 1873), I, 644, Appendix D, No. 17.

107. The modern French word *bourse* in the sense of "fellowship" comes from this mediaeval term.

108. Gabriel, *Student Life*, p. 221.

109. R. Busquet, "Etude historique sur le Collège de Fortet (1394-1764)," *Mémoires de la Société de l'Histoire de Paris et de l'Île de France*, XXXIV (1907), 143.

110. E. Pellegrin, *La bibliothèque de l'ancien Collège de Dormans-Beauvais à Paris* (Paris, 1947), p. 54. Published originally in the *Bulletin philologique et historique* in 1944-45.

111. Trois-Evêques or De Cambrai gave 6 sol. (Félibien and Lobineau, *op. cit.*, I, Part I [II], 602).

112. J. Launois, *Regii Navarrae Gymnasii Parisiensis Historiae*, in *Opera omnia* (Cologne, 1732), IV, Part I, 293.

113. Feret, *op. cit.*, III, 634-35. For the student in medicine, this meant 5 sol. for 12 consecutive weeks, and 6 sol. each week for the rest of the year.

114. Statutes of Oriel College (1326), in *Oxford Statutes*, I, 7.

115. Statutes of 1341, in *Oxford Statutes*, I, 16.

116. Fournier, *op. cit.*, II, 545-46, No. 1430.

117. *Cambridge Colleges*, II, 441.

118. A. Clark (ed.), *The Colleges at Oxford: Their History and Traditions* (London, 1892), p. 143.

119. Félibien and Lobineau, *op. cit.*, II, Part III [VII], 607-10.

120. *Ibid.*, II, Part III [VII], 616-17, 623-29.

121. Archives Nationales MM. 334¹, p. 33. Cf. Jaillot, *op. cit.*, V, 13-14. Cf. Félibien and Lobineau, *op. cit.*, II, Part I [IV], 490-505.

122. "Sub mysterio decursus Christi et Apostolorum in terris, Sociorum dictae aulae initialis numerus inchoetur, tredecim personas [master and twelve fellows]."—*Oxford Statutes*, I, 7.

123. Bulaeus, *op. cit.*, IV, 82.

124. Félibien and Lobineau, *op. cit.*, I, Part I [IV], 372-78.

125. J. Du Breul, *Le théâtre des antiquitez de Paris* (Paris, 1612), pp. 692-93; C. Jourdain, *Index chronologicus chartarum pertinentium ad historiam Universitatis Parisiensis* (Paris, 1862), pp. 287-89.

126. Chapotin, *op. cit.*, pp. 54-60, 73-80; Du Breul, *op. cit.*, pp. 717-18.

127. According to E. F. Jacob, some 146 to 150 secular members of the University out of the total of some 1200 members of the Oxford Community of scholars were accommodated in colleges (E. F. Jacob, "English University Clerks in the Later Middle Ages: The Problem of Maintenance," *Bulletin of the John Rylands Library*, XXIX (1946), 313-14.

128. *Oxford Statutes*, I, 2.

129. G. Zaoli, "Lo Studio Bolognese e Papa Martino V (Anni 1416-20), "*Studi e memorie per la storia dell'Università di Bologna*, III (1912), 163-88 (Fundatio, Dotatio ac Constitutiones et Regulae Collegii Gregoriani); F. Baldasseroni, "Registri Vaticani e Avegnonesi di Gregorio XI," *Chartularium Studii Bononiensis*, II (1913), 289-313 (Statuto del Collegio Gregoriano).

130. Charles Thurot, *De l'organisation de l'enseignement dans l'Université de Paris au Moyen-Âge* (Paris, 1850), p. 127.

131. Gabriel, *Student Life*, pp. 227, 358-59, Statute No. 104.

132. Astrik L. Gabriel, "The Preparatory Teaching in the Parisian Colleges during the XIVth Century," *Revue de l'Université d'Ottawa*, XXI (1951), 34-39; J. A. Corbett, *The "De instructione puerorum" of William of Tournai*, O.P. ("Texts and Studies in the History of Mediaeval Education," No. III [Notre Dame, Indiana, 1955]).

133. Astrik L. Gabriel, "Peter d'Ailly and the New Statutes of Ave Maria College," *Recueil de travaux offert à M. Clovis Brunel* ("Mémoires et documents publiés par la Société de l'Ecole des Chartes," No. 12 [Paris, 1955]), I, 476-89.

134. Gerson, *Opera omnia*, IV, 717-19.

135. *Ibid.*, p. 719C.

136. H. Jadart, *Jean de Gerson (1363-1429)*, (Rheims, 1881), pp. 230-58.

137. *Sermo de Officio Pastor*, in *Conc. Remensi*, Gerson, *op. cit.*, II, 549A; cf. *Tractatus de parvulis trahendis ad Christum, ibid.*, III, 277-96.

138. Félibien and Lobineau, *op. cit.*, II, Part III [VII], 674.

139. Statutes of the College of Cornouaille (1380), in *ibid.*, II, Part I [IV], 494-505.

140. D. W. Rannie, *Oriel College (University of Oxford College Histories* [London, 1900]), p. 37.

141. Statutes of the College of Narbonne (1379), in Félibien and Lobineau, *op. cit.*, II, Part III [VII], 663.

142. Clark, *op. cit.*, p. 78.

143. Statutes of 1341, in *Oxford Statutes,* I, 24.

144. "Ad auxilium provisoris vel universitatis recurratur."—Félibien and Lobineau, *op. cit.*, II, Part III [VII], 669; cf. the Statutes of the College of Narbonne, Paris (1379).

145. [J. B. L.] Crévier, *Histoire de l'Université de Paris* (Paris, 1761), II, 414; Bulaeus, *op. cit.*, IV, 349.

146. Date of foundation, September 22, 1370. Félibien and Lobineau, *op. cit.*, II, Part I [II], 671.

147. *Ibid.*, II, Part III [VII], 672.

148. *Cambridge Colleges*, II, 14.

149. Rashdall and Rait, *op. cit.*, p. 45.

150. Félibien and Lobineau, *op. cit.*, II, Part I [IV], 499*b*.

151. "De assumptione magistri . . . . Quandocumque vacare contingerit in dicta domo magistri seu rectoris officium, scholares omnes dictae domus . . . in capella seu aula dictae domus conveniant . . . . jurent ad sancta Dei Evangelia, quod nominabunt et eligent pura conscientia et bona fide de seipsis personam aliquam, quam credant idoneam."—Statutes (1366), No. 12, in Feret, *op. cit.*, III, 625.

152. "Item quod prepositus sic concorditer vel per maiorem partem electus collegiatorum."—E. Winkelmann, *op. cit.*, I, 109.

153. J. F. Hautz and K. A. Freiherrn von Reichlin-Meidegg, *Geschichte der Universität Heidelberg* (Mannheim, 1864), II, 371.

154. "Quociens ibi locus vacauerit, Theologi si ibi fuerint et omnes Magistri conueniant, et ille Magister arcium in quem maior eorum pars consenserit, recipiatur."—R. Kink, *Geschichte der kaiserlichen Universität zu Wien* (Vienna, 1854), II, 62.

155. *Passim* in *Auctarium Chartularii Universitatis Parisiensis*, ed. C. Samaran and Ae. Van Moé (Paris, 1935); *Reformatores* elected in 1474 (*Auct.* III, p. 285, line 30); in 1480 (*Ibid.*, p. 455, line 27); in 1484 (*Ibid.*, p. 561, line 17); in 1490 (*Ibid.*, p. 729, line 24).

156. Statutes of New College (1400), rubric No. 33, in *Oxford Statutes*, I, 59; cf. Rashdall and Rait, *op. cit.*, p. 62.

157. Guiot de Provins, *La Bible Guiot*, in Charles V. Langlois, *La vie en France au Moyen-Âge de la fin du XIIe au milieu du XIVe siècle d'après les moralistes du temps* (Paris, 1926), II, 83.

158. Gabriel, "Robert de Sorbonne," p. 481; P. Glorieux, *Les origines du Collège de Sorbonne* ("Texts and Studies in the History of Mediaeval Education," No. 8 [Notre Dame, Indiana, 1959]), pp. 13-14.

159. Gilson, *op. cit.*, pp. 517-18, 795.

160. L. Salembier, *Le Cardinal Pierre d'Ailly chancelier de l'Université de Paris, évêque de Puy et de Cambrai 1350-1420* (Tourcoing, 1932), p. 344.

161. E. Buron (ed.), *Ymago mundi de Pierre d'Ailly* (Paris, 1930), I-III; cf. Vol. II, Plate XV.

162. A. Franklin, *La Sorbonne, ses origines et sa bibliothèque* (Paris, 1875), pp. 225-26.

163. F. M. Powicke, *The Mediaeval Books of Merton College* (Oxford, 1931), p. 25; Pantin, *op. cit.*, pp. 136-140.

164. A. C. Crombie, *Augustine to Galileo: The History of Science A. D. 400-1650* (London, 1952), pp. 250-58.

165. "Sic etiam ego quondam, commorans in domo Cardinalis Monachi, vidi cum pluribus aliis sociis cadere fulmen super capellam."—*Questiones super libros Meteorologicorum Aritotelis*, III, 2, in *Histoire littéraire de la France*, XXXVIII (1949), 468.

166. *Ibid.*, p. 551.

167. "Sophismes d'Albert, de Climeton et l'une partie de Helebrich," Pellegrin, *op. cit.*, p. 30.

168. "Nullus admittatur ad licentiam . . . nisi . . . aliquos libros mathematicos audiverit."—Denifle and Chatelain, *op. cit.*, III, 145, No. 1319. Cf. the text of the oath taken by the bachelors at Paris in the fourteenth century: "Item, quod audivistis centum lectiones de Mathematica ad minus."—*Ibid.*, II, 678, No. 1185 (14).

169. "Pro legendo de scienciis mathematicis licitis . . . . Quorum unus leget in vico straminum diebus legibilibus . . . . Et alter leget . . . in aula artistarum dicti collegii [Magistri Gervasii]."—Feret, *op. cit.*, III, 635.

170. Master Sunon of Sweden gave a course on the *Sphera* in his house "in domo sua diebus festivis" (*Auct.* I, p. 44, line 13). Cf. the Statutes of the Faculty of Arts in Vienna (1389), in Kink, *op. cit.*, II, 196, No. 12.

171. P. Guerrini, "Guglielmo da Brescia e il Collegio Bresciano in Bologna," *Studi e memorie per la storia dell'Università di Bologna*, VII (1922), 95, No. 11.

172. Statutes of the College of Maître-Gervais (1378), in Feret, *op. cit.*, III, 633.

173. Thurot, *op. cit.*, p. 83; Bulaeus, *op. cit.*, IV, 893.

174. A. Lecoy de la Marche (ed.), *Anecdotes historiques, légendes et apologues tirés du recueil inédit d'Etienne de Bourbon*, ("Publications de la Société de l'Histoire de France," No. 185 [Paris, 1877]), p. 212, No. 249.

175. The anecdote was written down in 1470 by a former student of the English-German Nation in Paris, Johannes Jencz, who is mentioned around

1460 in the records of the Nation (*Auct.* II, p. 929, line 39; also in the *Liber receptorum*, Archives Nationales H. 2587, fol. 125r). He composed it at the request of Peter of Göttingen, master of arts in Leipzig. The text has been published by H. Leyser in *Zeitschrift für Deutsches Alterthum*, II (1842) 362-66.

176. The anecdote, as told by Henry of Kalkar in 1406, was published by L. Delisle, *Bulletin de la Société de l'Histoire de Paris*, II (1875), 101. Cf. *Histoire littéraire de la France*, XXXVIII (1949), 473-75.

177. Gilson, *op. cit.*, p. 516.

178. Testament XL, verse 341, *François Villon—Oeuvres*, ed. L. Foulet (Paris, 1932), pp. 22-23.

179. Translated by George P. Cuttino, *I Laugh through Tears: The Ballades of François Villon* (New York: Philosophical Library, 1955), p. 3.

180. "Et si contingat *extraneos* ad istas disputationes venire, si sint honeste persone, . . . si arguere voluerint, preferantur."—Denifle and Chatelain, II, 555, No. 1096; translated in Thorndike, *op. cit.*, p. 199.

181. K. Michalski, "Les courants critiques et sceptiques dans la philosophie du XIVᵉ siècle," *Bulletin international de l'Académie Polonaise des Sciences et des Lettres* (1925 [printed 1927]), Part II, pp. 194-95, 197; *Histoire littéraire de la France*, XXXVIII (1949), 497.

182. Siger of Courtrai made great use of this pedagogical method. Cf. G. Wallerand (ed.), *Les oeuvres de Siger de Courtrai* (*Les philosophes belges*, No. 8 [Louvain, 1913]), p. 29; M. Grabmann, *Mittelalterliches Geistesleben: Abhandlungen zur Geschichte der Scholastik und Mystik* (Munich, 1926), I, 116.

183. Félibien and Lobineau, *op. cit.*, II, Part I [IV], 442b.

184. *Oxford Statutes*, I, 15; cf. J. R. Magrath, *The Queen's College* (Oxford, 1921), I, 46.

185. Lemoine: "Item statuo et ordino quod semel ad minus in septimana disputetur in dicta domo, et quod omnes intersint, nisi legitimum habeant impedimentum."—Félibien and Lobineau, *op. cit.*, II, Part III [VII], 610a n. 33; New College: "quaestiones seu problemata disputare"—*Oxford Statutes*, p. 56; Oriel: *Oxford Statutes*, p. 14; Bayeux: "Item qualibet septimana fiat collatio de aliqua quaestione inter illos qui sunt ejusdem facultatis."—Félibien and Lobineau, *op. cit.*, II, Part III [VII], 628 n. 38; Cambray: *ibid.*, II, Part I [IV], 434 art. 20; Narbonne, 1379: "Poterunt etiam diebus festivis post comestionem disputare ex improviso per modum collationis aliquod dubium, ut sic habilitentur et materia novorum inutilium evitetur."—*Ibid.*, II, Part I [IV], 669a n. 28; Cornouaille: "Ut possit tenere singulis hebdomadis vel in feriis sextis, in quibus scholares communiter non canunt, unam disputationem inter illos qui audient logicam et physicam, et alios qui dictas scientias noverint; et respondebit unusquisque qui ad hoc aptus erit, in ordine et turno suo et alii circa eum arguent."—*Ibid.*, II, Part I [IV], 499b.

186. Chaucer, "The Nun's Priest's Tale," *The Complete Works of Geoffrey Chaucer*, ed. F. N. Robinson (New York, 1933), VII, 243, lines 3237-38.

187. Statutes of the College of Lemoine (1302); see n. 185, above.

188. K. Michalski, *op. cit.*, p. 194.

189. "Quaestiones super Aristotelis librum *de sensu et sensato* collectae Parisiis per Albertum de Rychmersdort, pronunciatae Pragae in quadam bursa": Munich, MS. Clm 4376 [1057], fol. 151, ca. 1365-67.

190. K. Michalski, "Le criticisme et le scepticisme dans la philosophie du XIVᵉ siècle," *Bulletin international de l'Académie Polonaise des Sciences et des Lettres* (1925 [printed 1926]), Part I, pp. 55-56, 64, 69-70.

191. *Ibid.*, p. 68.

192. J. Lappe, *Nicolaus von Autrecourt: Sein Leben, seine Philosophie, seine Schriften (Beiträge zur Geschichte der Philosophie des Mittelalters,* Vol. 6 [Münster, 1909]), p. 34*.

193. Martène and Durand, *op. cit.*, II, 1619C; cf. 1173F: "qui tales viri . . . insidiantibus seu insidiari volentibus incutient timorem."

194. Statutes of Queen's College (1341), in *Oxford Statutes,* I, 30-31.

195. Statutes of New College, Oxford (1400), rubric No. 1, in A. F. Leach, *Educational Charters,* 354-55.

196. Statutes (1416), in F. Zarncke, *Die Statutenbücher der Universität Leipzig* (Leipzig, 1861), p. 179, No. 22.

197. Statutes of the College of Maître-Gervais, in Feret, *op. cit.*, III, 633.

198. Statutes written before August 15, 1274, in Denifle and Chatelain, *op. cit.*, I, 505-14, No. 448 (translated by Thorndike, in *University Records,* pp. 88-98, No. 42); Statutes of around 1321, in Feret, *op. cit.*, pp. 593-99.

199. Text (1274) published in *Oxford Statutes,* I, 23-39.

200. "Tres pecias seu lauchias panis in qualibet scutella."—Gabriel, *Student Life,* p. 330, Statute No. 27.

201. "Lotrices etiam cameras scholarium vel habitantium quorumcunque in dicta aula non intrent, sed per eorundem barbitonsorem capita eorundem laventur."—*Oxford Statutes,* I, 33; cf. J. R. Magrath, *op. cit.*, I, 49.

202. Collège du Fortet, Archives Nationales, MM. 397, fol. 3; R. Busquet, *op. cit.*, XXXIII (1906), 187-290, XXXIV (1907), 1-136; Michel François, "Les plus beaux manuscrits à peintures conservés aux Archives Nationales," *Les trésors des bibliothèques de France,* VI (1938), 175-77, Plate LIX.

203. Archives Nationales, MM. 406, fol. 6ʳ to 11ᵛ; reproduced by Michel François, "Les statuts du Collège de Hubant à Paris: Manuscrit des Archives Nationales," *Les trésors des bibliothèques de France,* Fascicule 26 (1946), 97-106; and Gabriel, *Student Life,* Plates XIV-XXIII. A most beautifully illustrated statute book, that of the *Collegium Sapientiae* (1497) at the University of Freiburg, in Breisgau, belongs to the fifteenth century. A magnificent reproduction has been published by Josef H. Beckmann, director of the University of Freiburg in Breisgau Library, in *Johannes Kerer, Statuta Collegii Sapientiae* (Lindau and Constance: Jan Thorbecke Verlag, 1957), I, II.

There is an English translation of this work: *The Statutes of the Collegium Sapientiae in Freiburg University* (Lindau and Constance: Jan Thorbecke Verlag, 1957).

204. Dacre Baldson, *Oxford Life* (London, 1957), pp. 70-71.

205. H. P. Stokes, *op. cit.*, p. 30.

206. Henderson, *op. cit.*, pp. 44-45.

207. *Oxford Statutes*, I, 18.

208. Félibien and Lobineau, *op. cit.*, II, Part I [IV], p. 397 n. 19.

209. "Panem filiorum hominum canibus ad manducandum"—Statutes of Queen's College (1341), in *Oxford Statutes*, I, 18.

210. Statutes of New College, in *Oxford Statutes*, I, 48.

211. Félibien and Lobineau, *op cit.*, II, Part I [IV], 442*b*.

212. From a drawing by Warden Chandler in the manuscript *Life of Wykeham*, reproduced in A. F. Leach, *The Schools of Medieval England* ("The Antiquary's Books" [London, 1915]); also in Th. Fr. Kirby, "On Some Fifteenth-Century Drawings of Winchester College; New College, Oxford; etc.," *Archeologia*, LIII (1892), 230 and Plate XIV.

213. "Ad pilam vel ad crossiam"—Statutes of the College of Narbonne (1379), in Félibien and Lobineau, *op. cit.*, II, Part III [VII], 670*a*, No. 44.

214. "Causa recreactionis alicujus socii infirmi"—Statutes of the College of Cornouaille (1380), in *ibid.*, II, Part I [IV], 502.

215. Winkelmann, *op. cit.*, I, 112, line 24.

216. Félibien and Lobineau, *op. cit.*, II, Part III [VII], 670.

217. Statutes of New College (1400), rubric No. 18, in *Oxford Statutes*, I, 41.

218. "Indebito tempore intrantibus et exeuntibus, currentibus et recurrentibus hinc inde"—Winkelmann, *op. cit.*, I, 111, lines 36-37.

219. "Luctationes, choraeas, tripudia, saltus, cantus, clamores, tumultus et strepitus inordinatos, aquarum, cervisiae, aliorumque liquorum omnium effusiones, ludosque tumultuosos"—Statutes of New College (1400), rubric No. 63, in *Oxford Statutes*, I, 100. Cf. Rashdall and Rait, *op. cit.*, p. 61.

220. Hillairet, *op. cit.*, I, 515.

221. Cambridge, Pembroke College, MS 155, fol. 2^v: the commentary of William Whetley on *De disciplina scholarium*.

222. Zarncke, *op. cit.*, 179, No. 17.

223. *Oxford Statutes*, I, 19.

224. J. Dauvillier, "Origine et histoire des costumes universitaires français," *Annales de la Faculté de Droit de Toulouse*, VI (1958), 3-41; E. C. Clark, "English Academical Costume (Medieval)," *Archeological Journal*, L (1893), 73 ff.; and L. H. Dudley Buxton-Strickland Gibson, *Oxford University Ceremonies* (Oxford, 1935), pp. 19-29.

225. "Sedeantque de praedictis Sociis omnes Doctores in theologia et in decretis, tam in prandio quam in caena, singulis anni temporibus, in aula communi, propter status sui honestatem ac vestis et sanguinis Domini conformitatem, in palliis purpureis ad colla scissis, nigro fururatis bugeto."—*Oxford Statutes*, I, 14. Cf. Magrath, *op. cit.*, I, 55.

226. Statutes of New College, in *Oxford Statutes*, I, 46; Leach, *Winchester College*, p. 73.

227. Bulaeus, *op. cit.*, IV, 92: "de bruneta nigra"; cf. Statutes of the College of Boissy (1366), in Feret, *op. cit.*, III, 630 n. 14; Statutes of Boncour (1353), in Félibien and Lobineau, *op. cit.*, II, Part I [IV], 442; Statutes of Bourgogne (1331), in *ibid.*, II, Part III [VII], 641*b;* Statutes of Du Plessis (1326), in *ibid.* II, Part I [IV], 372.

228. "De panno azurino bruno et simplicis coloris"—Sorbonne, Archives, Reg. 96 fol. 252ᵛ. Cf. Chapotin, *op. cit.*, p. 6, and Du Breul, *op. cit.*, p. 717.

229. Félibien and Lobineau, *op. cit.*, II, Part III [VII], 725. Gray was also worn at the College of Rheims: "Capas grisias omnes habeant caeteras vestes non habeant coloratas."—Statutes of the College of Rheims (1245), No. 13, in E. Cauly, *Histoire du Collège des Bons-Enfants de l'Université de Reims* (Rheims, 1885), p. 656.

230. Rashdall *et al.*, *op. cit.*, I, 202, No. 3. Compare the somewhat mitigated rule in the 1648 Statutes of the College of Spain, p. 58, dist. 5, No. 2 (see note 59).

231. W. A. Pantin, "Architecture," in *Handbook to the University of Oxford* (Oxford, *s.d.* [1957]), pp. 92, 83-119.

232. Cf. Royal Commission on Historical Monuments, *An Inventory of the Historical Monuments in the City of Oxford* (London, 1939), p. 84.

233. For the plan of Dormans-Beauvais, see E. Raunié, *Epitaphier du vieux Paris (Histoire générale de Paris* [Paris, 1890]), I, 333; for that of the Collège des Bernardins, the Frontispiece in *ibid.*, II (1893); for that of the Collège de Cluny, *ibid.*, III (1901), the illustration facing p. 117; and for that of Lisieux, Archives Nationales, S 1607.

234. At 24, Rue de Poissy (Hillairet, *op. cit.*, I, 572-74).

235. We may wonder whether some scholastic exercises, such as the disputations, had an influence on the college architecture. There is a theory that the T-shaped plan of the chapel, with an ante-chapel occupying the cross bar, was adopted because it could function as a site for disputations. See Pantin, *Architecture*, p. 95.

236. A. Vallance, *The Old Colleges of Oxford: Their Architectural History Illustrated and Described* (London, *s.d.* [1912]), pp. 36-37 (New College); pp. 19-20, Plate IX (Merton).

237. J. Bonnerot, *La Sorbonne, sa vie, son rôle, son oeuvre à travers les siècles* (Paris, 1927), p. 5. Du Breul, *op. cit.*, p. 624.

238. Built in honor of Saint John the Evangelist, it is found today at 9, Rue Jean-de-Beauvais (Hillairet, *op. cit.*, I, 480; Chapotin, *op. cit.*, pp. 85-102).

239. Gabriel, *Student Life,* p. 170, Plate XXI.

240. E. Pellegrin, "La bibliothèque du Collège de Fortet du XV⁰ siècle," *Mélanges dédiés à la mémoire de Félix Grat* (Paris, 1949), II, 293-316.

241. "Id est, boni Libri faciunt bonos clericos."—Gerson, *De laude scriptorum,* in *Opera omnia,* II, 700A.

242. Charles E. Mallet, *A History of the University of Oxford* (London, 1924), I, 295 n. 4.

243. Franklin, *La Sorbonne,* pp. 41-44.

244. A. Franklin, *Les anciennes bibliothèques de Paris (Histoire générale de Paris* [Paris, 1867]), I, 389, 409, 411. See also Pellegrin, *La bibliothèque de Dormans-Beauvais,* p. 60 n. 2; and Gabriel, *Student Life,* pp. 166-70. For the statutes governing the library of the College of Bayeux, see Félibien and Lobineau, *op. cit.,* II, Part III [VII], 628a.

245. Statutes of the College of Bayeux (1315), in Félibien and Lobineau, *op. cit.,* II, Part III [VII], 628a.

246. See miniature No. 26, depicting the inspection of books, in Gabriel, *Student Life,* p. 167, Plate XXI.

247. *Cambridge Statutes,* II, 432.

248. P. Feret, *L'abbaye de Sainte-Geneviève et la Congrégation de France: Précédées de la vie de la patronne de Paris* (Paris, 1883), I, 165.

249. A. Franklin, *Les bibliothèques de Paris,* I, 210, 239.

250. Pellegrin, *La bibliothèque de Dormans-Beauvais,* p. 60 n. 2.

251. "Vinum autem provisori et subpriori interdicimus, quamdiu aliquis liber extra librariam aliter fuerit."—Franklin, *Les bibliothèques de Paris,* I, 210 n., 211.

252. Powicke, *op. cit.,* p. 10.

253. Franklin, *Bibliothèques de Paris,* I, 238-39.

254. Alain, *Propos,* ed. Maurice Savin ("Bibliothèque de la Pléiade," No. 116 [Paris, 1956]), 796.

255. A. F. Leach, *Educational Charters,* pp. 354-55.

PHILOSOPHY AND POLITICAL THOUGHT IN THE FOURTEENTH CENTURY

ALAN GEWIRTH

Introduction: The Problem of Philosophy and Politics

In the fourteenth century, as in many other centuries, theoretical and practical reflection on the political and social order developed in intimate contact with philosophy. The great names in the history of fourteenth-century political thought were either themselves philosophers who, amid their common theological concerns, had written on technical problems of logic, metaphysics, or epistemology, like Egidius of Rome, John of Paris, James of Viterbo, Augustinus Triumphus, William of Ockham, and John Wycliffe, or else they were learned in and imbued with philosophic ideas, like Dante and Marsilius of Padua. It might seem a rather straightforward project, then, to determine either the philosophical foundations of fourteenth-century political thought or the political implications of fourteenth-century philosophy, or both.

The question of the relation of philosophy and political thought in the fourteenth century cannot, however, be dealt with so directly. For it involves not only historical but also logical problems, and not only problems about specific connections between particular philosophies and particular political ideas but even problems about the very relevance of philosophy to politics. We are all familiar, for example, with the widely divergent answers currently offered to the question of the philosophic basis of liberal democracy. According to Bertrand Russell, this basis is found in the empiricism of Locke and Hume; according to Dewey, it is the experimentalism of the scientific method; according to Maritain, it is the natural law of the scholastic tradition; according to Niebuhr, it is the Calvinist doctrine of original sin.[1] Nor is this all; the divergence goes even deeper; for there are many philosophers today who declare that political ideas or institutions have no philosophic bases at all, and that philosophy has nothing to do with political beliefs.[2] And when in this context we also remember

125

that the political conflicts of our time are often described as conflicts of rival philosophies, our perplexity is bound to be great.

The issues that are involved in a discussion of the connection
between philosophy and political thought are many and complex,
and there are many ways of dealing with them. We might ask what
we mean by "philosophy," by "philosophic basis," and by "politics," or what are the many different things which men have meant
by them, and we might then attempt by logical analysis to elicit
the variety of relations between philosophy and politics which
result from those meanings. Or we might study how, and in what
senses, actually held philosophies or philosophic ideas have affected
the course of actual political events, as, for example, Jefferson's
knowledge of Locke and other philosophers influenced him in
writing the Declaration of Independence. Or, conversely, we
might also study how political events or attitudes have affected the
thought of philosophers, as, for example, in the cosmologies or
ontologies of Plato, Aristotle, Leibniz, Alexander, Whitehead, and
Russell.[3] All of these are legitimate ways of dealing with some
aspect of the question. But there is another way which, if not
logically prior to these in all respects, nevertheless would seem to
afford a means of coping with a fundamental aspect of the problem which is not dealt with by the other approaches. This is to
select a concrete historical period, in which political conflicts took
a very sharp form and evoked an extensive body of writings at once
theoretical and polemical from men who were philosophers as well
as publicists, and to ask what the relation was between what these
men said as philosophers and what they said as publicists. The
point of this last approach is that it should enable us to consider
the logical relations between philosophic and political ideas in a
practical context, with a large enough sample to make clear what
were some of the possible variations in the relations in question.
It is by this method that I wish to approach the problem of the
relation between philosophy and political thought in the fourteenth century. To do this is not, of course, to overlook the fact
that the century's political thought was subjected to many influ-
ences that were primarily non-philosophic from canon and civil
law and from developments in political institutions themselves,
and that important work relevant to politics was done by the
civilians and canonists, including Bartolus, Baldus, and John
Andreae. But the question of the relation between philosophy and
political thought is sufficiently complex and important of itself,

both logically and historically, without for the present introducing such additional considerations.

The fourteenth century is peculiarly suited to the kind of inquiry here proposed. Its nearest analogue is perhaps the seventeenth century, where names like Hobbes, Spinoza, and Locke figure as prominently in political thought as they do in philosophy. Yet even in these men, intensely concerned as they were with the political issues of their time, there was not the same degree of direct personal involvement as in the fourteenth-century political philosophers. It is easier to trace the practical alliance between Egidius of Rome and Pope Boniface VIII, or between Marsilius of Padua or William of Ockham and Emperor Ludwig of Bavaria, or between John Wycliffe and the Lollards, than it is between the seventeenth-century philosophers and the political figures or movements of their time. Whether this is because the decline of the Church led to a lessening of the political influence of philosophers and theologians as counselors to the wielders of political power, or for some other cause, is not our present concern; nor is it our concern to trace the direct ways in which Egidius may personally have influenced Boniface, or Marsilius, Ludwig. Our point is rather that the direct practical involvement of leading philosophers of the fourteenth century in the burning political issues of their time is one of the considerations which makes that century a peculiarly apt one for examining the perennially significant problem of the relation between philosophy and political thought.

Historical Parallelisms

Before entering directly on our topic, I wish to suggest from a rather different direction something of the contemporary relevance of a concern with the development of philosophy and of political thought in the fourteenth century. In both areas tendencies begun in the late thirteenth century were carried to such new heights of logical rigor, technical power, and explanatory fruitfulness that the results may well be described as revolutionary; and these achievements resemble modern developments to such an extent that historians have had to exercise exceptional critical restraint in order to point out underlying differences. In logic, William of Ockham, Richard Swineshead, John Buridan, and Albert of Saxony, among others, worked out doctrines of supposition, signification, *consequentiae*, and *insolubilia* which closely resemble recent developments in mathematical logistic and semantics, including, for example, De Morgan's law and the logical paradoxes.[4] In epistemology, Nicholas of Autrecourt, John of Mirecourt, and others set forth probabilistic and skeptical interpretations of empirical knowledge and causal inference which anticipate Hume's famous critique, as well as current emphases in such doctrines as the distinction between analytic and synthetic propositions.[5] In natural philosophy, men like Buridan, Thomas Bradwardine, William Heytesbury, Albert of Saxony, Marsilius of Inghen, and Nicholas Oresme did work on the latitude of forms, maxima and minima, the mathematical analysis of proportions of velocities, and the motion of the earth which has important continuities with the achievements of Copernicus, Galileo, and other giants of modern physics and astronomy.[6]

In the field of political thought, the picture is similar. The fourteenth was a century of intense political conflicts, from the struggles between Philip the Fair and Pope Boniface VIII and between Ludwig of Bavaria and Pope John XXII in the first half of the century to the intermittent strife of the Hundred Years' War, the peasant revolts, and the Great Schism in its latter half. These events called forth a polemical literature of unparalleled intensity and depth, in which, as has already been said, philosophers played a leading part. The first decade of the fourteenth century saw in Egidius of Rome's *De ecclesiastica potestate*[7] a work which wove together many strands from antecedent publicists, canonists, and theologians into a coherent and massive doctrine of what Egidius called the papal "plenitude of power," which historians have only with difficulty been able to avoid calling by such modern names as "sovereignty" and "totalitarianism." In the same decade, a theory very similar to Egidius' was presented with copious argumentation in James of Viterbo's *De regimine Christiano*.[8] Again in the same decade, these papalist theories were given a reply of considerable intellectual force in the *De potestate regia et papali* of John of Paris,[9] whose position, with its careful balancing of the temporal and spiritual authorities, has been declared by a leading Catholic theologian to correspond to "the contemporary doctrine and practice of the Church."[10] In the first decade, too, elaborately argued proposals for world government under secular auspices were set forth in the *Monarchia* of Dante and by such writers as Engelbert of Admont and Pierre

Dubois.[11] The decades immediately following, embroiled in the struggle between Ludwig of Bavaria and Pope John XXII, saw not only the production of further comprehensive works in favor of papal absolutism by Augustinus Triumphus [12] and Alvarus Pelagius,[13] but the devastating reply of the *Defensor pacis* of Marsilius of Padua,[14] who, for his theory of the people's legislative authority and the complete subjection of the priesthood to the secular state, has been likened by scholars to nearly every modern political thinker from Machiavelli, Hobbes, and Luther to Rousseau and Marx. Marsilius' work was followed within a few years by the voluminous political writings of William of Ockham,[15] whose doctrines of the natural rights of the individual, the general council, and the limitation and balancing of royal and papal powers have evoked comparisons to, among others, Locke and the modern natural-rights tradition. In the remainder of the century, so far as we now know, no works equal in stature to these were produced. Yet in the writings of Lupold of Bebenburg, Konrad of Megenberg, John Wycliffe, Henry of Langenstein, and Conrad of Gelnhausen,[16] much further work was done which has clear connections not only with the conciliarism of the following century but with other institutional and doctrinal developments leading both to the Reformation and to the modern sovereign state.

I have stressed the similarities to modern developments in this brief outline not because I think that this is the only or the chief ground on which to evaluate these works, but because it serves to underline the parallelisms between the historical status and contributions of philosophy and of political thought in the fourteenth century. Of course, this approach has omitted such other significant figures in fourteenth-century philosophy as the German mystics Eckhart, Suso, and Tauler. But even if we could fit these, too, into a scheme of parallelisms to political thinkers and similarities to modern developments, the fact remains that, for our present problem, to note these historical relations is only the beginning. What we are concerned with is the conceptual or logical relation between the two developments; specifically, what was the intellectual contribution which philosophy made to political thought in this period? Yet even this question is insufficiently precise for our present purpose. The philosophic and political ideas of the fourteenth century were propounded in so many complex forms, and in writings so voluminous in quantity, that to attempt the task of analyzing their logical interrelations without setting up many initial restrictions would be to doom the inquiry from the start. We can illustrate this point, and derive some relevant suggestions for our procedure, if we initially consider the case of the logical relation between philosophy and politics in just one fourteenth-century thinker, William of Ockham.

William of Ockham

Ockham's voluminous writings, both philosophical and political, with their massive intricacies of technical terminology, distinctions, and argumentation, must still be read in largely inaccessible editions.[17] Nevertheless, scholars over many generations have engaged in a continuing debate about the relation between the philosophical and the political aspects of Ockham's work. The chief contemporary proponents of the view that there is a close logical relation between Ockham's doctrines in logic, epistemology, physics, metaphysics, and theology on the one hand, and his politics on the other, are two Frenchmen, Lagarde and Baudry, each of whom is presently engaged, and has been for some decades, in writing a multi-volumed study of Ockham's philosophy and politics.[18] The proponents of the opposite view, that Ockham's philosophy and his political doctrines are two logically independent bodies of thought, include Boehner (who until his recent death did a very large amount of work in elucidating and editing Ockham's logical works) and such other scholars as Scholz and Morrall.[19]

If we examine carefully this scholarly debate over the relation between Ockham's philosophy and his politics, we find that what the two sides are arguing about is primarily a logical question rather than a psychological or sociological one. They are not asking what there was in Ockham's personal psychology which led him from his philosophic views to his political ones, or how it was that a man holding his philosophic views would be motivated, given the conditions of his time and place, to hold certain political views. The question of the debate seems to be rather whether, quite independently of the accidents of Ockham's personality or society, there is some sort of intrinsic, logically "inevitable" connection between his philosophic ideas and his political ones. If, now, we scrutinize the logic of the debate itself, we see that the two sides are not in as much disagreement as at first appears. To a large extent, the difference between them seems to derive from two points: first, the fact that they are considering two different phases or aspects of Ockham's political ideas; second, the fact that they start from opposite ends of the question.

In the first place, then, we must note that a complex system of political thought like Ockham's has two different phases or aspects, which we may call practical and theoretic. The practical aspect consists in specific recommendations on matters of policy; for example, as to how much power the pope should have in temporal or in spiritual affairs, or what the rights and duties of kings, popes, and private citizens are in respect to property. The theoretic aspect consists in elucidations of basic social and political concepts like "state," "people," "law," "property," and in general doctrines about the nature of social and political relations, as well as in the analysis of the intellectual methods used or referred to in dealing with these concepts or doctrines. To be sure, in a coherent political thinker like Ockham these two phases are often closely connected, in that he will appeal to his theoretic definitions and doctrines in support of his practical recommendations.[20] Yet, that there is no necessary or logical connection between these is suggested by the fact that other thinkers may propound the same practical political recommendations without Ockham's theoretic political doctrines, or even with opposed ones.[21]

Now the difference between those scholars who affirm and those who deny that there is a logical connection between Ockham's philosophy and his politics rests in part on this difference between the theoretic and the practical phases of his political thought. Baudry and Lagarde center attention on Ockham's general political definitions and theoretic doctrines, and they try to show how these are explicated by such of his philosophic ideas as his voluntaristic theory of God's absolute omnipotence, his nominalistic theory of terms and relations, and his theory of knowledge.[22] Boehner and Morrall, on the other hand, center attention on Ockham's practical political recommendations, and they have no difficulty in showing how these are logically independent of Ockham's logic or metaphysics.[23]

The second difference underlying the two divergent views on the relation between Ockham's philosophy and his politics consists in the direction in which the argument is made to run. Boehner and Morrall begin from Ockham's practical political recommendations—for example, his opposition to the papal plenitude of power —and they ask whether these recommendations logically imply Ockham's general philosophic doctrines. They reply in the negative, because, as has been said, the political recommendations can go hand in hand with many different and even opposed philosophic doctrines. Lagarde and Baudry, on the other hand, begin from Ockham's general philosophic doctrines, and they ask either how the political doctrines follow from these or how they are elucidated by the philosophy. And since Ockham, being a systematic thinker, does use his general philosophic concepts, methods, and doctrines to elucidate his political doctrines, although in ways not always reducible to a simple syllogistic pattern, Lagarde and Baudry are able to show that in this direction there *is* a logical connection between Ockham's philosophy and his politics. But these two positions are not at all contradictory. If I say that p implies q, and you say that q does not imply p, we are not contradicting one another. Nor are we contradicting one another if I say that the terms of q, and even q itself, are contained in or explained by p, and you say that q could nonetheless be understood and asserted without p.

I have gone into these questions of the interpretation of Ockham not only for the sake of understanding his own thought but also in order to derive suggestions as to how to proceed in examining the relation of philosophy to political thought in the fourteenth century. From what we have found, it seems plausible that, at the very least, the philosophy will clarify the methods and the theoretic concepts and doctrines of the political thought. But for our present problem let us restrict ourselves to the practical phase of political thought. Our question, therefore, concerns the sense in which, and the extent to which, there was a logical connection between philosophy and practical political recommendations in the fourteenth century. In view of the difficulties and disagreements over the interpretation of Ockham, the best mode of approach would seem to be to take a fairly simple yet basic philosophic doctrine and see how it is related to an issue in practical politics which was argued by political thinkers. The most famous such political issue in the fourteenth century was that concerning the distribution of authority between the spiritual and temporal powers. Fortunately, there is available a major attempt to deal with the very question of the relation between the positions taken on this issue and a basic philosophic doctrine. We shall take our point of departure, then, from an interpretation advanced by Martin Grabmann, whose extensive researches have contributed very considerably to our knowledge of fourteenth-century philosophy.

Grabmann's Correlations

In a famous and influential monograph published in 1934,[24] Grabmann took over the view, previously advanced by Mandonnet and Gilson,[25] among others, that on the fundamental question of the relation between reason and faith mediaeval philosophers were divided into three different doctrinal schools; and he correlated these schools with three different positions of mediaeval political thinkers on the relation between the state and the church. In the first place, there were the Christian Aristotelians, such as Thomas Aquinas and Albert the Great, who held that reason and faith are each self-sufficient in their own respective spheres, and that reason and worldly knowledge must be subordinated to faith only where they touch on questions with which faith is concerned. With this, Grabmann correlated the political position of Aquinas and John of Paris which held that state and church are autonomous in their own spheres, and which accorded the pope only an "indirect power" in temporal affairs, so that the pope could intervene only when spiritual issues were at stake. Secondly, there were the Latin Averroists, including Siger of Brabant and Boethius of Dacia, who regarded reason as completely self-contained in its ultimate goal and who either cared nothing for theological dogma and faith or else viewed them from the standpoint of the so-called two-fold truth, according to which reason and faith often yielded mutually contradictory conclusions. Grabmann correlated this doctrine with the political position of Marsilius of Padua, who made the secular power completely independent of the papacy, so that the latter not only had no power, direct or indirect, over the former, but came under the control of the secular power even in spiritual affairs. Thirdly, there were the traditionalist Augustinians, like St. Bonaventura and Henry of Ghent, who completely subordinated reason to faith, holding that reason is powerless unless aided by faith. Grabmann correlated this doctrine with the political position of Egidius of Rome, James of Viterbo, and other papalists, according to which the pope has a "direct power" in temporal affairs.

Without going into the technicalities of "direct" and "indirect" powers, and into the possible ambiguities of terms like "state," "church," "spiritual," "temporal," "secular," and so on, we may agree that what Grabmann has here presented seems plain enough. He has presented correlations which have an attractive symmetry because they take the form of a proportion: as faith is to reason in a given philosophy, so is the spiritual power to the temporal power in that philosophy's political offshoot. Nevertheless, this seems like an anomalous undertaking. For the terms of the correlations are a set of epistemological doctrines—doctrines about the relative abilities of human cognitive faculties (using "cognitive" in the sense in which both reason and faith were regarded as at least possible means of obtaining valid knowledge)—and a set of political doctrines. But we might well ask: What have the respective cognitive powers of reason and faith to do with the respective political powers of the emperor and the pope? It might seem that the anomaly would be removed only if the political struggle were viewed as in some way also a cognitive struggle—as if, for example, the debate over the relative political superiority of emperor and pope were made to hinge on the relative superiority of a rational faculty to which the emperor appealed and a fideistic or religious faculty to which the pope appealed. But this seems much too simple. Did not the emperor also proclaim his adherence to religious faith? And did not the pope also appeal to reason? Moreover, how could conclusions about matters as specific as those concerning the relative powers of emperor and pope be deduced from considerations as general as those concerning the relative powers of reason and faith? For the latter, like other epistemological issues, apply to a much broader range of subject matter than the political. Whether faith and reason are independent, or contradictory, or arranged hierarchically, is a question which bears on all the possible objects which could be known by faith or by reason or both; hence it seems difficult to grasp how such a general question can serve to differentiate positions to be taken on the specific issue of relative political power. And in addition to these considerations, there is another, perhaps even more obvious one. To set up such a correlation as we have been considering between cognitive faculties and political powers would appear to convert the political struggle into a purely theoretic affair far removed from the conflicts of passions and values which it actually involved. It would seem to make it possible to settle, or at least to define, political disputes solely by means of an appeal to "factual" considerations of what reason and faith, respectively, can do.

These last two objections are recurrent items in current debates on the relation between philosophy and politics. The latter objection is sometimes referred to as the "naturalistic fallacy" in that one of its many versions in which it would consist not in trying to define a value term by means of non-value terms, but in trying to draw a value conclusion from factual premises which do not, as such, contain value expressions. In this guise, the objection would be: Even if, for example, faith is superior to reason, how from this does it follow that the pope ought to be superior to the emperor?

However hackneyed this example, it does suggest at least the beginnings of an answer to the objections; for the issue of the relative status of faith and reason was suffused with value considerations for all mediaeval thinkers. This was so for many reasons; one of them was that among the matters held to be objects of faith or reason or both was that of the proper mode of life for man, his true end. What this meant was that faith and reason were conceived not only as theoretic faculties but as practical ones: their deliverances bore not only on facts and causes but also on what men ought to be and do. Consequently, if faith is cognitively superior to reason, in that reason must be validated by faith and cannot attain to objects as important as those of faith, then the end of life which only faith can grasp, that of supernatural beatitude in the future world, is superior to the purely natural happiness which is all that can be grasped by reason. From this in turn it follows that the value-status of the pope is superior to that of the emperor, because of the superior value of the end provided for by the pope over that provided for by the emperor. And in a context where value considerations of relative moral dignity or worth were regarded as decisive arguments for the allocation of relative political power, the conclusion necessarily followed of the pope's absolute superiority, even in temporal affairs.

There were many other ways in which the papalists used the superiority of faith over reason to establish their conclusion. But they all involved the same principle of hierarchized value considerations. Hence, it was inevitable that first John of Paris, and, more drastically, Marsilius after him, should emphasize that secular government involves urgencies and necessities of its own, and that these have nothing to do with the value considerations adduced by the papalists.[26] These emphases were important steps toward what we might call a pure science of politics—that is, the concentration on specifically political conditions of power and government, as against the moral and religious goals which they might serve and by which they might therefore be evaluated.

From the considerations so far adduced, we can also see how the other two kinds of epistemological doctrines mentioned by Grabmann are correlated with the respective political doctrines. If, as with the Christian Aristotelians, reason and faith are autonomous in their own spheres, then the values or ends of life which they respectively establish are likewise autonomous (even though the temporal end is ultimately ordered toward the spiritual), and so too are the respective political authorities. This was, roughly, the means by which Aquinas and John of Paris arrived at their moderate conclusions concerning the normal autonomy of the spiritual and temporal powers, and the intervention of each in the sphere of the other only in exceptional circumstances.[27] With the Averroist type of epistemological doctrine, the sequence is less clear. This is not only because the Averroists did not explicitly dwell on questions about the relative cognitive adequacy of reason and faith, but because by their doctrine of the so-called double truth they declared that faith alone reached truth, while reason, when it conflicted with faith, as it often did, attained at best only what was probable on the basis of sense experience. But in denying the power of reason to demonstrate many religious doctrines, such as eternal life, in asserting the contrariety of rational and religious doctrines, and in proclaiming that they as philosophers were proceeding by reason alone without regard for the deliverances of religious faith, the Averroists cut the ground out from under the Augustinian papalists' procedure of discussing within a single universe of discourse the relative values of faith and reason, of the goods of the next world and of this one, of the authority of the spiritual and the temporal powers. The way was thus left open for a politics based on rational considerations alone—and this was what Marsilius of Padua set forth in the first, and determining, portion of his political treatise.[28] Having by this means set up a state dedicated to this-worldly values alone, he could then fit priesthood and papacy into it without serious alterations.

We are now in a position to ask somewhat closer questions about the correlation of philosophic doctrine with political thought in the fourteenth century. "Correlation" is, of course, a vague word: it can refer to anything from an accidental conjunction to a logically necessary connection. What kind of correlation, then, was there between the relative status of reason and faith on the one hand and of the temporal and spiritual powers on the other? [29] Grabmann himself said that the correlation holds "only with certain limitations and reservations and only in broad outline." [30] This suggests that the correlations are not completely logical ones; that is, that to be a Christian Aristotelian, an Averroist, and an Augustinian, in the senses defined above with respect to the relation of reason and faith, did not entail simply by definition that in politics one was, respectively, a parallelist, an antipapalist, and a papalist. And this in turn suggests that it would not be logically contradictory to find Christian Aristotelians and even Averroists who were papalists, as well as Augustinians who were antipapalists. Now the first and third of these logical possibilities actually existed in the fourteenth century, and the second came closer to being realized than is generally known. I shall now deal with each of these "variants" in turn, in order to outline somewhat more fully the complex structure of this phase of the interrelations between the century's philosophy and its political thought.

Christian Aristotelianism and Papalism: James of Viterbo and Others

It will be recalled that Grabmann defined the Christian Aristotelians as those who, following Aquinas and Albert the Great, upheld the self-sufficiency of both reason and faith in their respective spheres. Now in Aquinas himself, reason and faith were correlated with nature and grace as the bases of their respective spheres of application.[31] And the relative autonomy of reason and faith did not remove the fact that the objects and values dealt with by faith were "higher" ones to which reason and its objects and values must be subordinated whenever there was intellectual or practical contact between them, although this contact was not conceived as regular or usual. To express this complex relation Aquinas used the formula "grace does not abolish nature but perfects it." [32] The relative autonomy of reason, then, meant the relative autonomy of natural, secular values; and one of the chief of these values was political society. To set forth this relative autonomy of the values of the secular political order, Aquinas

repeated the Aristotelian dicta that the state exists by nature and
that man is by nature a political animal.[33] This meant that the
state existed not as a consequence of sin, or of any cause accessible
primarily to faith or religion, but rather as an answer to certain
inherent needs of men, ascertainable by reason, which they would
have had even in the absence of sin.[34]

Now this Aristotelian doctrine of the naturalness of the state
was upheld by many papalists, including James of Viterbo, Augustinus Triumphus, Alexander of St. Elpidius, and Alvarus Pelagius.
Thus, for example, James of Viterbo, writing of the three communities—the family, the city, and the state—declares:

> The establishment of these communities or societies proceeded
> from men's natural inclination, as the Philosopher showed in the
> first book of the *Politics*. For man is naturally a social animal
> living in a multitude, which comes from natural necessity, because
> one man cannot sufficiently live by himself but needs to be helped
> by another. Hence too speech has been given to man, whereby
> he can express his thoughts to other men and thereby communi-
> cate and live more advantageously with others. Because there-
> fore it is natural to man to live in society, there resides in men a
> natural inclination toward such communities . . . .[35]

It was in a similar vein that Augustinus Triumphus, having raised
the question "Whether the pope can justly remove lordships and
jurisdictions from pagans," went on to reply: "No, because according to the Philosopher in the first book of the *Politics* the lordship
of one man over another is counted among natural benefits . . . .
But not only from believers but even from demons natural benefits
have not been removed." Augustinus went on to underline further this autonomous value of the natural: "Infidels deserve to
lose the power and liberty of grace, but not the power of nature.
Consequently the natural order of governance which derives from
the law of nature is not removed from them." [36]

The question which now arises is this: How could these papalists recognize the naturalness, the independent legitimacy, of the
secular state, and still be papalists? For, as papalists, they held
that the pope, being God's vicar, is endowed with plenitude of
power in the sense of containing all power, temporal as well as
spiritual, so that no other power is legitimate unless subjected to
it. This in turn meant that the temporal ruler is at most the

"executive" or "minister" of the pope, requiring to be established and judged by the pope, and requiring also that his laws be examined and approved by the pope. And when in the pope's judgment the ruler deserved it, the pope could depose him.[37]

Nevertheless, it is not difficult to see how these far-reaching claims could be made consistent with the papalists' Aristotelian doctrine of the relative autonomy of reason, nature, and temporal government. For the papalists, like Aquinas himself, held that reason and nature are only *relatively* autonomous. In this connection, the second clause in Aquinas' phrase "grace does not abolish nature but perfects it" is highly significant. A typical papalist interpretation of it was given by James of Viterbo as follows:

> The temporal power is established materially and in point of origin from men's natural inclination, and through this from God insofar as the work of nature is the work of God; but formally and in point of perfection the temporal power is established by the spiritual power, which is derived from God in a special way. For grace does not abolish nature but perfects and forms it; and similarly that which is of grace does not abolish that which is of nature, but forms and perfects it. Hence, since the spiritual power is in respect of grace, while the temporal power is in respect of nature, it follows that the spiritual power does not exclude the temporal but forms and perfects it. Indeed, all human power is imperfect and unformed unless it is formed and perfected by the spiritual. But this formation is approval and ratification.[38]

What this approval involves is shown by James's subsequent statement that "the temporal power must not use laws unless they have been approved by the spiritual power." [39] Moreover, James asserts, the spiritual power "can and must correct and direct the temporal power, and inflict on it not only spiritual but also temporal punishment by reason of its crime or delict, extending even to the temporal ruler's deposition if the quality of his delict requires it." [40] In a similar vein, Augustinus Triumphus, despite his denial of the pope's authority to remove political power from pagans, on the ground of the natural basis of such power, can nevertheless go on to deal in papalist fashion with the question "Whether the pope can deprive Jews of lordship over Christians." He first makes the Christian Aristotelian objection that "natural right cannot be abolished by the pope . . . . But the lordship of one man over another is from natural law." To this Augustinus makes the fol-

lowing reply: "All unbelievers by reason of their infidelity deserve
to lose power over those who are adopted sons of God. Consequently, the pope can deservedly deprive all unbelievers of such
power." [41]

The papalists, then, could accept the Christian Aristotelians'
doctrine of the relative autonomy of reason and nature and yet
subsume it under the ultimate control of faith and grace. There
was, of course, always an at least latent instability in the equi-
librium which Aquinas, John of Paris, Dante, and others tried to
set up between the two spheres; for as Christians they had to admit
the ultimate moral superiority of the realm of faith and grace.
It was this instability which the papalists exploited in making explicit the hierarchic implications of such superiority.

Augustinianism and Antipapalism: John Wycliffe

Let us now turn to a second correlation set up by Grabmann:
that of the Augustinian doctrine of the complete subordination of
reason to faith with the political espousal of the direct, plenary
power of the pope over the temporal ruler even in temporal affairs.
In our examination of how the philosophic doctrine of Christian
Aristotelianism was compatible with papalism, we might be said
to have reached a conclusion not too different from at least the
principle of Grabmann's correlations, the proportion whereby, as
faith is to reason, so is the spiritual power to the temporal. For
when the papalists moved from the autonomy of nature and grace
to the papal plenitude of power, this did ultimately involve the
subordination of nature to grace, and hence of reason to faith. But
when we consider how philosophic Augustinianism was correlated
not with papalism but with antipapalism, we find that this very
principle is completely overturned: the superiority of grace and
faith over nature and reason now leads to the political superiority
not of the pope but of the temporal ruler. History provides, in
fact, abundant examples of this contrary correlation, both before
and after the fourteenth century: for example, in the writings of
Gregory of Catino [42] and the Norman Anonymous [43] in the elev-
enth century, and in Luther and Calvin in the sixteenth. However, to remain within the confines of the fourteenth century, we
find a conspicuous example of this contrary position in John
Wycliffe.

That Wycliffe belongs to the Augustinian philosophic tradition is quite clear. He declares that men can have no knowledge without divine illumination, so that reason is completely subordinated to faith.[44] As against the Aristotelians, he holds that civil *dominium* is a consequence of sin.[45] Like the papalist Egidius of Rome at the beginning of the century, Wycliffe also holds that no just *dominium* is possible without grace, and indeed, that without faith and grace there is neither king nor kingdom nor people; moreover, civil law is contained in divine law or at least presupposes it.[46]

Nevertheless, in his political thought Wycliffe uses these ideas in a way which leads to conclusions sharply opposed to those of the papalists. He is emphatic, for example, that the pope has no power in temporal affairs,[47] that his claims to such power are those of an antichrist,[48] that the temporal ruler can legitimately take away from the clergy their temporal goods [49] and can intervene in the governance of the church to correct abuses.[50] The bishops have jurisdiction in spiritual cases by authority of the king.[51] Moreover, one is not required to believe that the pope is head of the Church,[52] nor is subjection to him necessary for salvation.[53]

It is not difficult to see how Wycliffe's antipapal ideas are consistent with his philosophical Augustinianism. Like the antipapalists of the investiture controversy three centuries earlier, Wycliffe simply claims for temporal rulership at least as much, and even more, divine sanction than he grants the papacy, so that the force of the papalists' elaborate justifications of papal power by appeal to God is either denied, or is divided between pope and king, or is ascribed more fully to the king. Thus he holds that the king as well as the pope is vicar of God—the one in temporal, the other in spiritual affairs; [54] the king, moreover, is God's chief (*praecipuus*) vicar; [55] he bears the image of Christ's divinity, the priest only that of his humanity, so that the king must rule the priest.[56]

Averroism and Quasi-Papalism: John of Jandun

Let us now turn to the third correlation set up by Grabmann: that of Averroism with antipapalism. The sole instance of this correlation cited in his above-mentioned monograph is Marsilius of Padua, whose Averroism has long been stressed by commentators. While many Averroist writings on ethics have been discovered, from the hands of such philosophers as Siger of Brabant,

Boethius of Dacia, Egidius of Orleans, and Antonius of Parma,[57] Grabmann declares that no political work from an Averroist other than Marsilius has yet been found, and he stresses the importance of overcoming this lack in order to be able to see more clearly the relation between Marsilius' political ideas and the Latin Averroism of the Paris faculty of arts.[58]

There is, however, another fourteenth-century Averroist from whom we have copious discussions of political problems. This is none other than John of Jandun, long alleged to be the co-author of the *Defensor pacis*.[59] In his *Questions on the Metaphysics* [60] we find lengthy disquisitions on political philosophy which, so far as I have been able to ascertain, have completely escaped the notice of commentators.[61] These political discussions are embedded in such *quaestiones* as "Whether purely speculative philosophers should be permitted in the state," [62] "Whether human happiness consists in wisdom," [63] "Whether metaphysics is the principal science," [64] "Whether metaphysics is a free science," [56] "Whether speculative habits are more honorable than practical ones," [66] "Whether custom in youth is the strongest impediment to the knowledge of truth," [67] "Whether there should be one ruler in the whole world." [68] I have dealt elsewhere with some of John's doctrines as they are presented in these questions; [69] here I wish to consider them only in so far as they are relevant to the correlation of Averroism with antipapalism.

It will be recalled that Grabmann defined Averroism by its view of reason as self-contained in its ultimate goal and by its doctrine of the so-called double truth, whereby reason and faith often yielded contrary conclusions. Now John of Jandun is notoriously of this school, and in the *Questions on the Metaphysics* which we are now considering, we find copious examples of it. Thus, for instance, on the question "Whether eternal substances other than the first one depend upon the first as on an agent and efficient cause," [70]—a question involving the Christian belief in God as the omnipotent creator of all reality—John first presents detailed arguments in the negative, based on the Aristotelian doctrine that there are many eternal substances, and these, *qua* eternal, could not be caused by an efficient cause. But then John concludes as follows:

> This is what must be said to the question in accordance with the intention of Aristotle and the Commentator, who posit besides the

first substance other eternal substances. And if this were true these others would not depend upon a true efficient cause acting through motion. But nevertheless it must be said in accordance with faith and truth that nothing beside the first substance is eternal, but all [other] things have begun to be anew, and consequently have been produced by the first principle as by an agent through creation out of nothing, at least abstract substances. And this creation is not motion nor generation taken in a univocal sense like the motion of inferior things, but is a different, supernatural production, which cannot be proved from sensible things and from the natural things whence proceed the philosophers who speak in a natural mode. But I only believe this firmly and know it, not by reason arising from sensible things, and this firmly makes me assent with reverence to the teachers of Scripture. Hence, since I do not know how to demonstrate this from sensible things, nor can it be demonstrated because it is above sensibles and nature, it follows that in simply and faithfully believing this I have merit. And in this too is proved the superiority in power of creation and salvation over any natural agent.[71]

Several points must be noted about this and many similar passages in which John of Jandun distinguishes sharply between what must be said "according to Aristotle and the Commentator" and what must be said "according to faith and truth." [72] In the first place, John holds that philosophic propositions contradict those of the Christian religion. Sometimes, to be sure, this contradiction is mitigated by his noting of the different bases and methods of philosophy and religion, but usually his position is that philosophy and religion are dealing with the same questions or propositions, and are giving contradictory answers to these questions. In the second place, as has often been noted,[73] John of Jandun, like the other Averroists, does not simultaneously assert the *truth* of the contradictory propositions of philosophic reason and of religious faith. He declares, rather, that only the latter are "true," even though they cannot be demonstrated from empirical or natural bases; while the propositions of philosophy, even though they can be thus demonstrated, he does not call "true" when they contradict faith. In the third place, consequently, there is a sharp difference between this Averroist view and that of the Christian Aristotelians. The latter uphold both a harmony and a separation of reason and faith: harmony, in the double sense that reason can demonstrate the "preambles" of faith, such as the existence and

unity of God, and is never in conflict with faith; separation, in that
the bases and objects of reason are different from those of faith,
which is why the two are never in conflict. Thus while both
Thomas Aquinas and John of Jandun sometimes say that philosophic reason cannot demonstrate some religious doctrine, the as-
sumptions of such statements are different. For Aquinas, they
mean that a strictly philosophic argument can demonstrate neither
the doctrine in question *nor its contradictory;* while for John of
Jandun they mean that a strictly philosophic argument *can* demonstrate the contradictory of the religious doctrine in question.
Moreover, Aquinas has no interest in pursuing or attempting
proof of propositions contrary to faith, except in so far as they
may bring out more clearly a truth of faith; while John of Jandun's
dominant concern is with the philosophic propositions themselves,
and if these contradict faith they are still elaborated with great
care and for their own sake, with but a brief disclaimer to the
effect that in such cases the "truth" lies rather with faith. Whether
or not Jandun was "sincere" in these disclaimers seems impossible
to ascertain with any significant degree of conclusiveness. The
salient point, however, is that he accepts such contradictions, and
is concerned with the pursuit of philosophic reason for its own
sake regardless of its impact on religious faith.[74]

Now on Grabmann's correlation of reason-faith and temporal
power–spiritual power, it might have been predicted that (parallel
to the unresolved contradictions between reason and faith) John
would hold that there is a sharp political conflict between the temporal and spiritual powers, and that (parallel to the obvious preference he evinces for pursuing philosophic reason for its own sake
regardless of religious faith) John would tend to an antipapalist
position, affirming not only the complete autonomy of the temporal power but also its superiority in political authority over the
spiritual power. Yet, in fact, John's political position is quite different. He is very far from being an antipapalist, and indeed he
goes far toward conciliating the papalists. His complete doctrine
on this matter is rather complicated, but we may note, to begin
with, the way in which he deals with the question "Whether
there should be one ruler in the whole universe." He sets forth
as an *argumentum a contrario* the consideration that the macro-
cosm should be like the microcosm, but "in the microcosm there
are several rulers who are equally primary . . . such as the king

and the supreme pontiff, because neither wishes to be subject to the other." [75] John's reply is as follows:

> . . . We must say that in the whole universe there should be one ruler. And when you say that it is neither the king nor the supreme pontiff, it must be replied that it is the supreme pontiff, and although the king is not subject to him in temporal affairs, yet he is subject to him in spiritual affairs and in virtue. But you will say that this is spoken inadequately, because it applies only in the law of the Christians and not in the other laws. It must be replied that insofar as it is a matter of merit and of natural law, all men, of whatever custom or law, must be under the law of the Christians, which is proved with evidence and certainty by evident miracles, which belong to no one except to the maker of the law of the Christians. Hence too insofar as it is a matter of merit all men should be subject to the supreme pontiff, even though they are not. Indeed, the more they resist the Christian law, the more they err and fall away from reason. [76]

It will have been noted that in this passage there is no attempt to derogate from the papacy, that, in particular, there is none of Marsilius' effort to draw a sharp distinction between the merits and prerogatives of Christ and the Christian religion on the one hand and of the pope on the other. The evidence of Christ's miracles is used to support the position that all men should be subject to the pope. In saying that the king should be subject to the pope in spiritual affairs, John resembles the Christian Aristotelians, but he goes beyond them in adducing natural law (*de jure naturali*) as the basis for the subjection of the king and of all men to the pope and the Christian religion.

The question hence arises: How can John, as an Averroist, regard reason as self-contained, and as contrary to faith on propositions of theology, including miracles, and yet endorse the king's subjection to the pope in spiritual affairs? This, as we shall see, is not an easy question to answer. At least part of the answer, however, is to be found in the intellectualist emphasis which John shares with many other Averroists. [77] He says that the highest good is "theoretic happiness" or wisdom, "which consists in the operation of the theoretic intellect in respect of the noblest object," and he equates such happiness with the love and contemplation of God, which he conceives in the Aristotelian manner as this-worldly θεωρία or contemplation of "abstract principles." Moreover, John

puts this theoretic happiness into a practical context, for he makes
it the necessary condition for the morality of a society:

> The wisdom which consists in the contemplation and knowledge
> of God and the other abstract principles is necessary for com-
> munity and good living together, because without a knowledge
> of God men cannot formally operate well, although they can
> materially. Hence in order that the legislator may make his citi-
> zens good he needs to have knowledge of God either through him-
> self, as through the habit of wisdom joined to himself, or through
> another wise man who will tell him and demonstrate God to him,
> in order that he may be able to instruct others. Hence too politi-
> cal happiness is ordered to theoretic happiness as its end.[78]

As this passage suggests, John makes it the function of the ruler
to inculcate such knowledge of God in his subjects. Since the
proper act of the ruler is to command, the ruler's political happiness consists in commanding the love and contemplation of God:

> . . . Among all the acts of man the noblest is to know God, and
> in the act of commanding this consists political happiness in the
> ruler operating toward the knowledge of God, just as theoretic
> happiness consists in the contemplation of God. And this doc-
> trine is marvelously close to the doctrine of the most pious legisla-
> tor our lord Jesus Christ, who when he was asked what is the
> first commandment in the law, replied "Love thy God with all
> thy heart," and then the most pious legislator added: "and thy
> neighbor as thyself." Therefore political happiness consists in the
> act of commanding that men operate toward the love of God.[79]

The ruler does not himself have the knowledge of God. Hence
he must receive it from someone else. But this can only be the
"theoretic philosophers who teach the knowledge of God." [80] Without such philosophers "the fulfillment of political happiness cannot be had." [81] Consequently, the theoretic philosophers are "the
final cause of the other parts of the state, just as . . . political happiness is ordered to theoretic happiness, and all the men in the
state are ordered to the contemplation of God." [82]

Having thus exalted the philosophers, John goes on to suggest
that at least ideally the philosophers would be priests. The theoretic philosophers, he writes,

> are presupposed by the priests, because it is necessary for the
> priests to know God, and they must be theoretic, because in

Greek priests are called the elders, who must be wise. You say that
the theoretic philosophers [etc.].[83] It must be replied that indeed
the philosophers would wish to be priests if they were treated as
they would deserve to be, but this is not done because prebends
and benefices are given to low characters. Hence the priest must
necessarily be wise and have knowledge of God . . . . The priests
do not add anything over and above the theoretic men in regard
to the contemplation of God except external acts . . . .[84]

The philosophers, then, are priests in all but official status, because their function is to lead men to the knowledge of God. This
near equation of priests and philosophers has an at least general
background in the Aristotelian tradition; [85] it is even found in
Marsilius of Padua.[86] But when Marsilius classifies the philosophers as priests, this in no way leads to the political hegemony
of the priesthood, because his criteria for the allocation of political
superiority are not intellectual ones. In John of Jandun, on the
other hand, the philosopher-would-be-priests appear as the power
behind the ruler's throne because of the theological-intellectual
values of which they are the teachers, just as for the papalists the
priesthood has ultimate political superiority over the temporal
ruler because of the higher values subserved by the former. John's
argument differs from that of the papalists in that the values to
which he appeals are not supernatural but this-worldly and intellectual; yet, as we have seen, he readily equates these with the
tenets of Christianity. He uses the Averroist intellectualist ideas
to set the philosopher, and hence the priest and pope, over the ruler
even in so far as the structure of values in this world is concerned.
In saying that the secular ruler's commands must be guided by the
theoretic philosopher acting as teacher of the "knowledge of God,"
John opens the way for precisely that papal claim to judiciary control over temporal laws which was the target of Marsilius' chief
polemics. There is, then, a close connection between John's Averroism and his exaltation of the pope, the chief priest.

However, this combination of Averroism and quasi-papalism
raises a serious problem. As an Averroist, John of Jandun frequently emphasizes, as we have seen, the contrariety between the
philosophic reason which proceeds by demonstrations derived from
sense experience and the religious truths to which he adheres by
faith. But as a quasi-papalist upholding the political influence of
the theoretic philosopher-priests, he also frequently claims that

"philosophy" and "reason" *support* the superiority of the Christian religion over other religions.[87] Thus he says that "the more men resist the Christian law, the more they err and fall away from *reason.*" [88] Again, he writes that

> all laws [89] besides the law of the Christians are with an admixture of error, such as the law of Mohammed that after this life there is had a life of pleasure and delight. Hence this is contrary to *reason.* But in a second way a particular law arises from a universal law without an admixture of error, so that nothing in it is contrary to *reason,* as in our law, the Christian.[90]

Similarly, he says that

> faith can be referred to two things. In one way it can be referred to false laws, and in this way the faith of the vulgar is stronger, because they believe more in false laws than in philosophy, because they have not seen many things and do not know how to distinguish the true from the false . . . . In another way faith can be referred to the true laws, and in this way the faith of the philosophers is stronger than the faith of the vulgar, because philosophers believe more in what is *true* than do the vulgar. And when the Commentator said that the faith of the vulgar is stronger than the faith of the philosophers, he meant in false laws and not in true ones.[91]

In such passages as these, John of Jandun is indicating a different relation between reason and faith than that which is characteristic of the Averroists. As an Averroist, he views the pair reason-philosophy as contradictory to the pair faith-truth. But in the above passages reason and philosophy are in agreement with faith, and truth consequently characterizes the former as well as the latter. However, there would be an insuperable difficulty here only if John of Jandun held that philosophic reason is always in contradiction to religious faith, and can never demonstrate anything pertaining to faith. Yet on the basis of the passages where he does affirm such contradiction and indemonstrability in particular questions, there is no need to interpret him as meaning that these relations hold on all questions. It is possible further to mitigate any seeming inconsistency in John's position by noting that the questions on which he asserts the contradiction and indemonstrability are theoretic ones of metaphysics, physics, and psychology; while the questions on which he declares the agreement of reason and faith are rather the practical ones bearing on the kinds of "laws," characters, and ends or values with and by which men ought to live. In Marsilius of Padua, likewise, reason and faith are in agreement on some kinds of questions, in separation on other kinds, and in contradiction on still other kinds. But in his case the agreement bears on political questions, the separation on metaphysical and cosmological questions, and the contradiction on moral questions.[92]

To what extent, then, do these complexities in John of Jandun's view of the relation of reason and faith affect Grabmann's correlation of Averroism with antipapalism? Since Averroism was defined in terms of the contrariety of reason and faith, does not John's view that reason and faith are in harmony on practical matters separate him, to that extent, from the Averroist position? And since John's quasi-papalism seems to be necessarily connected with this harmonizing strand of his philosophy, does not this remove or at least strongly mitigate the "refutation" here suggested of Grabmann's correlation? For it appears that John's view that the philosopher-priest with his knowledge of God is the final cause of the state depends upon precisely that phase of his doctrine wherein reason and faith are *not* in contradiction. For if they were in contradiction, then the philosopher's knowledge of God could not be utilized by the priest, and the ruler would be faced not with a single theology most ably presented by the philosophers, but with a double one, the "true" one presented by the Christian priests "according to faith and truth" and a "rational" one presented by the philosophers "according to Aristotle and the Commentator."

Nevertheless, these very points emphasize the difficulties in the way of attempts like that of Grabmann's correlation. For the fact that a philosopher may hold one view of the relation of reason and faith in theoretic questions and another view in practical questions, suggests that it is not from his view on theoretic questions alone that his practical political conclusions can be inferred. More generally, any attempt to derive political conclusions from general epistemological doctrines must always presuppose an extension of those doctrines to the very political concerns which are at issue. Consider, for example, Russell's view that empiricism, because of its tentativeness and its consequent opposition to rationalist dogmatism, provides the philosophic basis of the tolerance characteristic of liberal democracy.[93] This view assumes that the empiricist's tentativeness will always be translated into the democrat's tol-

erance; but such a translation would involve many specifically
practical questions of moral character and of political institutions,
and these in turn are by no means identical with the epistemological trait itself. Similarly, John of Jandun could hold that on
theoretic questions philosophic reason and religious faith were in
contradiction, and yet he could find what seemed to him adequate
grounds for not translating this theoretic contradiction into a practical political opposition. This non-translation need not by any
means be considered an incoherence in his total doctrine; instead,
it may have reflected his conviction that the requirements of
practical political institutions are different from those of theoretic
philosophy.

The question of John of Jandun's position also involves some
deeper problems about the interpretation of the Averroist tradition. From Averroës himself there stemmed a rhetorical conception of both politics and religion as based on considerations of
social utility rather than of ultimate truth.[94]

> For law exists not in order that we may have knowledge but in
> order that we may become good. And the reason for this is that
> the perfection of man is acquired only through assemblages of
> men in states, and the assemblage, i.e., the state, will be perfect
> only because of goodness, and not because of knowledge.[95]

This was echoed by Siger of Brabant when he wrote that

> the legislator does not lay down rules about first principles accord-
> ing to his opinions but according to what is more beneficial to
> men and according to the ways in which he can give more guid-
> ance to the good; but sometimes men may be made good through
> what is false and frivolous.[96]

John of Jandun, in his *Questions on the Metaphysics,* quoted at
least four times Averroës' dictum that "the assemblage, i.e., the
state, will be perfect only because of goodness, and not because of
knowledge." [97] Hence, it would not be anomalous, but rather
quite in keeping with the Averroist tradition, for John to hold
as a theoretic philosopher that reason and faith are in contradiction, while at the same time holding as a practical political philosopher that the view to be taken of the relation of reason and faith
must reflect what is needed not "in order that we may have knowledge" but "in order that we may become good."

Conclusion

What, then, is the upshot of our inquiry? We have tried to examine some of the ways in which philosophy was related to political thought in the fourteenth century, using Grabmann's influential correlations as a point of departure. And we have seen that these correlations are not logically necessary. While an explicit definition of "logically necessary correlation" has not been presented here, we have been assuming at least a criterion of the absence of such necessity: the correlation of the two items A and B is not logically necessary if A is found accompanied by the opposite of B, and vice versa. The logical pattern of our argument has thus resembled a negative application of the method of difference: we have shown that (where A is an epistemological doctrine about the relation of reason and faith, and B is a practical political position) B can be had even when A is removed and replaced by the contrary of A, so that there is no logically necessary connection between B and A.

The bulk of our discussion has been concerned with the variant correlations themselves. However, the reasons or grounds for those variations have been at least implicit in our discussion of them. Most generally, there is the distinction between the theoretic and the practical which was emphasized near the end of our preceding section in connection with John of Jandun. Men may agree in philosophy while disagreeing in politics, as well as conversely, because of the different objects, bases, and ends of theoretic philosophy and practical politics. This need not mean that practical political views cannot be based on "truth"; but the truths and methods relevant to politics are not necessarily the same as those relevant to theoretic philosophy.

A specific instance of this general point appeared in the case of Wycliffe. He agreed with the Augustinian papalists both in his philosophic doctrine about the relation of reason and faith and in his theoretic political position that political superiority belongs to God's chief vicar. But the minor premise which Wycliffe subsumed under this major premise was the opposite of that of the papalists, for he held that the king, not the pope, is God's chief vicar. In the case of James of Viterbo, in a somewhat similar way, the pattern was that of a shift from initial agreement with the Christian Aristotelians on their major premise, to a specification of the meaning of that premise which involved a disagreement.

For when he said that "grace does not abolish nature but perfects it," he upheld, like the Aristotelians, the autonomy of the "secular" state; but he so interpreted the concept of "perfection" that the secular state came under the papal authority for the fulfillment of its own values.

It may, however, be objected that our "disproof" of Grabmann's specific correlations proves little or nothing about the general relation between philosophy and politics. For if two philosophers have the same philosophic doctrine but differ in political views, there is always the possibility that one of them has not fully understood the meaning or "implications" of his philosophic doctrine, or has not argued from it correctly. A further objection may be derived from the familiar way of treating the idea of a "plurality of causes"—the idea that an effect may be the result of many different causes. This idea is usually refuted by the argument that if the effect is subjected to a sufficiently careful analysis, the alleged plurality disappears: the specific effect in question always has one, and only one, kind of specific cause. Similarly, it may be held that the political "effects" or "conclusions" with which we have dealt here, and which we have shown to follow from or accompany different "causes" or philosophic doctrines, have been too gross; if they were analyzed more carefully, they would be seen to stand in a one-to-one relationship with appropriate philosophic antecedents.

To the first of these objections I would reply that while the possibility always exists that a philosopher has not argued correctly from his premises, the burden of proof always rests on the objector to show where this is so. I think it would be difficult to show this in the cases of James of Viterbo, John Wycliffe, and John of Jandun, with whom we have dealt here. The second objection has, I think, more point. There is, indeed, a need for more precise analysis of doctrines, both philosophic and political, in order to see their possible logical relations. The bulk of this paper may, in fact, be viewed as further confirmation of the view which recent historians have been developing that the traditional classifications of mediaeval philosophers under such rubrics as "Augustinian," "Christian Aristotelian," and "Averroist" are too gross to be very helpful. For the assumption of such classifications is that various doctrines occur together and may hence be grouped under a general name like "Augustinianism," and, moreover, that this "togetherness" is logically necessitated. What we have seen in this paper is that the assumption underlying such general classifications is untenable in the case of Grabmann's correlations. But precisely for this reason it may be held that, if we analyze Augustinianism and the other general philosophic "positions" into more carefully selected components, there may still remain a tight correlation between at least some of the latter and political doctrines. However, is not the view taken on the relation between reason and faith such a component? Whether or not one defines "Augustinianism," "Averroism," and so on, by the view taken on this relation, the traditional idea that there were these different views has not been refuted. To be sure, further analysis of the views on this relation itself has led us to see that some thinkers may uphold a contrariety between reason and faith on some questions, a mere separation or distinction on other questions, and a harmony or agreement on still others. But even so, and notwithstanding the other possible views on the relation between reason and faith, we have seen no grounds for holding that there might be a logical connection between any such analyzed views and practical political doctrines; and we have seen abundant grounds for holding that there is not such a logical connection.

Moreover, if we turn to the political side of such alleged correlations, and if we make the same demand that the political doctrines in question be more fully analyzed, there is always the danger that a political idea will in this way be analyzed out of its practical relevance. The idea that the pope should be politically superior to the king, or conversely, was a living, practically cogent fact in the fourteenth century. Of what relevance would it be to analyze this idea to the point where what emerged was something quite different from what men actually believed and acted on? We have here another difference between "effects" or "consequences" in theoretic science and in practical politics: in the latter, the phenomenal, including the ideas which men consciously uphold, is the real in a far more irreplaceable sense than is the case in the domain of theoretic science.

Nevertheless, it would be wrong to conclude, from our negative examination of Grabmann's correlations, that philosophy is irrelevant to practical politics. For a philosophy consists of more than a series of discrete propositions such as those about the relation of faith and reason which we took as isolated units for the purpose of our inquiry. It consists in a whole interconnected pattern of ideas which emerge more or less directly in the way men look at the world. And practical politics consists not merely in overt acts or patterns of behavior but in processes of thought and volition that accompany and, in part, are considered to justify the behavior. Consequently, for men to agree in practical politics involves more than that they subscribe to an isolated position such as that the king should be politically superior to the pope, or conversely. It involves in addition the set of values, including ways of looking at the world, which is considered to justify the position. At what point the insistence on these values would remove or make impossible practical political agreement in action is a serious and complex question. But there can be little doubt that even though an Averroist like Marsilius and an Augustinian like Wycliffe agreed on the need for restricting the papal power and ensuring the "secular" ruler's supremacy, life in a Wycliffian state would be a far different thing from life in a Marsilian state. The Augustinian principles of Wycliffe, with their emphases on a religiously based righteousness, would force men to live with ideas and institutions quite different from those of the less moralistic, far more secular Averroism of Marsilius. To judge properly the logical relations between philosophy and politics, then, would require taking each of these relata in a far broader scope than the analytic method of this paper has permitted.

Moreover, to view the relation between a philosophic doctrine and a political belief exclusively in respect of their logical connection is insufficient for grasping how philosophy actually operates in political action. Such operation always occurs under definite historical conditions; consequently, the meaning of a philosophic doctrine, so far as its relation to politics is concerned, depends on the historical circumstances in which it is propounded. It is the variety of these circumstances which accounts, at least in part, for the multiple correlations that we have found between philosophic doctrines and political views. An adequate account of the bearing on fourteenth-century political thought of the philosophic ideas of the period, then, would have to deal with more than the logical relations between concepts. It would have to concern itself also with what philosophers thought they were trying to accomplish by their ideas, and with the historical factors that conditioned both their thought and their accomplishments.

1. Cf. Bertrand Russell, *Philosophy and Politics* (London, 1947), (reprinted in *Unpopular Essays* [London, 1950]); John Dewey, *The Public and Its Problems* (New York, 1927); Jacques Maritain, *Scholasticism and Politics* (New York, 1940); Reinhold Niebuhr, *The Children of Light and the Children of Darkness, a Vindication of Democracy and a Critique of Its Traditional Defense* (New York, 1944).

2. Cf. T. D. Weldon, *The Vocabulary of Politics* (London, 1953); P. Laslett (ed.), *Philosophy, Politics, and Society* (Oxford, 1956); F. Oppenheim, "Relativism, Absolutism, and Democracy," *American Political Science Review*, XLIV (1950), 951-60; A. Quinton, in symposium on "Philosophy and Beliefs," *The Twentieth Century*, CLVII (June, 1955), 495 ff. For contemporary proponents of the opposite view, that there is a logical connection between philosophic doctrines and political ideas (although they may disagree on just which doctrines and ideas are thus connected), see, in addition to those cited in note 1, I. Berlin, S. Hampshire, I. Murdoch, in the same symposium on "Philosophy and Beliefs" in which Quinton took part (see above, this note); H. Kelsen, "Absolutism and Relativism in Philosophy and Politics," *American Political Science Review*, XLII (1948), 911 ff. (reprinted in Kelsen, *What is Justice?* [Berkeley, Calif., 1957], pp. 198-208); J. W. N. Watkins, "Epistemology and Politics," *Proceedings of the Aristotelian Society*, LVIII (1957-58), 79-102.

3. For a discussion of how political attitudes (or at least political analogies) have influenced philosophic theories, cf. L. S. Feuer, "Political Myths and Metaphysics," *Philosophy and Phenomenological Research*, XV (1955), 332 ff.

4. For references to the texts, see P. Boehner, *Medieval Logic: An Outline of Its Development from 1250 to c. 1400* (Chicago, 1952); Boehner, *Collected Articles on Ockham* (St. Bonaventure, N. Y., 1958); E. A. Moody, *Truth and Consequence in Mediaeval Logic* (Amsterdam, 1953). The works listed in this note and in the two following notes are only a very small part of the rich historical materials dealing with these subjects.

5. For extensive references to the texts (with, however, not always reliable interpretations), cf. the monographs of K. Michalski: "Les courants philosophiques à Oxford et à Paris pendant le XIVᵉ siècle," *Bulletin international de l'Académie Polonaise des sciences et des lettres,* Classe de Philologie, Classe d'Histoire et de Philosophie (Cracow, 1922-24), pp. 59-88; "Le criticisme et le scepticisme dans la philosophie du XIVᵉ siècle," *ibid.* (1927), pp. 41-126; "Les courants critiques et sceptiques dans la philosophie du XIVᵉ siècle," *ibid.* (1927), pp. 192-242. See also J. R. Weinberg, *Nicolaus of Autrecourt* (Princeton, 1948).

6. For references to the texts, see the classic works of P. Duhem: *Etudes sur Leonardo da Vinci, ceux qu'il a lus, ceux qui l'ont lu* (3 vols.; Paris, 1906-13); *Le système du monde; histoire des doctrines cosmologiques de Platon à Copernic* (10 vols.; Paris, 1913-59). See also the series of studies by A. Maier under the general title of "Studien zur Naturphilosophie der Spätscholastik" (Rome: Edizioni di Storia e Letteratura): *Die Vorläufer Galileis im 14. Jahrhundert*, 1949; *Zwei Grundprobleme der scholastischen Naturphilosophie,*

1951; *Auf der Grenze von Scholastik und Naturwissenschaft*, 1952; *Metaphysische Hintergründe der spätscholastischen Naturphilosophie*, 1955. See also E. A. Moody, "Laws of Motion in Medieval Physics," *Scientific Monthly*, LXXII (1951), 18-23; "Galileo and Avempace," *Journal of the History of Ideas*, XII (1951), 163-93, 375-422; and, for the methodological development, J. H. Randall, Jr., "Development of Scientific Method in the School of Padua," *Journal of the History of Ideas*, I (1940), 177 ff.

7. Edited by R. Scholz (Weimar, 1929).

8. Edited by H. X. Arquillière under the title *Le plus ancien traité de l'Eglise: Jacques de Viterbe, "De regimine Christiano" (1301-1302)* (Paris, 1926).

9. Edited by J. Leclerq in *Jean de Paris et l'Ecclésiologie du XIIIᵉ sciècle* (Paris, 1942).

10. J. C. Murray, "Contemporary Orientations of Catholic Thought on Church and State in the Light of History," *Theological Studies*, X (1949), 212.

11. The *Monarchia* is found in *Tutte le opere di Dante Alighieri*, ed. E. Moore (Oxford, 1924), pp. 339-76; there are several English translations. Engelbert's *Liber de ortu, progressu, et fine Romani Imperii* is in *Maxima bibliotheca veterum patrum* (Lyons, 1677), XXV, 363-78. Pierre Dubois' *De recuperatione Sancte Terre* is edited by C. V. Langlois (Paris, 1891); there is an English translation by W. Brandt (New York, 1956).

12. *Summa de ecclesiastica potestate* (Augsburg, 1473).

13. *De planctu ecclesiae*, in *Bibliotheca maxima pontificia*, ed. J. T. Roccaberti (Rome, 1698), Vol. III.

14. There are two critical modern editions, one by C. W. Previté-Orton (*The Defensor Pacis of Marsilius of Padua* [Cambridge, 1928]) and one by R. Scholz ("Marsilius von Padua, *Defensor Pacis*," in *Fontes juris Germanici antiqui* of the *Monumenta Germaniae historica* [Hanover, 1932]). There is an English translation by A. Gewirth: *The "Defensor Pacis": Translated with an Introduction*, which is Vol. II of *Marsilius of Padua, the Defender of Peace* (New York, 1956).

15. A critical edition of Ockham's political works is in course of publication; so far only two volumes have appeared: *Guillelmi de Ockham opera politica*, ed. J. G. Sikes *et al.* (Manchester, 1940 [Vol. I], 1956 [Vol. III]). Ockham's longest and most important political work, *Dialogus*, must still be read in the old edition of M. Goldast, *Monarchia sancti Romani Imperii* (Frankfurt, 1611-14), II, 398-967. His *Breviloquium de principatu tyrannico* has been published in a critical edition by R. Scholz (*Wilhelm von Ockham als politischer Denker und sein Breviloquium de principatu tyrannico* [Stuttgart, 1944]) and in an edition based on one manuscript by L. Baudry (Guillelmi de Occam, *Breviloquium de potestate papae* [Paris, 1937]).

16. Lupold of Bebenburg's *Tractatus de juribus regni et imperii* is found in *De jurisdictione, auctoritate, et praeeminentia imperiali ac potestate ecclesiastica*, ed. S. Schard (Basel, 1566), pp. 328-409. Three works of Konrad

of Megenberg—*Planctus ecclesiae in Germaniam, De translatione Romani Imperii,* and *Tractatus contra Wilhelmum Occam*—are edited by R. Scholz, *Unbekannte Kirchenpolitische Streitschriften aus der Zeit Ludwigs des Bayern* (Rome, 1914), II, 188-391. For Wycliffe's political thought, see *De dominio divino,* ed. R. L. Poole (London, 1890); *De civili dominio,* ed. R. L. Poole (4 vols.; London, 1885-1904); *De officio regis,* ed. A. W. Pollard and C. Sayle (London, 1887); *De potestate papae,* ed. J. Loserth (London, 1907); *De ecclesia,* ed. J. Loserth (London, 1886). Henry of Langenstein's *Consilium pacis de unione ac reformatione ecclesiae* is found in *Opera omnia Joannis Gerson,* ed. L. du Pin (Antwerp, 1706), II, 809 ff.

17. For the still very incomplete critical edition of Ockham's political works, see n. 15. A critical edition of his non-political works is now being prepared: *Gulielmi Ockham opera omnia philosophica et theologica,* ed. E. M. Buytaert *et al.* (St. Bonaventure, N. Y., and Paderborn).

18. G. de Lagarde, *L'individualisme ockhamiste,* comprising Vols. IV-VI of Lagarde's still unfinished work *La naissance de l'esprit laïque au déclin du moyen âge* (Paris, 1942-46). See also Lagarde's "L'idée de représentation dans les oeuvres de Guillaume d'Ockham," *Bulletin of the International Committee of Historical Sciences,* IX (1937), 435-51; L. Baudry, *Guillaume d'Occam: Sa vie, ses oeuvres, ses idées sociales et politiques,* Vol. I (Paris, 1950). See also Baudry's "Le philosophe et le politique dans Guillaume d'Ockham," *Archives d'histoire doctrinale et littéraire du moyen âge,* XIV (1939), 209-30. The view that Ockham was a political "individualist" and a legal "voluntarist" because he was a philosophical "nominalist" is, of course, an old tradition of scholarly interpretation. Cf., for example, O. von Gierke, *Political Theories of the Middle Age,* trans. F. W. Maitland (Cambridge, 1900), pp. 172-73.

19. P. Boehner, "Ockham's Political Ideas," *Review of Politics,* V (1943), 462-87 (reprinted in Boehner's *Collected Articles on Ockham* [St. Bonaventure, N. Y., 1958], pp. 442-68); R. Scholz, *Wilhelm von Ockham als politischer Denker und sein Breviloquium de principatu tyrannico* (Stuttgart, 1944), pp. 18-28; J. B. Morrall, "Some Notes on a Recent Interpretation of William of Ockham's Political Philosophy," *Franciscan Studies,* IX (1949), 335-69. See also M. A. Shepard, "William of Occam and the Higher Law," *American Political Science Review,* XXVI (1932), 1009 ff.

20. Cf., for example, the discussion of how Ockham uses the concepts of *epieikeia, bonum commune,* and *necessitas* to deal with such practical problems as the canonical obstacles to the marriage of Ludwig of Bavaria's son, the secular ruler's competence to impose on the clergy extraordinary taxes in time of war without papal consent, and various other issues about the relations between the temporal and spiritual powers, in C. C. Bayley, "Pivotal Concepts in the Political Philosophy of William of Ockham," *Journal of the History of Ideas,* X (1949), 199-218.

21. To support this statement adequately would require a comparative study far more extensive than can be undertaken here. Examples of what is meant are likely to be misleading unless relevant qualifications are introduced. With this warning, however, reference may be made to the ways in

which Ockham, John of Paris, and Marsilius of Padua, amid their divergences in theoretical political definitions and doctrines, yet agree in their conciliarism and their opposition to the papal plenitude of power. To be sure, this agreement is not complete; there are also differences on these practical matters. Nevertheless, (a) it is doubtful whether these differences outweigh the similarities in political recommendations which distinguish all three thinkers from, for example, the papalists; (b) it is also doubtful to what extent these differences can be traced back to differences on the level of theoretical politics; (c) it is also doubtful to what extent their practical agreements can be traced back to agreements on theory. In discussing this whole question, it is important to avoid making the concept of "theoretical political doctrine" part of the meaning of "practical political recommendation," so that the proposition "There can be agreement in practical political recommendations amid disagreement in theoretic political doctrines" would become false by definition.

22. Thus, for example, Lagarde holds that from Ockham's view that the will is the essential attribute of all rational beings, both God and man, there follows his reduction of all law to will (La naissance . . . , VI, 91-92, 185, 212); Lagarde also believes that there is a "rigorous parallelism" between the epistemological characteristics which Ockham ascribes to the concepts whereby theoretic reason apprehends reality and those which he ascribes to the precepts which the practical reason apprehends as "natural laws" of morals and politics (ibid., VI, 141 ff.). (I am doubtful about the extent of the legal "voluntarism" and "irrationalism" which Lagarde attributes to Ockham.) Likewise, both Lagarde and Baudry emphasize how Ockham's nominalist doctrine that only individuals are real, and that relations and composites are real only in virtue of the individuals related or compounded, eventuates in his attacks on the reification or personification of social groups as entities distinct from their members (Lagarde, "L'idée de représentation . . . ," pp. 436 ff.; Baudry, "Le philosophe et le politique . . . ," pp. 211 ff.).

23. Cf. Boehner, "Ockham's Political Ideas" (Collected Articles on Ockham, p. 446): "Ockham's political ideas in their great outlines could have been developed, so far as we can see, from any of the classical metaphysics of the thirteenth century . . . . "

24. M. Grabmann, "Studien über den Einfluss der Aristotelischen Philosophie auf die mittelalterlichen Theorien über das Verhaltnis von Kirche und Staat," Sitzungsberichte der Bayerischen Akademie der Wissenschaften, Philosophisch-historische Abteilung, 1935, Heft 2.

25. P. Mandonnet, Siger de Brabant et l'averroïsme latin au XIIIᵉ siècle (2d ed.; Louvain, 1911); E. Gilson, Etudes de philosophie médiévale (Strasbourg, 1921), p. 51.

26. Cf. A. Gewirth, Marsilius of Padua (New York, 1951, 1956), I, 104-9; II, xlvii-liii.

27. Thomas Aquinas Summa theologica II. ii. qu. 60. a. 6. ad 3; qu. 147. a. 3. Resp.; De regimine principum I. xiv; Commentum in quatuor libros sententiarum Lib. II. Dist. xliv. qu. 2. a. 3. Expositio textus, ad 4; John of

Paris *De potestate regia et papali* cap. v, x, xii ff. (Leclerq, pp. 183-85, 194-201, 209 ff.).

28. Cf. *Defensor pacis* I. i. 8; I. iv. 2; I. v. 10, 11; I. ix. 2, 3; I. xii. 1.

29. In his initial presentation of the correlations, Grabmann uses such general expressions as the *Bedeutung* or the *Einwirkung* of the Aristotelian philosophy *für* or *auf* the mediaeval theories of the relations between church and state, and refers to his own procedure as one of *setzen* the political positions *zu* the philosophical doctrines (*op. cit.*, pp. 5-7).

30. *Ibid.*, p. 7.

31. Cf. *Summa theologica* I. qu. 1. a. 8. ad 2; qu. 2. a. 2. ad 1; II. i. qu. 109. a. 1.

32. *Ibid.* I. qu. 1. a. 8. ad 2: "Cum enim gratia non tollat naturam, sed perficiat, oportet quod naturalis ratio subserviat fidei . . . . "

33. *De regimine principum* I. i.

34. *Summa theologica* I. qu. 96. a. 4. Resp.

35. *De regimine Christiano* I. i (Arquillière, p. 91). See also II. iii, vii (pp. 176-77, 232). Cf., to the same effect, Alexander of St. Elpidius *Tractatus de ecclesiastica potestate* II. viii, in *Bibliotheca maxima pontificia*, ed. J. T. Roccaberti (Rome, 1698-99), II, 24; and Alvarus Pelagius *De planctu ecclesiae* I. xli, in Roccaberti, III, 69.

36. *Summa de ecclesiastica potestate* qu. 23. art. 3.

37. See James of Viterbo *De reg. Chr.* II. iv, vii, viii, ix, x (Arquillière, pp. 208, 234-35, 260-61, 273, 283, 295); Augustinus Triumphus *S. de eccl. pot.* qu. 1. aa. 1, 3, 4; qu. 44. a. 4; qu. 46. a. 2; Alexander of St. Elpidius *Tract. de eccl. pot.* II. cap. iv-ix (Roccaberti, II, 18-27); Alvarus Pelagius *De planctu eccl.* I. xxiv (Roccaberti, III, 33).

38. *De reg. Chr.* II. vii (Arquillière, p. 232). See, similarly, Alexander of St. Elpidius *Tract. de eccl. pot.* II. viii (Roccaberti, II, 24).

39. *De reg. Chr.* II. vii (Arquillière, p. 234).

40. *Ibid.* (pp. 234-35).

41. *S. de eccl. pot.* qu. 24. a. 6.

42. *Orthodoxa defensio imperialis*, in *Monumenta Germaniae historica, Libelli de lite*, II, 534-42.

43. *Tractatus eboracenses*, in *ibid.*, III, 645-87.

44. *Sermo XXV*, in *Sermones*, ed. J. Loserth (London, 1887), I, 171-72; *De dominio divino* I. xi (Poole, 86); *Tractatus de apostasia* xvi, ed. M. H. Dziewicki (London, 1889), p. 217.

45. *De civili dominio* I. viii. (Poole, I, 127); *De officio regis* xi (Pollard and Sayle, p. 247); *De ecclesia* xiv (Loserth, p. 321).

46. *De civili dominio* I. i, xxiii, xlii (Poole, I, 1 ff., 156, 349); *De officio regis* iv (Pollard and Sayle, p. 72). Cf. Egidius of Rome *De ecclesiastica potestate* II. iv, vii, viii (Scholz, pp. 48 ff., 70 ff.).

47. *De officio regis* vi (Pollard and Sayle, p. 146); *De potestate papae* vii (Loserth, p. 138).

48. *De potestate papae* xii (Loserth, pp. 326-28).

49. *De civili dominio* II. v (Poole, II, 36); *De ecclesia* xv, xvi (Loserth, pp. 337 ff., 376-77, 384 ff.); *De officio regis* vi (Pollard and Sayle, p. 120).

50. *De officio regis* vii (Pollard and Sayle, p. 186).

51. *Ibid.* vi (p. 119).

52. *De ecclesia* xix (Loserth, p. 464); cf. i (p. 5).

53. *Ibid.* ii (p. 31).

54. *De officio regis* i (Pollard and Sayle, p. 4); *De ecclesia* xiv (Loserth, pp. 314-16).

55. *De officio regis* iv (Pollard and Sayle, p. 79).

56. *Ibid.* i (pp. 13-14).

57. See Siger of Brabant *Quaestiones morales,* ed. F. Stegmüller, in *Recherches de théologie ancienne et médiévale,* III (1931), 172-77; Boethius of Dacia *De summo bono sive De vita philosophie* and *De sompniis,* in M. Grabmann, *Mittelalterliches Geistesleben* (Munich, 1936), II, 200-24. See also Grabmann, "Der lateinische Averroismus des 13. Jahrhunderts und seine Stellung zur christlichen Weltanschauung," *Sitzungsberichte der Bayerischen Akademie der Wissenschaften,* Phil.-hist. Abt., 1931, Heft 2; and R. A. Gauthier, "Trois commentaires 'averroïstes' sur l'Ethique à Nicomaque," *Archives d'histoire doctrinale et littéraire du moyen âge,* XVI (1947-48), 187-336.

58. Grabmann, "Studien über den Einfluss . . . ," p. 46; and "Die mittelalterlichen Kommentare zur Politik des Aristoteles," *Sitzungsberichte der Bayerischen Akademie der Wissenschaften,* Phil.-hist. Abt., 1941, Heft 10, pp. 24-25. Cf. Lagarde, *La naissance* . . . , III, chap. ii. No trace has been found of Siger of Brabant's lectures on Aristotle's *Politics* (which Pierre Dubois reported hearing; see *De recuperatione Terre Sancte* 132 [Langlois, p. 121]).

59. For reasons why John is not co-author, see A. Gewirth, "John of Jandun and the *Defensor Pacis,*" *Speculum,* XXIII (1948), 267-72.

60. *Quaestiones perspicacissimi peripatetici Joannis de Gandavo vulgo cognominati de Janduno in duodecim libros metaphysice iuxta Aristotelis et magni commentatoris intentionem ab eodem exactissime disputate* . . . . (Venetiis . . . sumptibus heredum . . . Octaviani Scoti . . . 1525). (To be abbreviated hereinafter as *Quaest. in metaphys.*)

61. Thus, for example, Grabmann writes: "Das einzige Werk, in welchem Johannes von Jandun sich über politische Dinge äussert, ist die soeben genannte Schrift De laudibus Parisius, die aus dem Jahre 1324 stammt" ("Studien über den Einfluss . . . ," p. 51). N. Valois, in his brief review of John's *Quaest. in metaphys.,* does not mention these political discussions, despite the light they shed on his position that John was co-author of the *Defensor pacis* ("Jean de Jandun et Marsile de Padoue, auteurs du *Defensor*

Pacis," *Histoire littéraire de la France* [Paris, 1906], XXIII, 528 ff., at pp. 556-58). See, similarly, M. de Wulf, *Histoire de la philosophie médiévale* (5th ed.; Paris, 1925), II, 217.

62. Lib. I. qu. 18.

63. Lib. I. qu. 1.

64. Lib. I. qu. 21.

65. Lib. I. qu. 22.

66. Lib. I. qu. 17.

67. Lib. II. qu. 11.

68. Lib. XII. qu. 22.

69. Cf. my article cited above, n. 59. For other references to, and discussions of, John's political ideas, consult the entry "John of Jandun" in the Index to my *Marsilius of Padua,* I, 333; see also II, 435-42.

70. *Quaest. in metaphys.* Lib. II. qu. 5 (fol. 26N ff.): "Utrum substantiae aeternae aliae a prima dependeant a prima tanquam ab aliquo agente et efficiente."

71. *Ibid.* (fol. 28A-B): "Hoc modo dicendum est ad quaestionem secundum intentionem Aristotelis et Commentatoris ponentium citra primam aliquas substantias aeternas. Et si hoc esset verum non dependeret a vero agente per motum. Sed tamen dicendum secundum fidem et veritatem quod nihil citra primum est aeternum, sed omnia incoeperunt de novo esse, et per consequens producta fuerunt a primo principio tanquam ab agente per creationem ex nihilo, saltem substantiae abstractae, et illa creatio non est motus nec generatio univoce dictus cum motu inferiorum, sed alia productio supernaturalis quae non potest convinci ex sensatis et ex naturalibus ex quibus procedunt philosophi naturaliter loquentes. Sed tantum firmiter hoc credo et scio, non de ratione orta ex sensatis, et hoc firmiter facit scripturae doctoribus reverenter assentire. Unde ex hoc quod nescio demonstrare ex sensatis, nec potest quia est super sensibilia et naturam, tunc simpliciter credendo et fideliter habeo meritum, et in hoc etiam probatur creationis et salvationis excellentia vigoris super agens quodlibet naturale."

72. Cf. John's discussions of the eternity of the world (*ibid.* Lib. I. qu. 16 [fols. 11E-13B, esp. at fol. 13A-B]); the human intellect's knowledge of God (*ibid.* Lib. II. qu. 4 [fols. 22M-26M, esp. at fol. 25O-Q]); the infinite regress in the accidental orders of efficient, material, and formal causes (*ibid.* Lib. II, qus. 6, 7, 9 [fols. 28B-29I, 30C-O, esp. at fols. 28N, 29H, 30I]); whether God has a passive potentiality or only an active one (*ibid.* Lib. V. qu. 37 [fol. 77C-M]); the real separability of accidents from substances (*ibid.* Lib. VII. qu. 1 [fols. 87L-88O, esp. at fol. 88G]); the immortality and plurality of the human intellect (*ibid.* Lib. XII. qu. 4 [fols. 129F-130C]); whether God understands anything other than himself (*ibid.* Lib. XII. qu. 21 [fols. 142C-143H, esp. at fol. 143A-B]).

73. Cf. Gilson, *op. cit.,* pp. 51-75.

162   ALAN GEWIRTH

74. These differences seem to me to receive perhaps insufficient attention in the interesting discussion of John's position by S. MacClintock, *Perversity and Error: Studies on the "Averroist" John of Jandun* (Bloomington, Indiana, 1956), pp. 69-99.

75. *Quaest. in metaphys.* Lib. XII. qu 22 (fol. 143I): "Sed in minori mundo sunt plures principes aeque primi, sicut in homine sunt plures dominantes quorum unus non est sub alio nec obedit sibi: ut rex et summus pontifex, quia neuter vult esse subjectus alteri."

76. *Ibid.* (fol. 144C-D): "Unde ad propositum debemus dicere quod in toto universo unus debet esse princeps. Tu dicis quod non est rex nec summus pontifex. Dicendum quod summus pontifex, et licet rex non subsit sibi in [spiritualibus, immo in] temporalibus, tamen in spiritualibus et virtute. Sed dices, quod insufficienter loqueris, quia tantum in lege christianorum et non in aliis. Dicendum quod inquantum est de condigno et de jure naturali omnes homines cujuscumque moris et legis debent esse sub lege christianorum, quae est probata evidenter et certitudinaliter per evidentia mirabilia, quae nulli competunt nisi legis factori christianorum. Unde etiam inquantum est de condigno omnes debent esse sub pontifice summo, quamvis non sunt. Immo plus errant et deficiunt a ratione, quanto plus resistunt legi christianae." (I have bracketed the three words *spiritualibus, immo in* since the passage does not make sense otherwise. It is to be noted, however, that these three words also occur in the Venice editions of 1554 and 1586, the relevant passages from which I have consulted in microfilms from the Bibliothèque Nationale and the British Museum, respectively. I have not been able to consult the manuscripts). It is interesting to note, in comparison with this passage where John holds that the *summus pontifex* should be the single ruler over the whole world, that in the *De laudibus Parisius* John holds that it is rather the king of France who should be the ruler: "Illustrissimis et precellentissimis Francie regibus monarchicum totius orbis dominium, saltem ex native pronitatis ad melius jure, debetur" (*Tractatus de laudibus Parisius* II. 8, in *Paris et ses historiens*, ed. LeRoux de Lincy and L. M. Tisserand [Paris, 1867], p. 58). This work was completed on November 4, 1323 (cf. the *explicit,* p. 78), probably a decade or more after the *Quaest. in metaphys.*

77. Cf. Lagarde, *La naissance* . . . , III, pp. 54-55; Gewirth, *Marsilius of Paduu,* I, 64, including n. 71.

78. *Quaest. in metaphys.* Lib. I. qu. 1 (fol. 1F, 2A): " . . . Sapientia quae est in contemplatione et cognitione Dei et aliorum principiorum abstractorum necessaria est ad communicationem et bonum convictum, quia sine cognitione Dei homines formaliter non possunt bene operari, licet materialiter: unde ad hoc quod legislator suos cives faciat bonos, opus quod habeat cognitionem Dei per se ut per habitum sapientie sibi adjunctum vel per alium sapientem qui dicat sibi et demonstret sibi deum, ut possit alios instruere, unde etiam felicitas politica ordinatur ad felicitatem speculativam, sicut ad illud quod est finis, et sic ad illud."

79. *Ibid.* Lib. I. qu. 18 (fol. 14N-O); " . . . Inter omnes actus hominis nobilissimus est cognoscere Deum, et in illo actu praecipiendi consistit

felicitas politica in principe operanti ad cognitionem Dei, sicut etiam felicitas speculativa consistit in speculatione Dei. Et haec doctrina mirabiliter propinqua est doctrinae piissimi legislatoris domini nostri Jesu Christi, qui cum ab eo quaereretur quod est primum mandatum in lege, respondit, Dilige Deum tuum ex toto corde tuo, et postea subdit piissimus legislator: et proximum tuum sicut teipsum. Ergo in actu praecipiendi operari ad dilectionem Dei consistit felicitas politica."

80. *Ibid.* (fol. 15C): " . . . Felicitas politica consistit in nobilissimo actu practico, scilicet, in praecipere, et praeceptum est cognoscere et diligere Deum, et hoc praeceptum princeps facere non potest nisi per cognitionem Dei per se vel quia recipiat cognitionem Dei ab alio qui hoc sciat, et hoc est per speculativos philosophos qui docent cognitionem Dei."

81. *Ibid.* (fol. 15A): "Illi debent permitti in civitate ex praecepto et ordinatione deliberata sine quibus non potest haberi complementum felicitatis politicae. Haec est manifesta quia finis necessitat alia, cum sit optimus. Sed sine viris speculativis secundo modo dictis non potest haberi complementum felicitatis sufficienter . . . isti philosophi cum permittuntur in proprio opere ut speculari et doctrinari ita quod non molestantur per opera politica et artes, tunc maxime prosunt ad complementum humanae felicitatis, ut intendere et docere ad cognitionem Dei et substantiarum abstractarum, ad quas sic se habet intellectus noster sicut oculus noctuae ad lumen solis. Et sic ex praecepto permissi in civitate melius possunt cognoscere ardua et nobilissima et docere aliquos cognitionem talium, quia non sunt intricati aliis operibus prudentiae et artis."

82. *Ibid.* (fol. 15K): "Dicendum quod speculativi viri sunt finis aliarum partium civitatis gratia cujus, quia sicut omnes homines sunt propter speculativos viros tanquam gratia cujus, sic tota civitas propter illos, et felicitas politica ordinatur ad felicitatem speculativam, sicut omnes homines in civitate ordinantur ad speculationem de Deo."

83. This refers to the *argumentum a contrario* (fol. 14F-G) that philosophers must not be permitted in the state because they fall under none of the six parts of the state listed in the seventh book of Aristotle's *Politics* (VII, 8. 1328b 3 ff.).

84. *Quaest. in metaphys.* Lib. I. qu. 18 (fol. 15I-K): " .. . Philosophi . . . praesupponuntur a sacerdotibus, quia sacerdotibus necessarium est cognoscere deum et debent esse speculativi, quia in greco sacerdotes dicuntur seniores, qui debent esse sapientes. Tu dices quod speculativi etc. Dicendum quod immo vellent sacerdotari si fieret eis sicut esset condignum, sed non sic fit, quia praebendae et beneficia dantur idiotis, unde sacerdos debet esse necessario sapiens et habere cognitionem de Deo. . . . Sacerdotes non addunt supra speculativos viros ad speciem speculationum Dei nisi actus exteriores."

85. Cf. Aristotle *Metaphysics* I. 1. 981b 20-24; *Nicomachean Ethics* VI. 7. 1141b 1 ff.; X. 7. 1177b 25 ff.; *Politics* VII. 9. 1329a 26 ff.

86. *Defensor pacis* I. vi. 9.

87. Marsilius, on the other hand, says that only "by faith alone" does he hold the Christian religion to be superior to other religions. Cf. *Defensor pacis* II. xxx. 4.

88. *Quaest. in metaphys.* Lib. XII. qu. 22 (fol. 144D), (quoted above, note 76).

89. By "laws" (*leges*) John of Jandun, like the other Averroists, means religions. Cf. the Introduction to my translation of *Defensor pacis,* p. xc.

90. *Quaest. in metaphys.* Lib. II. qu. 11 (fol. 35E): " . . . Omnes leges praeter Christianorum legem sunt cum admixtione erroris, sicut lex Mahumeti est quod post istam vitam habetur vita voluptuosa et delectabilis. Unde hoc est contra rationem. Secundo modo oritur lex propria a lege communi sine admixtione erroris, ita quod nihil est in ea contra rationem, sicut in nostra lege, ut Christiana."

91. *Ibid.* Lib. I. qu. 16 (fol. 14E): "Dicendum quod fides potest referri ad duo. Uno enim modo potest referri ad falsas leges, et sic fides vulgi est fortior, quia magis credunt falsis legibus quam philosophiae, quia non viderunt multa et nesciunt discernere verum a falso . . . . Alio modo fides potest referri ad verum, et sic fides philosophorum fortior est fide vulgi, quia philosophi magis credunt veris quam vulgares. El quando Commentator dixit quod fides vulgi fortior est fide philosophorum, intellexit in legibus falsis et non in veris."

92. Cf. Gewirth, *Marsilius of Padua,* I, 41-42, 68-84.

93. Bertrand Russell, *op. cit.,* p. 20.

94. See Averroës *Traité décisif sur l'accord de la religion et de la philosophie,* trans. L. Gauthier (Algiers, 1942), and *Commentary on Plato's Republic,* ed. and trans. E. I. J. Rosenthal (Cambridge, 1956). Cf. Gewirth, *Marsilius of Padua,* I, 84, including n. 45; II, 440-42.

95. Averroës *Metaphysicorum expositio media* II. iii (*Aristotelis opera cum commentariis Averrois* [Venice, 1560], VIII, 55D): "Lex enim non est ut sciamus, sed ut boni fiamus. Et causa est, quoniam perfectio hominis non acquiritur nisi per congregationes hominum in civitatibus, et congregatio, id est Civitas, non erit perfecta nisi propter bonitatem, et non propter scientiam. Quare, ut homines sint boni necessarium est lex, non ut sciant."

96. Siger of Brabant *Quaestiones in metaphysicam* Lib. II. qu. 16 (ed. C. O. Graiff [Louvain, 1948], p. 74): " . . . Legislator non ponit de primis principiis secundum quod opinatur, sed secundum quod magis conferens est hominibus, et secundum quod magis potest instruere bonis; aliquando autem per falsa et frivola possunt homines fieri boni."

97. *Quaest. in metaphys.* I. qus. 1, 17, 18, 21 (fols. 1C, 13C, 14E-F, 17P).

NOTES ON THE CONTRIBUTORS

HARRY BOBER is professor of the History of Art in the Institute of Fine Arts, New York University, and director of the International Center of Romanesque Art. Among his books are an edition of a work by F. Saxl and H. Meier, *Catalogue of Astrological and Mythological Illuminated Manuscripts of the Latin Middle Ages: Manuscripts in English Libraries*, *The Coronation Book of Charles IV and Jeanne d'Evreux*, *The Guennol Collection: Mediaeval Art* (soon to be published), and "Mediaeval Schemata" (in preparation). He has also written numerous articles and reviews in learned journals.

GEORGE P. CUTTINO, professor of history at Emory University, is the author of *English Diplomatic Administration, 1259–1339*, *The Gascon Calendar of 1322*, *I Laugh through Tears: The Ballades of François Villon*, *Le Livre d'Agenais*, and a number of articles in learned journals.

GRACE FRANK (Mrs. Tenney Frank), professor emeritus of Old French at Bryn Mawr College, sometime visiting professor at The Johns Hopkins University, Fellow of the Mediaeval Academy, and a frequent contributor to various learned journals, is the author of *The Medieval French Drama* and the editor of *La Passion du Palatinus*, Rutebeuf's *Miracle de Théophile*, *Le Livre de la Passion*, *La Passion d'Autun*, and (with Dorothy Miner) *Proverbes en Rime*.

ASTRIK L. GABRIEL is director of the Mediaeval Institute and professor of Mediaeval Civilization in the Graduate School, University of Notre Dame (Indiana). He is the author of many publications on the history of mediaeval education; among them are *Student Life in Ave Marie College, Mediaeval Paris*, which was awarded the Thorlet Prize of the Académie des Inscriptions, *The Educational Ideas of Vincent of Beauvais*, *Skara House at the Mediaeval University of Paris*, and *Index romain et littérature française à l'époque romantique*. He is co-editor with the Reverend Joseph N. Garvin, C.S.C., of the series "Texts and Studies in the History of Mediaeval Education."

ALAN GEWIRTH, professor of philosophy at the University of Chicago, is the author of *Marsilius of Padua and Mediaeval Political Philosophy* and the translator of *The "Defensor Pacis"* (with an Introduction), which is Volume II of *Marsilius of Padua, the Defender of Peace*.

FRANCIS LEE UTLEY is professor of English at Ohio State University. He is the author of *The Crooked Rib,* the *Ninth Supplement to Wells' Manual of the Writings of Middle English,* co-editor of *Studies in Biblical and Jewish Folklore,* and has published some one hundred articles in linguistics, folklore, and mediaeval literature.

DATE DUE

ICO 38-297